A Century of Trollope Criticism

A Century of Trollope Criticism

by

RAFAEL HELLING

KENNIKAT PRESS, INC./PORT WASHINGTON, N. Y.

Originally published in 1956
Reissued in 1967 by Kennikat Press

Library of Congress Catalog Card No: 67-27607

Manufactured in the United States of America

CONTENTS

                                                                          Page
Acknowledgements 5
INTRODUCTION 7
  The Time Limits of Trollope's Epoch 9
  Outlines of Trollope's Epoch and His Relation to It 12

Part I

THE HISTORY OF TROLLOPE'S REPUTATION 25

Part II

THE CRITICISM 71
  A. The Judgments by Trollope's Contemporaries 72
  B. Trollope in the Eyes of Posterity
      Some Comments on *An Autobiography* 126
      In Oblivion 133
      The New Judgment 138
      Mr. Cockshut's Critical Study 174
CONCLUSION 176
Bibliography 184
Notes 190
Index 197

Note. The letter *A* (*A*, 15) in the text refers to Trollope's *Autobiography,* see Bibliography. 'Sadleir' refers to his *Trollope: A Commentary* unless otherwise stated or inferable from the context.

ACKNOWLEDGEMENTS

In 1948 my attention was directed by Professor Ole Reuter to the subject of the present thesis, and I do not think a better suggestion could have been made to one who was interested in the Victorian period and literature. In the spring and summer of 1950 I had the privilege to attend some lectures on Victorian literature at King's College, London, and my conversations and later correspondence with Dr. W. Armstrong, one of the lecturers, have been profitable for my study. Without access to the British Museum Library the thesis could not have been written, but the Senate House Library of the University of London has been equally useful especially through its prompt delivery of photostats. Further I have to acknowledge help of various kinds from the British Council, the B.B.C., authors, publishers and editors in England, and especially from my friend Mr. Patrick Whitmore, who has not spared himself in getting for me all the books, articles and information I have wanted in the last year. I have further received books and articles, not otherwise available, through the kindness of some Americans. The courtesy of the librarians at the University Library of Helsingfors has facilitated my work. Professor O. Reuter and Professor R. Koskimies have read through my thesis. I beg to express my gratitude to all the persons and institutions mentioned.

Borgå, Finland,
October, 1955

Rafael Helling

Introduction

The purpose of the present study is to trace the main features of Anthony Trollope's reputation, chiefly in England, from the time his popularity was first established to the middle of the nineteen-fifties, and to analyse and synthetize the Trollope criticism, mainly English but largely American, too, during the hundred years now gone by since the publication of *The Warden.* I shall have to pay attention to good and bad opinions but more to the former, not only because appreciative interpretations are more useful generally but because my chief endeavour will be to establish the essence of Trollope's appeal, first to his contemporaries and then to posterity, as reflected in the criticism contained in reviews, essays, and books; his own statements about his work and art, especially in the *Autobiography,* must of course also be regarded. An inquiry into these things seems to be especially called for because of the exceptionally great swings of the pendulum of this novelist's reputation, which have often been wondered at but not fully explained nor hitherto investigated in one comprehensive attempt. By the present study I hope to be able to shed some additional light on these phenomena and to contribute in some measure to the appreciation of Anthony Trollope, the novelist, as well as to give a surveyable representation of the essentials of the criticism that has been applied to him and which should be interesting also for its own sake.

Several books on Anthony Trollope have by now been given to the world. After his death in 1882, however, the writer, once famous and popular, was practically forgotten or neglected for about twenty years till some publishers ventured to reissue a few of his novels thereby fanning into life a tiny flame of interest in them, which, in spite of several years of flickering, did not die, but eventually began to shine with a steady light. His first biographer, T. H. S. Escott, made a great effort to secure this interest by publishing, in 1913, his large book on Trollope, but only after the publication in 1927 of Michael Sadleir's famous *Trollope*:

A Commentary did the reputation of the writer begin really to revive in the English speaking world, and eventually grew in a manner almost without a parallel. »With the exception of Herman Melville», says Professor Bradford Booth, »no novelist has had a more singular career.»[1]

In his Introduction Sadleir calls Trollope »the Voice of an Epoch», i.e. the epoch he regards as the mid-Victorian age. This is, in the main at least, the 'Victorian' period *par excellence*, and Anthony Trollope has not only been considered as »a more typical Victorian than any of his famous contemporaries»[2] but, of all Victorian novelists, »the most faithful recorder of ordinary life and manners»[3]; we may add that he was the last of the Great Novelists of his period.

Considerable work has been devoted to the attempts to establish the significance of the Victorian age in the history of British civilization. Most books and essays written on Trollope in our own century also give some exposition of the spirit of that age; in fact, Anthony Trollope seems to draw out more comments on Victorianism than any other single novelist. We find that the increasing interest in the Victorian age of the last twenty or thirty years has grown simultaneously with the interest in Trollope, and the study of the period has no doubt stimulated the study of the writer, and *vice versa*.

Just as the mid-Victorian writers— and Trollope more than anyone else — were once disparaged, their whole period was looked down upon by the following generation. In the new century opinion gradually changed; about 1930 Cazamian even dared to predict that the Victorian age, including the end of the nineteenth century, would »probably come to be looked upon as the most powerful and the greatest among all the periods of English culture».[4] In 1945 R. P. Stebbins spoke of Trollope as »our most consummate interpreter of a whole glorious phase of Anglo-Saxon civilization».[5] Innumerable books on Victorian literature, thought, and culture in general have been written, and the age has been considered to be of so great an interest even to the general public that a great variety of its aspects have been made the subjects of talks broadcast by the B.B.C., subsequently published as *Ideas and Beliefs of the Victorians* (1949), a book comprising about 430 × 400 words actually spoken in the series.

In *Early Victorian Novelists* (1934) by Lord David Cecil we find the subtitle 'Essays in Revaluation'; the subtitle of *Ideas and Beliefs* is 'an historic revaluation of the Victorian Age'. In both cases the word 'revaluation' is suggestive of the attempts at dispassionate judgment in these books. But in some minds the 'revaluation' may even turn into a sentimental yearning for the earlier debunked century as for a promised land, in which »all that we now lack seems present in abundance.»[6] Studying these books and the countless other publications on this subject, we find that our attitude and judgment must be dependent on so many different facts, circumstances, aspects, and views that it seems impossible for anyone to master them all, and that we must content ourselves with a choice of views and facts to have any conception of this period at all. And a fairly comprehensive notion of the Victorian age is necessary for an adequate appreciation of a writer so deeply merged in it as Trollope; to be able to follow the ups and downs of his reputation such a notion is still more called for, which happily was perceived by Sadleir when writing his *Commentary*. His tendency to put so much stress on the relation of Trollope's reputation to social history and literary prejudices really forms the basis of the success of his book, »the Trollope Bible», as it has been called.

Sadleir's characterization of Trollope as »the Voice of an Epoch» is explained by the opening words of the *Commentary:* »When Anthony Trollope died, there passed not only the mid-Victorian novel but a social epoch also. This dual significance of Trollope — at once literary and social — sets him apart from the other novelists of his time.» The aim of Sadleir's book was to re-establish the novelist in the esteem of the world, a world which had only just had time to rally after the Great War, and was likely to listen to the voice of an epoch which seemed to take on the suggestion of an idyll, not in a dreamland, but in an England wonderfully real and more English than anything the war generation could remember if only the remains of the inherited prejudices against the mid-Victorians could be overcome. A better advocate for Trollope than Sadleir could hardly be imagined at least at that time and a better advocate for the mid-Victorians than Trollope himself could not be found. The world began to listen to his voice more willingly than ever before. Sadleir's *Commentary* is a biographical and critical study to which all subsequent writers on Trollope have been greatly indebted, a source on which the present study, too, will have frequently to draw.

The Time Limits of Trollope's Epoch

'The Voice of an Epoch' may sound somewhat like the caption of a publisher's advertisement but we find Trollope characterized in words to much the same effect already by his contemporaries. Especially when a

considerable part of his works had been published, his merits as a painter
of society, with all its conventions, prejudices, manners, and morals, and
as an interpreter of the spirit of the age was plainly recognized. In 1872
the *Dublin Review* expresses this recognition in words that are characteristic of Victorian self-confidence:

> The leading novelist of the day is its accurate representative, its faithful mouth-
> piece — not as regards its vulgar aspects but its real, permeating motives, its
> spirits, its aims, and its manners. It is impatiently inattentive to anything —
> unless it be within the sphere of scientific research, — which goes further back
> than yesterday; it shrinks from the trouble of bringing itself into *rapport* with any
> lives whose mechanical resources did not include railways and the electric telegraph,
> and which were destitute of dailies and weeklies. It has broken with the past more
> thoroughly than we can conceive any previous age to have broken with its past.
> There is an occasional chance for the antique, if it be well furbished up indeed, but
> there is none for the merely old-fashioned. There is such a difference between past
> and *passé*. Mr. Trollope meets, suits, gratifies this taste. He is the most entirely
> modern novelist, for, though he must perforce use the materials of which human
> lives have been made from the beginning, he handles and combines them exactly
> according to the latest fashions, and tells »the old, old story» with the newest
> notes, and, for all their shrewd ingenuity, with the most conventional comments.
> (Vol. 19, pp. 396—7.)

It seems to be necessary to try to ascertain what could be meant by
'the day' in this article, or rather what time limits could be regarded as
appropriate to the period in question. We find that there is no purely
literary period contemporaneous with the reign of Queen Victoria.
Legouis and Cazamian regard the years 1832—75 as characterized by
'The Search for Balance', which is followed by a period of 'New Divergencies' (1875—1940). Elton considers that the fifty years from 1830 to
1880 »form a real, not an artificial, period», i.e. not as regards ideas and
opinions, but »the history of the fine arts of writing.»[7] Cruse finds that
»that curious emanation known as Victorianism» lasted from 1837 to
1887 when »it began to weaken before the new influences brought to bear
upon the country.» In fact, there seem to be about as many opinions on
the most adequate way of dividing the nineteenth century into periods
as there are books on literature, thought, and social history.

Sadleir wants to divide the reign of Queen Victoria into three social
epochs: early Victorian, 1837—50, mid-Victorian, 1851—79, and late
Victorian »from about 1880 to the opening of the new century.» (Cecil,
however, includes George Eliot and Trollope in his *Early Victorian
Novelists*, thus, like most other literary historians, or critics, paying no
heed to any 'mid-Victorianism'.) Social historians are apt to put the end

of one period (whether called 'mid-Victorian' or not) some years earlier than Sadleir's limit between his last two epochs. S. M. Ellis considers the point in his review of the *Commentary*[8]; he regards its preface, called 'The Voice of an Epoch', as »an artful controversial bait», and does not agree with Sadleir's view that »on the death of Anthony Trollope in 1882 'there passed not only the Mid-Victorian novel but a social epoch also'.» According to Ellis »the particular social epoch depicted by Trollope had passed some years earlier, in the early 'seventies, and by 1882 an entirely new society had evolved.» But Ellis also objects to Sadleir's statement as to Trollope's literary significance, alleging that »at the same time the traditions and scope of the Mid-Victorian novel were being well maintained by many writers of the second rank, such as Blackmore, Wilkie Collins, William Black and Miss Braddon.» Today, at least, Trollope is commonly considered to have represented the traditions and scope of the Great Victorian Novelists in a different way than those writers of the second rank. His reputation has changed since Ellis wrote his review (1927).

In 1883 the *Dublin Review* (Vol. 40) finds that Trollope's most important works, his 'Chronicles of Barset', »are good photographs of clergymen and of their influence, lives and opinions during the two middle quarters of this century», and that in these novels »the representatives of the Anglican clergy of thirty years ago assume an altogether old-fashioned and old-world air, and (that) even their successors are passing out of date before that author takes final leave of them» (pp. 319—20). This statement by one of Trollope's contemporaries supports the opinion of Ellis in regard to the end of the social period referred to at least in the 'clerical' novels, or even puts it earlier.

The beginning of the period depicted in Trollope's novels seems to be vaguer. If they regard the point at all, Trollopians usually, like Sadleir, consider it to be the middle of the century. The opinion of the *Dublin Review*, however, which through its expression »the two middle quarters of this century» puts this beginning much earlier, is supported by the fact that Trollope was born in 1815, and was thus thirty-five by 1850; it seems very unlikely that his pictures of society could escape the influence of social conditions, or at least manners and conventions, prevalent in his formative years, even if, as Ellis thinks, such a henpecked husband as Mrs. Proudie's was not often to be found before the middle of the nineteenth century.[9] Still Trollope's setting is *intended* to be roughly contemporary, which is a check to his success when the social changes of the

Second Reform Era are setting in. In social history a mid-Victorian Epoch seems to be distinguishable, beginning, as Sadleir thinks, from about 1851, but ending about 1872, i.e. from the Great Exhibition to the social changes which will be referred to in Part I. With these limits the mid-Victorian period is, in the words of Sadleir (p. 14), Trollope's period 'to a peculiar degree'; but the preceding twenty-five years cannot be categorically excluded from his picture of life. To understand the background of Trollope's novels and the vicissitudes of his fame we have to consider the Victorian age from its beginning.

Outlines of Trollope's Epoch and His Relation to It

The Industrial Revolution, the most important cause of the changes of life in the nineteenth century (and today still in progress), had begun to be definitely perceptible already in the second half of the eighteenth century. The first fifty years of this Revolution entailed difficulties either not foreseen or not understood, anyway neglected by the authorities, and the consequent social misery and political perplexity were brought to a head by the beginning of the eighteen-thirties. The danger had to be coped with, and the result was the Reform Bill which was passed in 1832. This year is also regarded as the beginning of a new phase of the Industrial Revolution, 'the age of coal and iron', or 'the Railway Age', which put an end to the world of the stage-coaches, Pickwick's world.[10]

The 'thirties, so important to all England, was the decade when Trollope grew into manhood, from fifteen to twenty-five years of age. This decade saw the railway net beginning to spread, the first English steamship company for transatlantic traffic, and Fox Talbot's first photograph; it witnessed momentous parliamentary measures and Queen Victoria's accession to the throne.

The 'tempest of reform', which resulted in the first Reform Act, gave occasion to demonstrations of great animosity against the Anglican clergy. This public reaction was caused in part by the existence of »country gentlemen in orders, who rode to hounds, and shot and danced and farmed, and often did worse things», and the »pluralists who built fortunes and endowed families out of the Church»[11] — conditions still to be found among the clergy of Trollope's novels.[12]

Of all the social evils of this decade and the next the employment of children, even very young ones, in mills and mines seems to have been the worst. Although the sentiment of humanity then prevailing abolished slavery and gave birth to the Factory Act of 1833, it did not yet end the employment of little children, whose death rate was a grave accusation of society. Their fate in the mines, where the toll of lives was greater than in the mills, was described by the Commission of 1840—42 in a report »which shocked all England by its disclosures».[13] Writers and poets were roused to protest. *Oliver Twist* (1837—8) had already illustrated how cruelly children were treated in workhouses, an outcome of the New Poor Law of 1834. E. B. Browning published her poem *The Cry of the Children* (1843), a heart-rending appeal to the English nation. In the same year T. Hood in his *Song of the Shirt* complained against society on behalf of the overworked poor. Disraeli's novel *Sybil, or The Two Nations*, published in 1845, pictures not only the fate of poor children but the general conditions of the poor people at the beginning of Queen Victoria's reign.

The 'hungry 'forties' were a result of the unfortunate conditions beginning at the end of the preceding decade when the price of corn had risen and unemployment had become the constant trouble of the rapidly increasing population, condemning multitudes to workhouses and millions to starvation. These conditions and discontent with the suffrage regulations as well as with some questions concerning Parliament gave birth to the 'People's Charter' and the political movement hence called Chartism, which lasted from 1838 to 1848, ending with riots in Scotland and London and defeat of the Chartists. But for the revolutions in 1848 elsewhere in Europe, these riots would possibly not have occurred.[14] *Sybil* gives an account of the motives, the ideals, and the fights of the Chartists. In *Alton Locke* (1850) Charles Kingsley, too, »describes the aspirations of the Chartists, particularly the moral-force Chartists, with a familiarity that was the outcome of first-hand knowledge.»[15]

The book-title *The Two Nations* is often quoted as roughly indicative of the social state of early Victorian England: there were the poor and the rich, and the gulf between them was so wide, their conditions were so different, that they looked on each other as strange peoples. Writers who have held up the condition of the poor to the view of the public have often been praised on that account. Quiller-Couch thinks this concern with social evils is the reason why such names as Shelley, Dickens, Carlyle, Ruskin, and, from a later period, William Morris »live on the lips of men to-day» (1925).[16] If this were true there would not seem to be much to say for the future of writers not interested in *les miserables*. Still Quiller-Couch

himself, in the preface to the book quoted, predicts that Trollope »will
certainly come to his own some day.» And Trollope chose to write about
the other 'nation', the well-to-do, which did not seem to offer half so
much inspiration as the poor to a writer interested in social conditions.

The first novels of Trollope's that mattered to the public were
published comparatively late in his life, *The Warden* (1855) when he
was 40, and *Framley Parsonage* (1861), his first really great success,
when he was 45 years of age. Booth's statement that »he knew nothing
of society — social, intellectual, or literary — until 1861»[17] can only mean
that Trollope did not have much intercourse with persons of note until
that date. At the age of 40 any man may, however, be supposed to have
lived through the most receptive years of his life, and many of the
writers contemporary with Trollope had by that age been stirred by the
burning social events and conditions to write about them as has been
mentioned. Kingsley published his *Yeast* (1848) at the age of 29, *Alton
Locke* at 31, Dickens his *Oliver Twist* and *Nicholas Nickleby* (with its
Dotheboys Hall episode) at 26 and 27 respectively, while Disraeli
published *Coningsby* and *Sybil* in 1844 and 1845 at 40 and 41. Mrs.
Gaskell's novel *Mary Barton*, based on the industrial troubles of 1842—3,
was published in 1848 when the authoress was 38. It is a striking fact that
the social evils of his day practically left Trollope altogether cold although
his chief interest was society. Yet his name 'lives on the lips of men today'
more than those enumerated by Quiller-Couch with the exception of
Dickens.

A survey of part of Trollope's life will help us to place him in the social
picture of his period.

In the beginning of the 'thirties Anthony was still at school; on being
removed from Winchester he was sent to Harrow for the second time,
and stayed there till 1834. Being reduced to bankruptcy his father then
had to leave England, and migrated to Bruges where he was followed by
the rest of the family. In the autumn of that year Anthony went back
to England to become a junior clerk at the General Post Office in London.
There he stayed to August 1841 when he became a Postal Surveyor's
clerk in Ireland where his duty entailed frequent travelling about the
country. He married in 1844 and was promoted Surveyor in 1845. In
Ireland he remained till the Spring of 1851. After that he was transferred
to England for some years, went back to Ireland, made several journeys
abroad mostly on official business — to Italy, Egypt, and Palestine —

visited Scotland and the north of England, went back to Ireland, made a
journey to the West Indies in 1858, visited Spain in 1859 and was transferred from Ireland to England for good towards the end of the same
year. He visited the U.S.A. three times, Australia twice, and further
New Zealand, Ceylon, South Africa and Iceland.

Anthony's father, Thomas Anthony Trollope, was a lawyer whose
temper and manners made him unpopular with his clients and surround-
ings. He was singularly unpractical in his undertakings and the extravagant, cheerful irresponsibility of his wife, Frances, helped to ruin him.
He gave up his practice at the bar and took to farming, of which he knew
nothing, and devoted all the time he was not in the fields, or ill in bed,
to the compilation of an Ecclesiastical Encyclopaedia, which only resulted
in a useless manuscript, unfinished at his death in 1835. — If Frances
accelerated his bankruptcy, it was she who, from 1832 on, supported
the family by the money she made by her innumerable travel books,
novels, and essays. Her writing capacity and success must be regarded
as all the more wonderful as she was past fifty years of age when starting
on her career.

Anthony's school-time at Harrow in the 'thirties was not happier
than his earlier spell at that school. After an unfortunate business venture
in America Thomas A. Trollope had left most of his family there in 1830
and returned with his son Anthony to England, where he »took himself
to live at a wretched tumble-down farmhouse on the second farm he had
hired!» (A, 29.) From there Anthony was sent to school as a day-boarder.
He describes the first eighteen months of this time as the »worst period»
of his life:

> I was now over fifteen, and had come to an age at which I could appreciate at
> its full the misery of expulsion from all social intercourse. I had not only no friends,
> but was despised by all my companions. The indignities I endured are not to be
> described. As I look back it seems to me that all hands were turned against me —
> those of masters as well as boys. I was allowed to join in no plays. Nor did I learn
> anything — for I was taught nothing. (A, 29—30.)

The reason for his misery was partly the fact that day-boarders were
usually despised at Harrow, and partly the poverty of his home and the
oddity of his father. But, unlike Dickens, Trollope did not make use of
his experiences of school-life in his novels, nor did he caricature his
father in any of his heroes.[18]

Only as a junior clerk at the General Post Office (1834—41) did
Trollope come to know social conditions which he later thought interesting

enough as such to use as a background for a novel, *The Three Clerks* (1858).
In that position he tried to enjoy the gaieties of London on a scanty
salary and with no one to guide him in his ignorance of things. He was
in debt all the time. The novel gives us an idea of the life of such a clerk
at that period. Some of those experiences are repeatedly made use of
in his other novels, too.

Trollope's transference to Ireland for eighteen years (1841—59)
removed him from immediate contact with life in England, but it put
him in the midst of other living conditions which could not fail to rouse
in him something of the interest in social evils that was manifested by
those other writers mentioned above. In fact, his interest in both the
social conditions and the political state of Ireland never left him, perhaps
because the evils of the Ireland of his day were worse than anything in
the ruling country, and possibly also because it was only in Ireland that
Trollope came mentally of age. Nobody then living in that country could
remain unaffected by the »chronic starvation and frequent famine among
the potato-fed population, culminating in the disaster of 1847»[19], i.e. the
famine and pestilence which reduced the Irish population by about half
a million.[20] The pitiful state of things was partly due to the fact that »the
rural landlord of Ireland was a mere exploiter of other people's labour».[21]

Trollope's impulse to write novels on Irish subjects probably came
through Charles Lever, the successful Irish writer, whom Trollope met at
Cool Park, the house of Sir William Gregory, his old Harrow schoolfellow.[22]
The first two novels by Trollope, published in 1847 and 1848, were hardly
noticed at all, partly because they were the works of a beginner, and
partly because Irish subjects were unpopular. Only after he had become
known as the successful author of *The Warden* did reviewers begin to
give their opinions on his Irish stories, too. *Castle Richmond* (1859),
»the *locus classicus* in literature for description of the Irish famine»[23], and
The Landleaguers, unfinished at Trollope's death, are called by Sadleir
(p. 144) »sad accounts of wretched actuality in which characterisation
is submerged in floods of almost literal fact». These two books show that
social evils and political contention were subjects unsuited to his genius
as a novelist however persistently these Irish things haunted him all his
life. Still Ireland, the people he met there, his delight in the new kind of
work assigned to him, his mother's example as a successful novelist, and
finally his own ripening, all combined to wake the writing impulse latent
in him. On account of his Irish novels he may rank »as a capital document
for the social history of Ireland»[24], but, just as Sadleir (p. 144) points out,

it was fortunate that his discouragement in his first literary attempts and his chance transfer to England made him turn to other subjects.

Trollope himself tells us, in simple words as usual, about the germ of his success as a novelist:

> In the course of the job I visited Salisbury, and whilst wandering there one mid-summer evening round the purlieus of the cathedral I conceived the story of *The Warden,* — from whence came that series of novels of which Barchester, with its bishops, deans, and archdeacon, was the central site. (*A,* 95.)

This visit took place in 1851 some time after his transfer to the English provinces, but not until one year later did he start writing the novel, finished it in the autumn of 1853 in Belfast, and got it published in 1855. Like this 'first Trollopian novel' (Sadleir), the second one in this series, *Barchester Towers* (1857), was long in taking final shape, but when writing *Doctor Thorne* (1858) Trollope acquired his well-known working habits and began to turn out novel after novel with unbelievable rapidity.

The English clergy, regarded as nothing but individuals with social ambitions and ordinary human weaknesses and troubles, may be said to constitute the common theme of the Barsetshire novels, which therefore afford a peculiar interest to the social student of Victorian England. Something has already been said of the public animosity against the clergy displayed during the 'tempest of reform'. As a rule, however, the parish clergymen were respectable, and, in remote villages, even very useful in their manifold capacities as teachers, magistrates, and doctors, although they did not concern themselves much about religion.[25] Between 1836 and 1840 Acts of Parliament were passed that »removed the worst abuses in the distribution of endowments, and partially at least bridged the gap between rich and poor clergy — though not completely, as readers of Trollope's novels will remember.»[26]

Just as the reforms occasioned by the ever spreading Industrial Revolution spared England the political revolutions of other countries — making the English proud of their constitution — the reforms of the Church saved her from »the serious attack upon her that had been predicted alike by friend and foe.»[27] The Church Establishment had been unpopular not only because of its abuses and the old Toryism of many leading members of the clergy but also because of its antagonism to the religious movement of which John Wesley had been the greatest apostle. The Church, or at least many of its most influential leaders, renounced this religion as 'enthusiastic', but the movement did not stop outside the

Church among the Methodist sects of the poor; it penetrated into the very Establishment in the first decade of the nineteenth century and created the »powerful party of the Evangelicals».[28] Evangelicalism became rapidly the strongest moral force in English society, and is by Somervell (p. 101) said to have been »the principal ingredient in the state of mind which to-day (1929) we describe, contemptuously perhaps, as 'Victorianism'». Still the Evangelicals were not liked by some men of letters[29], among them Trollope, whose views, however, were tempered by his humour. Examples of the Evangelical or Low Church demand for strict 'Sabbath observance' are to be found in his novels, a demand he evidently regarded as uncalled for, but which the Evangelicals, by the middle of the century, were strong enough to enforce.[30]

The great social importance of religion in the nineteenth century is evident from the fact that politics then paid about as much regard to denomination as to class. Trollope's novels, however, give evidence of the subordination of the clergy of the earlier Victorian decades as can be inferred from Trevelyan's statement of conditions in the middle of the century: »In the more old-fashioned parts of England — let us say in 'Barsetshire' — the clergy were still under the patronage and influence of the upper class.» But elsewhere the Industrial Revolution had altered this order of things.[31]

Scarcely had Evangelicalism gained a firm footing within the Establishment when the Oxford Movement began to propagate the doctrine of the exclusively divine essence of the Church, which consequently was not to be subordinated to the State. After Newman's secession to Roman Catholicism in 1845, the movement manifested itself outwardly in candles and crucifixes on altars, in garbs and ritualism; and Puseyism became identical with ritualism. The movement was more generally called Anglo-Catholicism, a term which also came to be applied to the attitude of High Churchmen.[32] The Anglo-Catholic ideals of the 'fifties and 'sixties are also reflected in the Barsetshire novels.

Newman's secession to Rome gave an impetus to the Roman Catholic mission in England where the Church of Rome has ever since been gaining ground. But in spite of the Catholic Emancipation Act of 1829, this creed was by mid-century »still obnoxious to a strongly Protestant nation».[33] This is manifest in Trollope's reminiscences from the Ireland of the 'forties (*A*, 78), and in *The Landleagers*, too[34], although he wrote in 1876: »The religious enmity between the classes, though it is not yet dead, is dying out» (*A*, 78).

During Trollope's period »clergymen were being forced more and more to justify their position»[35] and a new field of activity was offered them by the new social conditions about the middle of the century. The 'Christian Socialism' of Charles Kingsley and F. D. Maurice was an attempt to apply Christian principles to industrial organization.[36] The 'Broad Churchmanship' of these men and others gave rise to severe controversies within the Church, which began in the 'fifties. But already much earlier a kind of Broad Church as well as a Christian Society had been among the leading ideas of Dr. Thomas Arnold, the great headmaster of Rugby (1828—42), »who changed the face of education all through the public schools of England».[37]

The cloth was, indeed, as the *North British Review* wrote in an essay on 'Mr. Trollope's Novels' in 1864 »a more glaring badge in these days than any other», and Trollope found that it was interesting enough to attract readers even if he used it as a mere setting for his pictures of life in a cathedral town and the small country parishes in England; it was enough if he took a wide range of clergymen into these pictures and made them recognizable as such through faithful indications of their manners and conditions, adding some light allusions to the controversies of the Church, whereas religion could be left entirely alone. Surely it is not too much to say that the intense life and great importance of the Church of his day, and its palpable reality to the general public, had a large share in Trollope's success.

However, the social interest in Trollope's stories comprises much more than the clergy both in the Barsetshire series and his other novels. This is the essence of his 'modernness' of spirit, appreciated so much in the passage quoted above (p. 10) from the *Dublin Review*.

The Victorian interest in its own age was a natural result of the material progress of which the Great Exhibition in 1851 was an imposing demonstration and, at the same time, a symbol of the raising of the general standard of life in England. The Exhibition could also be regarded as a confirmation of the fact that England had entered upon the period of prosperity which was one of the essential features of the mid-Victorian epoch. The causes of this prosperity were many; Halévy (p. 289) attributes it to the discovery of the Californian goldfield in 1848, which, through the influx of gold in the United States, increased the demand for goods from 'the workshop of the world'; but the demand could not have been met but for the adoption of free trade and the development of the railways and steamships.[38]

The tumultuous 'thirties had faded into oblivion; the 'hungry 'forties' with their Chartist riots were gone. The danger of revolution on the model of other European countries was happily past, and the fact could be looked upon as an evidence of the superiority of the »historic English way». »It is about this time that the word 'Victorian' was coined to register a new self-consciousness.»[39] In spite of the great aggregation of people in cities and industrial centres, British agriculture, too, was prospering in the 'fifties and 'sixties ;[40] there was no overseas competition as yet. »The basis of mid-Victorian prosperity — and, indeed, of society — was a balance of land and industry, an ever enlarging market for English manufactures, and a still restricted market for foreign produce.»[41]

The railways made it easy for townsfolk to reach even distant parts of the country for the purpose of shooting and riding to hounds, pastimes that Trollope made much of both in life and in his novels. But the countries of the Continent, too, attracted the Victorians; »Europe was the great playground of the English, who flocked abroad in thousands to spend their newly gotten wealth.»[42]

From 1850 foreign and colonial events began to draw more attention than domestic policy.[43] Such events were the gold discoveries in California and Australia, the *Coup d'État* of Napoleon III, Garibaldi's campaigns, Livingstone's journeys of exploration, and the American Civil War (1861—65), all of which had their share in the hopes and fears, thoughts and actions of the Victorians. The Crimean War entailed an improvement in nursing and hospital conditions owing to the energetic activity of Florence Nightingale. Fashion was also affected by this war: smoking returned to polite circles after a banishment of eighty years, beards after an absence of two centuries. »The typical mid-Victorian of all classes was a man with a beard and a pipe.»[44]

About mid-century the Crown, i.e. the Queen supported by Prince Albert, asserted itself as the centre of the State, a position it had not held for thirty years, but which was now based on a national goodwill it had not enjoyed for sixty years.[45] Both the Queen and Prince Albert were serious and virtuous just like the public spirit of the period, a spirit which the royal models, in fact, helped to encourage. »The typical man of the new age» manifested a »double anxiety to obey a given ethical code and to 'get on' in profitable business.»[46] Evangelicalism and Benthamism (Utilitarianism), however different in their pursuits, had combined to create the narrow conception of what Matthew Arnold called the 'Philistines'.[47]

Woman's position in Victorian society cannot fail to awake the special interest of readers of Trollope, whose novels are so much concerned with girls, love, and marriage. The crinoline alone could be regarded as symbolic of the mid-Victorian conception of the female[48] if only because it encumbered her motions. Herbert Spencer in his book on *Education*, published in 1861, gives us some idea of the ideal young lady about that time:

We have a vague suspicion that to produce a robust *physique* is thought un-desirable; that rude health and abundant vigour are considered somewhat plebeian; that a certain delicacy, a strength not competent to more than a mile or two's walk, an appetite fastidious and easily satisfied, joined with that timidity which commonly accompanies feebleness, are held more ladylike.[49]

And yet the early Victorian lady had been still more 'sheltered'; she had been too 'delicate' to work and even to walk more than a few steps. In the mid-Victorian period ladies still did not work, but they were allowed to walk and to partake with gentlemen »in the milder tournaments of the croquet lawn», and some even hunted as they do in Trollope's novels. These activities may be regarded as concessions to Victorian strenuousness and the general interest now displayed in outdoor diversions.[50]

The fact that a queen, not a king, was on the throne was no doubt inducive to the weaker sex to assert itself. The efficiency of Queen Victoria, Florence Nightingale, and other prominent women was inspiring. Voices began to be raised for the 'rights' of women, voices demanding for them: a share in work that could be done out of the home, better education, freedom from conventional restrictions as to manners and dress, and political influence. The demands gradually resulted in a considerable degree of emancipation towards the end of the nineteenth century.[51] Mill and Maurice were the most important early theorists who advocated an improvement in the education of women, and Mill's »little book *The Subjection of Woman* (1869) was the most important tract on the subject for a whole generation».[52] Just in the year before Trollope died the Married Women's Property Act was passed; till then a man had got the legal right to his wife's property at marriage.

Public opinion, however, was strongly against the Woman's Movement during the first decades of the Queen's reign. The Queen herself was, in theory, against the emancipation, »a process which may be truly named Victorian if only for the horror with which Victoria regarded it».[53] The prevalent idea of a wife's duty was expressed by a certain Mrs. Ellis thus:

It is the privilege of a married woman to be able to show by the most delicate attentions how much she feels her husband's superiority to herself — not by mere personal services ... but by a respectful deference to his opinions, and a willingly imposed silence when he speaks.[54]

Victorian fiction presents many docile heroines of this kind. The low level of feminine education — and it was very low, indeed, in the 'fifties — was chiefly responsible for this attitude. Little education or training for any useful work was necessary for the doll's part assigned to the wife in the rising middle class; her idleness was positively encouraged because as a mere ornament, chaste and observant of propriety, she was regarded as »a living testimony of her husband's social status».[55] And the mid-Victorian woman, gratefully as a rule, accepted such a position. Even up to the 'eighties »marriage to a man of their own or a higher social grade was the only recognised vocation for women not compelled to earn their own livelihood. It was this society life which absorbed nearly half the time and more than half the vital energy of the daughters of the upper and upper middle class», according to Mrs. Beatrice Webb's comment on 'The London Season'.[56] Mothers and daughters scheming to entrap young men into marriage is a subject that recurs in Trollope's novels with remarkable persistency.

The sexual relation between man and woman was a subject that the early and mid-Victorian members of the middle and upper classes could not refer to at all. The convention of prudery was an unbreakable law, and one of the things that later generations revolted against most fiercely.

The conception of the 'bourgeois rule' of Victorian England, entertained by Sadleir (p. 18) and others, is criticized by Trevelyan because, he says, the middle class »never had a party of its own outside commercial questions».[57] That is perhaps in part the reason why Trollope's novels, although six of them have actually been called 'political', display very little real interest in politics, which continued to be conducted by the aristocracy in spite of the democratic measures of the age.

Trollope's men and women mainly belong to the upper and upper middle class; his novels, apart from the 'Irish' ones, are very little concerned with the poor. The poor were still there, mostly in the slums of the big cities, but wages were raised, at least for the skilled labourer, in the 'fifties and 'sixties partly owing to »the prosperity of trade in those fortunate years when England was the workshop of the world», and partly for other reasons. Disraeli's division of the nation into only two classes could no longer be regarded as valid; a number of middle classes of

varying means had arisen.[58] The worst social evils had been alleviated,
and fiction as well as the public was concerned with 'progress' and the
brighter prospects of life.[59]

With the segregation of society into several classes came a keener
strife for precedence. Those immediately below tried to climb into at least
some sort of equality with those a little above, while those above were
trying to keep the distance, or attempted in their turn to reach the
next rung of the social ladder.[60] This strife belongs to Trollope's domain in
a special degree. It seems always to have afforded a great interest to
mankind both in life and fiction, but there probably never was a period
in English history when social precedence was so important to so large
sections of society as it was to Trollope's contemporaries. Even the earlier
unquestioned precedence of the aristocracy was in some danger now when
great fortunes amassed by business men seemed to equal 'blood', as
we find for instance in *Doctor Thorne*. But as a rule Trollope is even less
concerned with the aristocracy than with the poor. In his novels it is
usually »put in by way of contrast to the life of the gentry» and the
contrast favours the latter class.[61]

A few words must be said about the general level of education, the
improvement of which has contributed so much to democratizing society
and to other changes in it. In the 'thirties a large proportion of the working
classes could not even read, or write their names, and by the end of the
'fifties »a substantial proportion of the children were still not taught to
write».[62] From 1833 state grants were made to schools for the children
of the poor, schools set up by voluntary societies of different denomina-
tions who were hostile to each other. But the number of those schools was
insufficient. Only in 1870 was the Education Act passed which provided
for state schools to fill up the large gaps. The social importance of this
Act was indicated by the often quoted words of Robert Lowe: »We must
educate our masters.»[63]

For the middle classes the 'Public School' became the fashion through
Dr. Thomas Arnold's reforms in the 'thirties. But it was also the school
of the upper classes; it was expensive and »became a terrible self-imposed
burden on middle-class and professional families».[64] Other choices were
the grammar school and the day school. But most of the secondary schools
without university connexions »were turning out, at fifteen or so, the
boys who were to be the executive of the late Victorian industries and
professions, and could be fairly described as the worst educated class in
Europe». And in 1861 it was »found that the girls were even worse off

than the boys».[65] The harsh criticism of English secondary education
as the »worst in the world» originates from Matthew Arnold, who called
the aristocratic class the »Barbarians» to distinguish it from the »Philistine
proper, or middle class».[66] Arnold urged for state secondary schools for
the middle class, and the Education Act of 1902 may be regarded as the
posthumous result of his labours.[67] In spite of Arnold's criticism,
Trevelyan considers that »the higher culture of Nineteenth Century
England was varied, solid and widespread over a large proportion of the
community. The world is not likely», he says, »to see again so fine and
broad a culture for many centuries to come.»[68]

The improvement of the average reading ability was, of course, of
great importance to the press, the mouthpiece as well as the moulder of
public opinion. The press had steadily grown in bulk and power since
about 1770 when newspaper advertising began. The tax imposed since
Queen Anne's reign kept the price of newspapers high still in the early
decades of the nineteenth century, but in 1855 *The Daily Telegraph*
was established as the first penny London paper.[69] The Quarterlies,
marking a new feature in publishing, started with the *Edinburgh Review*,
founded in 1802. The *Quarterly* was founded in 1809, and the *Westminster*, by Bentham, in 1824. They chiefly contained essays on politics,
economics, and literature, and among the contributors were famous
writers and statesmen, such as Scott, Macaulay, Carlyle, Arnold, Can-
ning, and Gladstone. But by the middle of the century, according to
Somervell (p. 59), much of the earlier influence of the Quarterlies was
passing to the Monthly magazines; before the end of the century the
Monthlies were in their turn outstripped by the Weeklies, such as the
Spectator and the *Saturday Review*.

Periodicals — such as *Chamber's Edinburgh Journal* and the *Penny
Magazine*, both started in 1832 — were published for the working men,
too; some of them, like the miscellanies, contained short stories.[70] Novels
began to be published in shilling numbers or serials in journals, and no
single author did so much for the popularity of such publications as
Dickens. Already before the middle of the century the cheap periodicals
had millions of readers, according to Charles Knight.[71] In addition the
circulating libraries were catering for a great number of people. By that
time the writers could thus reach, entertain, and influence also the mass
of the working people and the lower middle classes.

During the mid-Victorian period new novels in book form were
usually published in three volumes at ten shillings and sixpence a volume,

which was the standard price since 'Scott and his business associates had imposed it' for *Kenilworth* in 1821.[72] Such books could only be bought by the wealthy, and this was one of the facts that had induced Mudie to start his famous lending library for the great middle class in 1840.[73] In the same year was founded the comic journal *Punch*, »the delight of every class»[74], but evidently most appreciated by the middle and upper classes. Trevelyan's statement of the level and range of Victorian culture is supported by the fact that this journal and Mudie's Select Library, both popular and still answering high moral and intellectual claims, could be ranged among the 'national institutions' before the end of the mid-Victorian period.

Thus, when Trollope started to make his name and for a good many years to come, the general prospects of success, fame and money were good for men of letters, and very good, indeed, for those writers who, like Dickens, Thackeray, Trollope, and Mrs. Gaskell, made social relations the themes of their works.

I

The History of Trollope's Reputation

Anthony Trollope is by Cazamian (p. 1200) placed, among the Victorian realists, in »one great group, relatively interconnected, that in which the desire for accuracy, stimulated by what is newest and keenest in the atmosphere of the time, claims as its justification the pleasure or the contentment inherent in the search for truth». As he began to receive due recognition, at first on account of *The Warden* (1855), and definitely after the publication of his *Framley Parsonage* (1861), he was frequently compared to the other writers of the group, especially to Thackeray and George Eliot. Often he was found to resemble Jane Austen, too, and sometimes Fielding. Even Scott, Dumas, and Balzac were referred to in the reviews of Trollope's books, though mostly only because of his similar prolificness. And although his contemporary Dickens is put in a different group by Cazamian, Trollope has often been compared to him ever since the name of Anthony Trollope began to be firmly established in the minds of his readers. Scores of lesser writers were mentioned by the reviewers just in passing to allow Trollope to soar so much the higher.

Of all these comparisons those to Thackeray, Eliot, and Dickens seem to be the most important as a measure of contemporary appreciation because these writers were the greatest of his contemporaries who treated somewhat kindred subjects. Often enough the comparisons were not unfavourable to Trollope but the general verdict was that, although he did not come up to their level, he, of all the contemporaries who could be compared at all, was next to these giants.

It has been alleged that Trollope's great merits were obscured by the competition of the many famous writers that happened to be his contemporaries; that he would shine with a brighter light if his age had been less crowded with great novelists because his real merits entitle him to a relatively higher rank among the novelists of England than is assigned to him in literary history. It is perhaps futile to discuss such a point, but a consideration of the actual competition he had to sustain will be a help to a correct perspective of his reputation.

Trollope's great period of writing began in 1855 and lasted for about twenty years, with seven years more of actual work but less fame. A chronological table of the writers working then, or just before, shows us the following points of interest. Charlotte Brontë died in 1855, Thackeray in 1863. George Eliot changed her style »when she left her 'Adam Bedes' and 'Silas Marners' for philosophical disquisitions in 'Middlemarch' and 'Daniel Deronda'», which the *Edinburgh Review* (Jan. 1884, p. 197), had »always regretted». (*Silas Marner* was published in 1861.) Dickens, who died in 1870, did not publish much in the 'sixties, having written the bulk of his best works long ago. Mrs. Gaskell, »the typical Victorian woman»[1] and Trollope's female equivalent though a lesser writer than he, still wrote a few stories in the 'sixties, but died in 1865, having given her best in the 'forties and 'fifties. Disraeli had written his famous trilogy already in the 'forties, but his *Lothair* was published in 1870. Charles Kingsley published four remarkable works of fiction between 1855 and 1865. Charles Reade and Wilkie Collins were the only writers of note who were in their prime still after 1865 simultaneously with Trollope; however, in the meticulous planning of their works and in their aims as 'sensationalists' (Phillips) they differed too much from Trollope to encroach upon his domain. Thus the 'literary competition' of the latter half of the 'fifties and the beginning of the 'sixties was rather keen, but the major part of the 'sixties and — if we do not consider George Eliot's 'philosophical' novels — the whole decade of the 'seventies left Trollope without any great living rival. George Meredith could have been one, but attained little recognition before the 'eighties, and even then failed to gain any great popularity.[2]

The competition of the dead writers, however, was not negligible. The statement of the *Dublin Review* in 1872 that there was little chance for 'the antique' and 'none for the merely old-fashioned' in literature (cf. above, p. 10) seems to limit the range of this competition to the recently dead, but that was serious enough, and as late as 1880 even the Waverley Novels were »among the books most frequently bought at railway stations».[3] Trollope's novels were compared with works that had enraptured their readers more than he could ever hope to enrapture his. In fact, very few of his novels enraptured readers; most of them were just quietly admired. »It's dogged as does it», the often quoted words of one of his characters[4], seem to be applicable to his own career as a writer. In his long and mighty flood of novels he was, as a rule, persistently sticking to his commonplace subjects and his pedestrian way of looking at things, conducting many of his best characters from volume to volume, or at least inserting them again occasionally in new novels, creating his Barsetshire — a new county, imaginary, but felt to be so entirely real and English that foreigners were enticed seriously to ask where it was — and interesting his readers as it were by virtue of his bulk just as much as by his art.[5] And critics began to compare him even favourably, in some respects, to the writers usually considered greater, but now dead or no longer popular or in their prime. He had the great advantage of being alive and of being able to remind his public of this fact by incessantly pouring out novels of approximately the same level.

* * *

Mudie's and *Punch* have been called 'national institutions'; so has Dickens, and, having stated this, Quiller-Couch (p. 5) remarks: »Our fathers of the nineteenth century had a way (perhaps not altogether a bad way) of considering their great writers as national institutions; Carlyle was one, Ruskin another. It was part of their stout individualism, nowadays derided.» In 1863 the *National Review* 'almost' conferred this distinction on Trollope, too, and the argument of the *Review* might be considered as so good an evidence of the writer's popularity at the time as to be quoted at some length:

Mr. Trollope has become almost a national institution. The *Cornhill*[6] counts its readers by millions, and it is to his contributions. in ninety-nine cases out of a hundred that the reader first betakes himself. So great is his popularity, so familiar

are his chief characters to his countrymen, so wide-spread is the interest felt about
his tales, that they necessarily form part of the common stock-in-trade with which
the social commerce of the day is carried on. — — — The characters are public
property ... More than a million people habitually read Mr. Trollope, and they
do so because the personages in his stories correspond to something in themselves:
the hopes, fears, and regrets, are such as they are accustomed to experience; the
thoughtfulness is such as they can appreciate; the standard of conduct just that
to which they are prepared to submit. (He is an author in whom a large) section
of the community sees as it were its own reflection, and who may himself unhesitat-
ingly be accepted as the modern type of a successful novelist. (XVI, 28—9).

In 1872 Trollope was considered by the *Dublin Review* as »the leading
novelist of the day» in the passage quoted on page 10. The beginning of
the article shows, however, that the critic was alive to Trollope's limitations, but liked him the better for them:

> Those who hold that the novelist's business is to delineate the manners of his
> own day, and to draw portraits of the people among whom he lives or whom he has
> opportunities of observing, those who, in fact, regard the novel as a product essent-
> ially distinct from the romance, will probably be disposed to agree with us in our
> estimate of Mr. Anthony Trollope as the first master of his craft now in existence.

As late as 1877 the *Edinburgh Review* (Vol. 146) gave thirty-four
pages to a very laudatory article on Trollope's novels, ranging from
The Warden to his latest, *The American Senator*. The article begins:
»We have little hesitation in asserting that the present generation owes
a larger debt of gratitude to Mr. Trollope than to any other writer of
fiction, living or dead.» His limitations are acknowledged, but, the
Review goes on, »unlike more eminent authors, Mr. Trollope has never
'written himself out', and, as we are glad to flatter ourselves, he shows
no signs of doing so».

Amy Cruse (Ch. XIII) enumerates among Trollope's admirers of the
'sixties and 'seventies several persons of a high literary or social standing:
Thackeray, R. L. Stevenson, Lord Rayleigh, Lady de Rothschield,
Walter Bagehot, Frederic Harrison, George Eliot, and FitzGerald, who
read *Barchester Towers* several times over, and, having tried in vain to
digest George Eliot, wrote in 1873, »Oh, for some more brave Trollope!»

As has been indicated, Trollope went on writing till his death in 1882,
whereas the social period to which his novels properly belong ended some
ten years earlier. A closer examination of his fame during the last dozen
years of his life seems to be called for.

* * *

According to Sadleir's minute exposition Trollope's reputation began somewhat to decline already about 1870, and definitely after 1876 when *The Prime Minister* had been published and considered a failure.[7] There had been failures before without injury to his general reputation.

> We have always the consolation of knowing (says the reviewer in the *Edinburgh*, 1877, Vol. 146, p. 458) that a *fiasco* more or less complete has no permanent significance. If we may forecast anything from a failure, it will be a reasonable expectation that the next piece of the author's work will be decidedly above his average. Mr. Trollope worked up by slow degrees to his present eminence, but there he has sustained himself ever since he reached it, and, for all we can see to the contrary, there he is likely indefinitely to remain.

A few years before, this optimism could have been reasonable. There were better works to come, and some worse, than *The Prime Minister*, but however well he might write, there did not seem to be any chance for Trollope any more to make such hits with the new generation as his clerical novels, or *Orley Farm*, had been long ago, or *The Eustace Diamonds* as late as 1872. And nothing less could have sustained him at his former height. The partisanship of Henry Reeve, the editor of the *Edinburgh*, 1855—95, was to little avail and apparently not much valued by Trollope himself.[8]

Reeve, who had probably himself written the article referred to above[9], spoke, of course, for the old generation. If a great many of Trollope's readers were still faithful to him in the 'seventies, when new subjects, a new mood, a new conception of society, and a new technique began to be adopted in literature, it was not only because these readers did not like the new fashion, but because they saw what Reeve calls the 'sterling merit' of Trollope 'in his special sphere'; and Reeve probably correctly expresses their satisfaction with the limits that Trollope had set himself, or that nature had set him, and with the things he specialized in, when he writes in the same article:

> He has seldom attempted to go beyond the powers he is conscious of, or to soar a sustained flight in an atmosphere too refined for his pinions. He has not the genius either of pathos, or of humour, or of satire, though he is very far from being deficient in any of these invaluable gifts. He has never written a great work of romance that will survive as the lasting monument of his fame; but then again, under the influence of too ambitious aspiration, he has never advanced to the brilliant authorship that chills and dazzles the reader with its cold, hard polish; or puzzles him with its perpetual mystery of inscrutable moral enigmas. (P. 455.)
>
> He seeks his unfailing sources of interest in his vivid pictures of English life, with their fresh yet realistic colouring. — — — He has never sent his ambition fluttering after the conception of strange and erratic genius, nor has he stooped to inventing deformities of moral perversity. (P. 461.)

As writers of 'inscrutable moral enigmas' Reeve could have had in mind the Brontës, George Eliot, and Meredith, to name a few of the greatest of Trollope's contemporaries in this field. When speaking of 'deformities of moral perversity', Reeve was perhaps thinking of part of the doubtful literature engendered by the 'rage for sensationalism'[10] that had set in already in the 'sixties beginning with *The Woman in White* (1860) by Wilkie Collins; he could have been thinking for instance of Hardy's *Desparate Remedies* (1871), one of the books influenced by Collins.[11]

Still, by the time Reeve wrote his article, Trollope had occasionally begun to try his hand at novels which in their centre of interest differed from his usual genre. Sadleir (p. 313) puts it like this for the time after 1870:

> He realised that he was regarded as *démodé*; that he had become a survival from the 'sixties . . . A little angrily he turned his immense dexterity to the fashioning of further novels — some in the new manner of psychological analysis, others to the new design of ruthless realism. They were very good novels — better than most of those they challenged; but they did not impress the revolutionaries so much as they displeased his former adherents.

Already in 1867 Trollope had begun the psychological novel *He Knew He Was Right*, which was published in 1869, the very year regarded by Sadleir (p. 298) as »the peak year of Trollope's reputation». The author himself was not pleased with this experiment (*A*, 280), but he had other reasons, too, for being disappointed about this time. According to Sadleir, Trollope greatly injured his reputation by his failure both as an editor of *St. Paul's Magazine* and as a candidate for Beverley about the same time, and by getting involved with various publishers of comparatively low standing when the Magazine failed. Of »these three misfortunes in 1868 and 1869» Sadleir (himself a publisher) apparently regards the »unlucky change of publishers» as the worst. Trollope then »became primarily a writer of novels for serial, of novels whose subsequent book issue was less important than their magazine appearances». »And this», says Sadleir (p. 301), »in an author of Trollope's capacity and achievement, is a sure mark of decadence.» This conclusion seems somewhat remarkable since Sadleir knows that »Charles Reade had this same experience and at about the same time», and that »Charles Lever also met a similar fate.» These two writers were very popular, too. — There seem to be good reasons for supposing that by this time, after the period of the cheapening of reading matter »from 1825 onward for about forty years»[12], the publishers had become more and more reluctant to issue as expensive three-volume novels such stories as had been serialised in cheap magazines in the preceding months.

In the slight fall of prices paid for Trollope's novels from 1870 to 1876 Sadleir sees an indication that the author was, in regard to his reputation, »in the first stage of decline. The second stage», says Sadleir (p. 299), »began in 1876, after which date the market sagged dangerously. From then to the end of his life there was rapid decadence.» By 'the market' Sadleir obviously means the market for Trollope's novels only, not for novels in general. But surely the state of the general book market must be considered if we are to infer anything from the prices paid to an individual writer. It is considered by the *Edinburgh Review*, Jan. 1884, which states that »the conditions of the market for novels have been revolutionised of late». The *Review* is »not speaking of writers of exceptional genius», but »of novelists of capacity and talent, who turn out such readable books as Trollope wrote»; it finds that the chief cause of the decline in prices paid to such authors is due to the circulating libraries with which the publishers have to deal before a new book can be published. »The pecuniary success of the best of books is stifled by the system.»[13] In some degree the book market was probably also influenced by »the economic frost which stole over England after 1873» and lasted to the end of the century; it was marked by a general fall of prices and by unemployment.[14] In view of these circumstances it is difficult to agree with Sadleir that the decline of prices for Trollope's novels, or even the preference publishers gave to the idea of serialising his novels, was *per se* any indication of a decline of his popularity.

One of the most interesting results of Trollope's experiments within new literary domains was *The Way We Live Now* (1875), by Hugh Walpole declared to be »one of the most remarkable of all English novels published between 1860 and 1890». Walpole (pp. 165—6) adds:

This novel, had it been written by anyone else or had it been published anonymously, would never have been allowed to pass out of English fiction, but because it came after a long series of novels by the same hand, and because its author had been for some years before its appearance far too readily »taken for granted» by the critics, its remarkable qualities remained unperceived.

Even Henry James 'took him for granted' to such a degree that he could write in 1883: »With Trollope we were always safe; there was sure to be no experiments.» To James *The Way We Live Now* was only a »copious record of disagreeable matters», a book testifying to the »savour

of bitterness» he had acquired »as he grew old and had sometimes to go
farther afield for his subjects».[15] — Anyway this book, like some others of
the novels of Trollope's last years[16], induces the suggestion that, had
Trollope been a younger man in good health, he could have definitely
and successfully adopted the new motifs and conceptions that began to
be appreciated in the 'seventies. Walpole (pp. 173—4) almost says as
much although he hesitates because of the occasional lapses »which
show the old Trollope sinking into a sort of ghostly repetition of his worst
literary self», and because Trollope is »fumbling and hesitating» in his
attitude to the new type of novel. The Stebbinses (p. 316) are more
positive of at least one side of his capability; in regard to some characters
in *Marion Fay* (finished in 1879) they write: ». . . all minor characters,
but frightful in their potentialities, showing how completely Trollope
could have dealt with morbid psychology had he not been deterred by the
wish to please his public and by his own scruples.» Thus the 'narrowness'
of the Trollope novel proper — with its clergy and country gentlemen,
its dutiful daughters and meticulous decorums — appears to be a deliberate concession to the mid-Victorian *Zeitgeist*, not an indication of any
narrowness of the author's mind.

According to Trollope's own declaration, *The Way We Live Now*
was written because »I was instigated by what I conceived to be the
commercial profligacy of the age», »a certain class of dishonesty», so much
so that he took »the whip of the satirist» into his hand. The accusations
were exaggerated for effect, and the author did not look upon the book
as one of his failures; »nor was it», says he, »taken as a failure by the
public or the press». (*A*, 307—310.) This statement contrasts sharply
with the conclusion of the Stebbinses (p. 291) who find that »an accumulation of unfavourable reviews» of this novel annoyed Trollope enough to
make him write his *Autobiography* in 1876 »in bitterness of spirit» »thus
heaping with his own hand the gloomy burial mound in which he was
to spend the decades following his death». I shall revert to the effect of
the *Autobiography* later. It is, however, difficult to imagine that Trollope
could have been foolish enough to let such bitterness prevail upon him
to write this book — which was to be published posthumously — as a
piece of polemical writing, as the Stebbinses assume. It might have been
written, as Charles Morgan (Introd. 7) points out, because at the time
the market was rather crowded with recent Trollope novels and he had
leisure for his memoirs and reflections, which he, like so many other men
of letters, had a natural wish to put down. At the same time it may be

taken as an indication of the fact that Trollope felt his physical powers
to be declining, which induced him to write this confessional book as
long as he was able to do so by his own hand. He had begun to suffer
from writer's cramp, and he needed more rest than during the many
previous years of overwork.

Though exacting less from himself, he still performed his daily task,
dictating most of his new works to his niece[17], but, as may be inferred
from the tone of the *Autobiography*, he hardly expected to be able to write
any new great successes, and did not much care except when, as has been
mentioned, *The Prime Minister* was so severely criticized (cf. note 7).
But he wanted to go on writing novels even if he was paid nothing for
them — »much rather than not write them at all», as he assures John
Tilley, his brother-in-law in a letter in April 1878.[18]

Trollope continued to be praised occasionally at least. As late as 1880
The Nation (Vol. 31) for instance, generally commending the author,
calls *The Duke's Children* »one of Mr. Trollope's most successful novels».
And about two months before his death he had the pleasure of hearing of
Cardinal Newman's good opinion of his novels.[19] But there is no denying
that his popularity was waning in his last years. *The Duke's Children*
caused the publishers a loss of £ 120, which Trollope offered to repay.[20]
In the *Saturday Review*, Jan. 22, 1881, he was compared to a cook that
had worked up »his comparatively limited materials» into a new compound
called *Dr. Wortle's School*. — The literary merits of *The Way We Live Now*
had been overshadowed by the displeasure it had caused; even Reeve,
in his article of 1877 quoted above, p. 28, had condemned the book[21],
and the accusation of the *Westminster Review* in 1875 that Trollope
resembled Lady Carbury (one of the characters in this novel) and, like her,
wrote up to »what may be called the paying point»[22] could very well have
been one of the seeds of aversion which the posthumous *Autobiography*
helped to develop into animosity.

To sum up so far, Trollope's reputation began to dawn with *The
Warden* in 1855, developed into brilliant daylight with the serialisation of
Framley Parsonage in the *Cornhill* from the beginning of 1860, was
strengthened by the diminished competition of other writers, especially
the death of Thackeray in 1863, reached its noon with *The Last Chronicle
of Barset* in 1867, and shone into the 'seventies, gradually declining, but
not yet expiring, towards the end of his life.

* * *

The Last Chronicle, commonly regarded as Trollope's best novel, was published in the very year of the Second Reform Act, »which created a new body of working-class electors equal in numbers to the whole of the old upper and middle class electorate».[23] The class whose life and manners supplied Trollope with his main subjects and included the majority of his readers, this very class made a decisive move — soon to be followed by others — towards raising the position of the workers just when Trollope was reaching the summit of his reputation. If the middle class by such moves »at the same time decreed (perhaps) its merging into another class»[24] or not, the outcome was a levelling by degrees, which was manifested by the spirit of revolt that had begun to permeate society by 1870, a spirit very much opposed to the conventions accepted in Trollope's novels, in which class distinctions were regarded as unchangeable.

This change of spirit is well described by Somervell (pp. 192—3), who quotes Bagehot as his authority. Before the Second Reform Act Walter Bagehot, in his treatise on *The English Constitution*, had »found that the secret of the success of our parliamentary system lay in the fact that we were 'a deferential nation'. The lower classes were content to be voteless, and to leave the franchise to their betters; the middle-class voters were content to elect upper-class members, and upper-class members to accept an aristocratic Cabinet. The masses, in fact, were hyponotized by 'what we may call the theatrical show of society'.» The idea of 'rebelling against the structure of Society' never suggested itself to those masses. If the 'deference' is exaggerated in Bagehot's picture, the element of truth in it is confirmed by Trollope's novels. — In the new edition of his book in 1872 Bagehot finds that the 'deference' has begun to recede, as he had feared it would, because of »a popular franchise, popular semi-education, and a cheap Press». The new attitude was not limited to the working classes as we find in Trevelyan's *Soc. Hist.* (p. 556): »In all ranks of life free debate of social customs and religious beliefs is taking the place of the settled creeds of the early Victorian era. John Stuart Mill in his *Liberty* (1859) preached the doctrine of revolt against the tame acceptance of conventional opinions, and a dozen years later such an attitude has become very general.»

Trollope is usually considered to have acquiesced in the conventions of his age more completely than any of his famous contemporaries[25], although the Stebbinses (p. 143) think his real »desire was to probe deep into human nature and to publish his discoveries, unrestrained by the

shabby-genteel limitations of his age». Whatever his original desire
was, in the novels that made his name he did abandon himself to the
ideas and beliefs of his age with a relish that amounted to an inspiration.
»Not only», says Sadleir (p. 368) »does he agree to the terms proposed by
life, but he glories in them», i.e. the terms of life in mid-Victorian England.
His tastes were identical with those of other Victorian gentlemen, as
Cecil (p. 246) points out; like them he »respected good birth; like them
he accepted unquestioningly the existing state of society. Indeed»,
Cecil continues, »his only quarrel with his age was that it questioned it
too much.»

This acceptance and acquiescence was all very well as long as the
period remained mid-Victorian, but according as the age was infused
with the spirit of revolt, in which he took no part, his popularity began to
suffer. In 1872 the *Dublin Review* could still aptly call him »the leading
novelist of the day»(cf. above, p. 10), but by that time his social standards
had begun to lose ground, and he was no longer »the most entirely modern
of novelists» that the same Review tried to make out. Such dashes of
superficial 'modernness' as occasional allusions to railways no longer
sufficed, nor could even such a recent novel as *Ralph the Heir* (1871) —
which contains much talk of socialistic ideas, but only to ridicule their
ignorant supporters — be regarded as complying with the new social
outlook of the 'seventies. (This novel is hardly noticed at all by the
important English reviews.) And, as has been stated, Trollope's experiments with the new style met with little success. The public of 'his period'
had been fond of looking into the mirror he held up to it[26]; now the readers
began to find that the picture no longer quite represented themselves
and they grew less interested. The faithful representation of contemporary
life and conventions had been one of Trollope's special attractions to his
readers; when that attraction began to fail, it must needs affect his
reputation.[27] In fact, Trollope had not been quite modern even in 1867
when *The Last Chronicle* was published (cf. above, p. 11). In his criticism
of Trollope in 1870, Friswell (p. 143) writes:

> Thank God, good people, whose goodness is confined to the fact that they do
> not swear, commonplace bishops and vinegary bishop's wives, squires and their
> educated do-nothing sons, girls who feebly intrigue as they play crocket for a good
> match, and are utterly regardless of good men, are passing away.

And the Stebbinses (p. 336) make out that Trollope was, at his death,
»twenty years behind his own times».

The Second Reform Act signified the dawn of a Second Reform Era

beginning with the enfranchisement of a large section of middle-class
people left without suffrage in 1832 and the working-men of towns.
Benthamite individualism and the *laissez-faire* attitude were being
abandoned and the result was an increasing number of collectivist
measures. But this result was perhaps as much due to the fact that
»the statesmen sought to attract the votes of the new electorate», which
was to be further enlarged by the Third Reform Bill of 1885.[28] England
continued to be ruled by the upper classes but they had to pay more
regard than before to other classes and the general tendency in politics
was clearly democratic and clearly marked off from the mid-Victorian
attitude. »The Education Act of 1870 was, for most English people,
the first sensible impact of the administrative State on their private
lives.»[29] The resulting School Board Elections gave to many people
their first experience, and aroused their first interest, in local government.
— Broad Church had been steadily gaining power in the aristocratic
Establishment; the demand for free thought in religious matters was
advocated by such publications as *Essays and Reviews* (1860), Bishop
Colenso's *Critical Examination of the Pentateuch* (1862—79), Seeley's
Ecce Homo (1865), and Matthew Arnold's *Literature and Dogma* (1873).
Through such writings the authority of the Church was questioned and
the belief in its creeds was shaken. *The Origin of Species* (1859) began a
new era in the history of science and religion, and was followed by
Darwin's second great book, *The Descent of Man* (1871), which caused an
equally great clamour among the scientists and the clergy.[30] Darwinism
helped to undermine the authority of the Church, and in some cases even
turned belief into disbelief. We notice that Mill's treatise *On Liberty*
and Darwin's first famous book were published in the same year, and the
effect of the works of these two men combined in encouraging freedom
of thought and discussion. The Church could no longer monopolize
Oxford and Cambridge, which in 1871 were made accessible to all irrespective of religious belief.[31] The Trade Unions became a force which could
no longer be ignored in legislation; in 1875 Parliament recognized their
rights. About the same time the laws as to women's property and personal
rights began to be reformed; the idea of the equality of the sexes, for which
Mill had pleaded in 1869 (cf. above, p. 20) — and to which Trollope was
strongly opposed[32] —, began to influence social thought and custom
already in the beginning of the 'seventies.[33]

In all the new collectivist measures of the time there was, however,
no common plan or purpose. They were brought about in a haphazard

manner, improvised according to momentary needs, or carried by one
party or the other to gain an advantage in political rivalry. Some
of the idealistic causes have been mentioned, but we must not forget the
further progress of the Industrial Revolution, which went on changing
the requirements and minds of people; it also changed the old rural
England which Trollope loved to depict.

»Victoria's England», says Trevelyan, »consisted of two strongly
contrasted social systems, the aristocratic England of the rural districts
and the democratic England of the great cities. The counties and the
market towns were still ruled and judged by country gentlemen to whom
all classes bowed.»[34] This state of things lasted until the collapse of
English agriculture in 1875 caused by failing crops and American competition in the corn market. The landed aristocracy was overthrown.
The Free Trade doctrine was the rule of the 'seventies and 'eighties and
nothing was done by the State to help the landlords and farmers »for their
day as the political rulers of England had gone by». The agricultural
labourers largely either migrated overseas or flocked into towns. In the
'nineties there was another agricultural depression.[35] — Rural life never
again became anything like that of the middle decades of the century.

The country life of Trollope's novels, the landed gentry with its
traditional routine, thus began to change and vanish after the middle
of the 'seventies. To the new generation which itself experienced the
change, whether with content or regret, Trollope's pictures could hardly
appeal very strongly. They no longer reflected contemporary conditions
in rural life; they were too recent to be regarded as social history; they
began to be looked upon as 'merely old-fashioned', the very thing the
Dublin Review, 1872, regarded as having no chance to interest his readers.
The English squires, so frequent in Trollope's stories, were becoming
insignificant as a class and therefore uninteresting to a period in which
other strata of society were in the ascendant. This is hardly noticeable
in the reviews of the time but the influence of social changes, when
observed at all by literary critics, are usually observed a good many years
after they have happened. (Friswell's statement about squires passing
away, above p. 35, is remarkable for its early date.)

Such great foreign events as the American Civil War (1861—65),
Bismarck's conquest of France (1871), and England's colonial wars,
besides the possibilities opened by the Reform Acts, combined to make
people more politically minded than before. But »political ferment kills
literature; prolonged war kills it; social agitation unnerves it; and still

more the uneasy sense of great and unknown change», says Harrison
(p. 30) in 1895 with reference to the constitutional agitations of both
English and American people »in this last twenty-nine years». The political
interest awakened about 1870 and after that continually increasing was
probably one of the reasons why new novels of the old life-embracing
kind were getting scarce, a fact which helped Trollope to preserve whatever he could preserve of his reputation. As has been said before (p. 26),
there was no living novelist of note who could seriously threaten his
place in popular esteem in the 'seventies, if we do not reckon with George
Eliot by virtue of her early novels. And even in the 'eighties there was no
one who could fill it immediately after his death.[36] There seems to have
been a lull in the production of novels for the mass of readers before the
»new sort of writing in the form of the romance was springing up to
enliven the dull hours», the romance originating from Stevenson.[37] The
publishers, sensitive to the reactions of the public, found that the readers
were dissatisfied, and tried to fill the void by novels written by beginners.
A passage from the *Edinburgh Review*, Jan. 1884, p. 211, presents the
situation thus:

'A novel by a new author' appears to be a favourite form of advertisement now.
In reality, a novel by a new man presupposes a poor and inartistic effort. The
publishers may possibly have hatched a swan, but the odds are infinitely in favour
of the swan, at all events in the beginning, being 'an ugly duckling'. It is to be
presumed, however, that the publishers are practically wise in their generation,
and know how to appeal to the popular taste; and in so far that form of advertisement is significant.

The dilemma of the publishers could perhaps be explained by »the
decline of the novel as an intellectual force acting on the great body of
public opinion», a decline considered to have begun with Meredith and
Hardy because »neither was as close to the common life of the people
he portrayed as his great predecessors were».[38] Whether, like Batho and
Dobrée, we consider George Eliot to have been »the last great novelist
to be read by the mass of readers», or look upon Trollope — whose literary
'greatness' is still a matter of controversy — as the last great novelist
with such a wide appeal, the fact remains that the novel about this time
began to cater for different strata of society. A survey of some currents
and tendencies in Victorian thought and literature will explain the fate
of Trollope's reputation immediately after his death.

In the 'seventies and after, the social and economic changes in
England, and very likely the growth of the political and economic

influence of Germany and America, undermined Victorian selfconfi-
dence. The religious discussions referred to above diverged into
the field of science through the theory of evolution, which became
public property after the publication of *The Origin of Species*. According
to Batho and Dobrée (p. 29) the 'unnecessary' battle between religion and
science went on from about 1860 to 1890. No doubt it prepared the public
for the implicit or outspoken paganism of Swinburne, Meredith, Hardy
and other writers which forms a striking contrast to the conventional
attitude to belief of the earlier writers. There was, in Cazamian's words,
a 'revolt against mechanism and the authority of reason', a 'craving for
renovation', a tendency to enthrone feeling, long restrained by conventional rules, and imagination, earlier employed 'as a mere assistant'; there
was, in short, a revival of Romanticism, which had prevailed at the
beginning of the century. If the new Romanticism, 'steeped to the core
in the keenest intellectuality', is the dominant trait of this period, from
about 1875 to the outbreak of the Great War, and in fact revolts against
realism, realism is, on the other hand, continued and even intensified in
several directions.[39]

The French doctrine of 'art for art's sake' had its most influential
English representative in Walter Pater, the master of the Aesthetic
Movement in literature. A collection of his essays, *Studies in the History
of the Renaissance*, was published in 1873 and caused intense discussion.
Mrs. Humphry Ward later recalled »very clearly the effect of that book,
and of the strange and poignant sense of beauty expressed in it, of its
entire aloofness also from the Christian tradition of Oxford, its glorifica-
tion of the higher and intenser forms of aesthetic pleasure, of passion in
the intellectual sense — as against the Christian doctrine of denial and
renunciation.»[40] The aesthetic cult in England had been prepared by
Ruskin, who gave the first impetus to it in the first volume of his *Modern
Painters* already in 1844. The cult grew stronger in the 'seventies when
Oscar Wilde became its most conspicuous promoter, began to decline
in the 'eighties, and died in the 'nineties. Within art Ruskin and Morris
aimed at improving the taste of the common people, but within literature
the movement could be appreciated only by a limited circle, excluding the
'philistines'.

The receding self-confidence was followed by a greater susceptibility
to foreign influence. The French school of novelists as represented by
Flaubert, Zola, Maupassant, Balzac, and even Victor Hugo and Turgeniev
influenced English writers, and »for the first time in history we have a

whole body of English novelists determined to write novels which should
be works of art». George Moore, Henry James, Joseph Conrad, and even
Hardy evince this influence.[41]

The difference between the old Victorian novelists and the new
writers was noted by the *Century*, an American journal, as early as 1882:

> The art of fiction has in fact become a finer art in our day than it was with
> Dickens and Thackeray. We could not suffer the confidential attitude of the latter
> now, nor the mannerism of the former, any more than we could endure the prolixity
> of Richardson or the coarseness of Fielding. These great men are of the past, they
> and their methods and interests; even Trollope and Reade are not of the present.[42]

The new kind of fiction was highly praised in 1886 by the poet G. M.
Hopkins in a letter, with reference to Hardy:

> The amount of genius and gift which goes into novels in the literature of this
> generation is perhaps not inferior to what made the Elizabethan drama.[43]

Trollope's »light-hearted attitude» in his declaration:

> When I sit down to write a novel I do not at all know, and I do not very much
> care, how it is to end (*A*, 228),

is by Q. D. Leavis (p. 168) contrasted with the implications of *Notes on
Novelists* by Henry James; and she finds that Trollope's attitude »meant
that no barrier was placed between the best novelists of the age and the
ordinary reader». Those who could read Dickens, »the Edgar Wallace of
his time», could also read George Eliot, Charlotte Brontë, Thackeray,
and Trollope, »the novelists of the educated», whereas »the conscious
cultivation of the novel as an art meant an initiated audience».

By the time of Trollope's death the literary code of the aesthetes had
begun to influence the critics and aggravate the fastidiousness of the
intellectual readers; and with the young romance readers he had no
chance.

»Already when he died in the winter of 1882», says Sadleir (p. 362),
»the dispraises of a new and rebellious generation were mingling with
the respectful compliments due to a vanished eminence». — As we have
seen above and shall further see in the next chapter, the dispraises
had begun much earlier, not only because of his occasional failures
but for his inveterate failure to comply with certain artistic principles. —
The obituary notices written by his friends were »sympathetic, sorrowful
and moving; but those briefer ones that recorded the death of a novelist

and not of a man, were at best tolerant, at worst contemptuous». Sadleir
quotes *The Times*, Dec. 7, 1882, as typical:

> He could not manage very deep passion and had the sense rarely to attempt it.
> He could still less manage intellectual difficulties and had the sense still more rarely
> to attempt them ... No deep riddles, no unconquerable troubles diversified
> Mr. Trollope's stories ... It would be rash to prophesy that his work will long be
> read; most of it lacks some of the qualifications which that stern official who draws
> up the passports for the Land of Matters Unforgot insists upon.

And Sadleir has found that »only the *Saturday Review* gave the dead man
true and generous credit for his qualities».

Because of the revolt of the then modern intellectuals against the
spirit of the previous age, temporary oblivion would have been Trollope's
fate in any case, but he had made matters worse by his *Autobiography*,
which was published a few months after his death in conformity with his
wish. It was a challenge to fashionable criticism and Sadleir (p. 364)
puts the effect of it into very strong words:

> The book is a compendium of all that was most offensive to the new modishness.
> ... a man who went out of his way to deny his literary caste, ... a man blatantly
> English. ... flouted every artistic prejudice. (Etc.)

To be more exact, Trollope denied the necessity of any inspiration
for the sort of fiction he wrote, he compared his work to that of a cobbler,
he wrote to the clock producing so and so many words an hour, and
admitted that he wrote to earn money entirely disregarding — in the
words of the *Quarterly Review*, July, 1932 — »the particular snobbery of
the mid-Victorians, the shame of everything that smacked of trade»,
a snobbery peculiar to the aesthetes, too. Besides, the publishers could
not be very pleased with his disclosures of the relation between author
and publisher, of the haggling and bargaining and the considerations
of the lengths of novels.

But however severely Trollope was condemned in some quarters, in
several eminent periodicals the reviews of the *Autobiography* were unprejudiced and sensible enough although some of them at least were evidently
not written by men who knew him personally.[44] The *Spectator*, Oct. 27,
1883, was perhaps least flattering, but still recognized him as 'a man
of genius'. Richard Littledale in *The Academy* (July—Dec. 1883, p. 273 ff.)
thought that Trollope's »theory of work had much to do with his failures»,
and that »it is certain that his own reputation will rest mainly on a
small group of figures in a few of his books». The general praise of the
Westminster Review (Jan.—Apr. 1884, p. 83 ff.) is all the more striking

as the journal »seldom troubled to notice him»[45] and had been very offensive in 1875 about *The Way We Live Now* (cf. above, p. 33); it finds that
»Trollope took a high view of his work as a novelist», and ends the article
with a feeling of »gratitude for the pleasure — in the case of his autobiography, for the instruction also — which he has afforded us». Some
half a dozen more journals of note in 1883 and 1884, though wondering
somewhat at his theory and mode of work, reviewed the *Autobiography*
dispassionately or even with admiration; among them we find the
Edinburgh Review, whose editor, Henry Reeve, was faithful and understanding as usual.

But this only meant an extra farewell to Trollope. The eminent
journals felt that they had done their duty and spoke of him no more.

As has been said already, Trollope's reputation had been declining
for various reasons some years before his death, and besides he had
written too much, as the Stebbinses say (p. 336), »not to have wearied
the reading world». The *Autobiography* could only be shocking to the
aesthetes and the sentimental public, and put the seal to Trollope's
doom. Charles Whibley, however, writing in 1923, finds that »a weightier
cause of his passing oblivion», than either the *Autobiography* or the fact
that he had published too much, »was the sad truth that Trollope was
dead. A rising generation can forgive anything more easily than bodily
extinction. For the young a living dog is always better and greater than
a dead lion.»[46] This simple explanation is in agreement with another
commonplace, viz. »Every great man must go through a period of un-
popularity not while he is alive, but shortly after he is dead.»[47] However,
Trollope aggravated his sin of dying by having his *Autobiography* published, as has been mentioned, a few months after his decease. There had
been the usual feeling of *De mortuis nil nisi bene*, not fully embraced in
all the obituary notices, it is true, but still suppressing inordinate harsh-
ness. The challenge of the book was felt to be bad enough by itself,
but coming from a recently dead man, whom common decency required
to be remembered with reverence or at least forbearance, it must have
been felt to be twice as offensive. The dead man took unfair advantage
of his position and furthermore, as Sadleir points out, disarmed criticism
of his attitude to his work by his modesty and by openly disclaiming
any pretensions to be regarded as a genius.

But the ardent spirits of the new generation could not let matters
stand at that. If the challenge of the *Autobiography* could not be retorted
to, there was the huge bulk of his work open to criticism at any time and

from innumerable points of view. And it was attacked before and after the space of oblivion into which Trollope sank a few years after his death.[48]

At his death Trollope had still had a large and faithful public which is seen from the fact that over thirty of his books (new editions and a few new books) were published in the first half of the 'eighties, according to the *Eng. Cat. of Books.* »Nevertheless», as Sadleir points out, »in five years he was seemingly forgotten».[49] Within that time the *Westminster Review* once more changed its mind and published in its Jan.—April volume of 1885 an article called 'English Character and Manners as Portrayed by Anthony Trollope', which is singularly hostile to him; it ridicules the virtues with which he had endowed his characters and finds these characters generally dull or unpleasant and deficient in intellectual qualities; even his famous hunting scenes are disapproved of in the article. Character, manners, and hunting scenes had always been regarded as particularly strong points in Trollope. The review devotes nearly fifty pages to the annihilation of any such conception. — In 1887 a reminiscence of Trollope was to be found in Julian Hawthorne's book *Confessions and Criticism* under the heading 'The writer of many books'. Hawthorne describes his first meeting with Trollope, which happened in 1879, and gives a very sympathetic and perspicacious analysis of his character, which is quoted by Sadleir. But Hawthorne further speaks of the *Autobiography* as »the most interesting and amusing book that its author has ever written» mainly because it is an »unconscious self-revelation», and proceeds to review it and Trollope's novels with many good observations. He finds the novels interesting although he is not blind to the author's limits and shortcomings; he is apparently not at all prejudiced, and gives the reader a perfect surprise by writing without a warning:

> The world has long ago passed its judgment on his stories . . . To the view of the present writer, how much good soever Mr. Trollope may have done as a preacher and moralist, he has done great harm to English fictitious literature by his novels . . . But Trollope the man is the abundant and consoling compensation for Trollope the novelist; and one wishes that his books might have died, and he lived on indefinitely.

The prejudice against Trollope's works appears by this time to have grown so strong among the literary critics that there seems to be no possibility of his revival. And after 1886 the publishers ceased to issue new editions of his books.

*   *   *

In 1887, when Trollope's name sank altogether below the notice of literary criticism, the Queen celebrated the fiftieth anniversary of her reign; Victoria »was hailed as the mother of her people and as the embodied symbol of their imperial greatness» as Strachey (p. 244) puts it. As imperialism grew it was attended with a suggestion of mysticism in the public conception of the destiny of England. The long reign of the Queen had seen the immense changes of the social structure of the country and the growth of its prosperity and power. This fact gave Queen Victoria a prestige which, increasing towards the end of the century, contributed, no doubt, to the sentiment of imperialism, the »climax of which the second Jubilee was the symbol», to borrow from Somervell (p. 186). But the pomp of the second Jubilee (1897) was also what Young (p. 182) calls »an Imperial defiance» because »an area of fifty times as large as Britain had in ten years been added to the Queen's dominions». The Imperialistic period was involved in a Titanic chaos, of which no survey can be attempted here.

Kipling, who is regarded as the greatest exponent of the imperialistic sentiment, published his first book of short stories in the year of the first Jubilee. He introduced into fiction new themes with action as a vital element and his characters are often men in the British Army. Batho and Dobrée (p. 100) appoint him »the greatest master of the short story in the language». Kipling became the moulder of the mind of his people, »the prophet of the imperial ideal», the doctrine of which was based on such facts, or assumptions, as that the British race had proved its superiority in the struggle with other races, that the conquering people had obligations towards the conquered, and that the Empire represented a great obligation, 'the white man's burden'.[50] Kipling's stories and poems, themes and ideas represent an important part of the divergencies within the literature of the 'eighties and 'nineties. And whatever divergencies there were, they were all imcompatible with Trollope's world.

About the same time as imperialism, another principle became noticeable in the life of the nation, a principle applied ever since and today more than ever. It has proved a force which has revolutionized the ideas of social relations and made them totally different from what they were in Trollope's day. The new principle was socialism. Socialism is perhaps mainly a consequence of the Industrial revolution, but oddly enough it was comparatively late in asserting itself in the country that for a long time had been the very 'workshop of the world'. There had been some socialistic activity in the first forty years of the century and none in the next four decades, but in the 'eighties socialism returned, drawing from the doctrines of the Continental socialists, especially those of Karl Marx, who, in fact, himself had studied the earlier British socialists. This return was caused by the industrial depression which began in the middle 'seventies (cf. above, p. 31). Democracy had been granted in politics; now it was demanded in the distribution of wealth. The people became more class conscious than before and discovered that a capitalist class and a working class stood against one another with very contrary ideas. The Trade Unions had lately been given a legal status (cf. above, p. 36), but their first activities were limited to the interests of skilled labour; the Trade Unions became democratic only after the Great Dock Strike in 1889.[51]

Earlier in the century the novels dealing with social questions had appealed to the sentiments of their readers. They had treated some particular evils, trying to awaken pity and a sense of duty to help the needy. Carlyle and Ruskin preached the gospel of the necessity to change society as a whole, appealing not to the heart but to the intellect of the public. But the first book that really gave an impetus to the revival of socialism was *Progress and Poverty* by Henry George, the American writer on political economy and sociology; it was published in America in 1879 and in England in 1881, and it pleaded for the nationalization of land. Its author went to Ireland in 1881 to lecture just when the trouble with the Land League was acute, and George was arrested.[52] — Here we are reminded of Trollope's persistent interest in the social evils of Ireland, for the last time coming to life in his *Landleaguers*, in which the professional agitator is a Yankee. — In the year of the Great Dock Strike the *Fabian Essays in Socialism* were published with Bernard Shaw as one of the contributors.

Some people thought that the socialistic books, lectures, and newspapers did the working man more harm than good. Among them we find George Gissing, whose novels, however, mainly deal with the lower middle class and expose its lack of intellectual interests and its sordidness of life. He was influenced by Dickens, but unlike his master he could not suggest, or did not believe in, any remedies for the diseases of society.

Owing to the County Council Act of 1888 — a radical means of promoting 'municipal socialism' — the conditions of life could be vastly improved during the last two decades of the century. Among the new amenities were baths and wash-houses, public libraries, and lodging-houses for the working classes. »Tramways, gas, electricity and water were in many places municipalised.» — The 'safety' bicycle of the 'nineties, displacing the high-wheeled bicycle of the 'eighties, as well as football and cricket, games now popularized and spreading to all strata of society, contributed much to the 'new look' of England at the *fin de siècle*.[53] Already in the 'eighties, after the disappearance of the earlier cumbrous dress of the ladies, »the active movements of lawn tennis took the place of croquet as the game for the encounter of ladies and gentlemen», an evidence of the progress of 'the equality of the sexes'.[54]

In the upper and middle strata of society, including part of the working classes, religion was now less prominent than in the mid-Victorian era, and this was partly due to the critical tendencies already mentioned (p. 36), and partly to the new entertainments of every kind. The daily paper and cheap publications of every description had ousted the Bible from many households.[55]

The consequences of the standardization of life were becoming evident. »The standards of Victorian 'respectability' were beginning to crumble. The balance maintained between tradition and democracy, which had been the essence of the Victorian age, was giving way.»[56] The levelling tendencies of the new circumstances had been evident already to Mill, who had given his famous warning against this menace to culture in his book *On Liberty*. And literature, largely yielding to journalism, could no longer be trusted, as Matthew Arnold had hoped, to prevent the vulgarization of society, or at least those sections of society which could not appreciate the superior sort of writing that had lost contact with life.

In 1887 when the critics and publishers had definitely given up Trollope, Thomas Hardy's twelfth novel was published, Meredith had become popular by his *Diana of the Crossways* (1885), Stevenson was at the height of his fame, Henry James was preparing to increase his, and Gissing, a pessimist like Hardy, was beginning to be known. Hall Caine and Marie Corelli wrote to entertain the masses and began by this time to gain a wide popularity with their sensational stories. But the earlier Great Novelists — Trollope, too — were still cherished by a great number of readers.[57]

As has been mentioned (p. 39) the aesthetic movement began to flourish in the 'seventies; it shot up into an excessive cult manifesting itself in a variety of eccentricities in dress, outward appearence and manners on the model of Swinburne and particularly Oscar Wilde. These eccentricities must at least in part be looked upon as demonstrations against the 'philistines' like the similar manifestations of romanticism in the beginning of the century especially in Germany. The literature produced by the aesthetes abounds in paradoxes and unusual words and phrases, and the writers themselves are numbered among the English 'decadents' of the 'nineties, a group not clearly to be defined but spiritually united by »the outbreak of the instincts which had been repressed by the constraint of the Victorian period». Some of the decadents at last rallied round a quarterly, the *Yellow Book* (1894—7), but a reaction against the movement with its »despair, nihilism, and vain revolts» already set in in 1895. The exertion of national will-power required for the Boer War finally brought decadentism to an end.[58]

Of the 'new prose' of the 'eighties and 'nineties Oliver Elton (II, 371) says: »The new writers incline to concentrate on minute felicities of form, and to tesselate their style like a mosaic, or to carve it like ivory. They are not happy till they have got the phrase.» Similarly Quiller-Couch (pp. 139—40) remembers: »Passions of faith we had: the first commanding us (poor fellows!) to agonize in search of the right or most expressive word; the second to keep ourselves out of any given story.» And the favourite models of 'those who were young in the 'nineties' were the French and Russian writers who had already influenced the somewhat earlier English generation (cf. above, p. 39).

Political and social change and literary fashion thus seemed to give the Victorian writers no chance of being appreciated by the young and modern spirits. For Trollope was not alone in his condemnation. Thackeray, whom he resembled more than any other of the Great Novelists, was especially condemned because of his 'preachiness'.[59] Dickens, who had outrivalled Thackeray in popularity, was also sneered at in the early 'nineties because he was regarded by the Smárt Set as »crude, catholic, and an apostle of the obvious».[60] All three were denounced for the names of many of their characters, names which »spoilt the verisimilitude of their novels».[61]

The year 1895 has been mentioned as the date of the first reaction against decadentism. It is perhaps not a mere coincidence that in that very year two prominent critics took it into their heads to write about Trollope, the one to denounce him, and the other in a shy attempt to revive him. The critics were Saintsbury and Harrison.

What George Saintsbury says of Trollope in his *Corrected Impressions* (pp. 172—7) is interesting mainly because it shows what an influence the aspiration and fashion of the *littérateurs* of the time had even upon a middle-aged, learned man (born in 1845), in fact one of England's most erudite critics, whom at least 'The Chronicles of Barset' had once »given great pleasure». (Our interest in this article is greatly increased when we learn that Saintsbury later once more corrected his impressions of Trollope.) Perhaps Saintsbury's attitude to Trollope is chiefly determined by »the revolt from plainness» which he sees as »quite the most distinct literary feature of the last quarter of the century» in his *Short History of English Literature,* p. 796.

In the *Corrected Impressions* Saintsbury considers the vicissitudes of Trollope's reputation to be less striking than those of George Eliot's[62] because she had genius while he had none. Trollope seems to Saintsbury to be »the most remarkable example we have yet seen of the kind of writer who I suppose is destined to multiply as long as the fancy for novel-reading lasts». He is nothing but an *amuseur* like Theodore Hook in the generation before Trollope's.

They are of the same general kind (Saintsbury continues), and the motto of their kind is *Mene, Tekel.* I do not even think that any one is ever again likely to attain even so high a rank in it as Mr. Trollope's. I do not know that I myself ever took Mr. Trollope for one of the immortals; but really between 1860 and 1870 it might have been excusable so to take him. He showed the faculty of constructing a thoroughly readable story. — — Perhaps there is never likely to be very much, and still less likely to be too much, of such work about the world. And yet even such work is doomed to pass — with everything that is of the day and the craftsman, not of eternity and art. It was not because Mr. Trollope had, as I believe he had in private life, a good deal of the genial Philistine about him, that his work lacks the certain vital signs. — — But it never has the last exalting touch of genius, it is every-day, commonplace, and even not infrequently vulgar. These are the three things that great art never is. — — There is a very short road to vulgarity; and I think since Mr. Trollope's time it has been pretty frequently trodden by those who are hastening to the same goal of comparative oblivion which, I fear, he has already reached.

When referring to Theodore Hook (who died in 1841) Saintsbury touches upon a point which may be regarded as one of the particular reasons why Trollope had sunk into 'comparative oblivion', only Saintsbury's opinion on this point is the exact opposite of Harrison's. »Hook is of course», says Saintsbury, »at a much greater disadvantage with a reader of the present day — at least with a reader of my standing — than is Trollope. Much of him is positively obsolete, while in Trollope's case the mere outward framework, the ways and language of society, the institutions, customs, and atmosphere of daily life, have not had time to alter very strikingly, if at all.» In Harrison's opinion Trollope had fallen into disfavour, after he had ceased to be modern, just because the world of his novels was not old enough — only old-fashioned.

Frederic Harrison was fourteen years older than Saintsbury and, unlike the latter, not professionally engaged in literature. These two facts make it rather natural that he should look upon Trollope with another eye than Saintsbury. His essay on Trollope, here quoted from his *Studies in Early Victorian Literature*, 1895[63], might be taken as an indication that the reaction against decadentism was more spontaneous outside the circle of professional critics than within it. In the article which introduces his *Studies* Harrison gives a survey of the state of literature in 1895, and some of its points are quoted here as reflecting the views of the old generation.

What sons of their own time were Fielding, Scott, Dickens, Thackeray, Trollope: how intensely did they drink with both hands from the cup of life. George Eliot, George Meredith, Louis Stevenson, Howells, James, look on life from a private box. We see their kid gloves and their opera-glass . . .

It is the lady-like age: and so it is the age of ladies' novels. — — Men, revolting from this polite and monotonous world, are trying desperate expedients. But they are all wrong; the age is against it. Try to get out of modern democratic uniformity and decorum and you may as well try to get out of your skin. — — But let us have no pessimism also. The age is against the romance of colour, movement, passion, and jollity. But it is full of the romance of subtle and decorous psychology. It is not the highest art: it is indeed a very limited art. But it is true art: wholesome, sound, and cheerful. The world does not exist in order to supply brilliant literature; and the march of democratic equality and of decorous social uniformity is too certain a thing, in one sense too blessed a thing, to be denied or to be denounced. An age of colour, movement, variety, and romantic beauty will come again one day. — — Let us accept what the dregs of the nineteenth century can give us, without murmuring and repining for what it cannot give and should not seek to give.

Here is an eminent intellectual who is not impressed with the motto *l'art pour l'art*, and does not believe in the search for *le mot juste*. Harrison, the leader of the English Positivist group, naturally regards literature as something that should not be disconnected with life and social circumstances. We notice, however, that life at that time did not seem to offer much inspiration in his opinion; the pessimistic mood of the period of new romanticism oppresses him, too, in spite of the 'cheerful romance of subtle and decorous psychology'. And this was another reason for him to appreciate Trollope.

The abyss of disgrace into which Trollope had been flung is suggested by the fact that, in the beginning of his essay on him, Harrison finds it necessary to excuse himself for writing of him at all:

Some of our younger friends who read the name which heads this essay may
incline to think that it ought to be very short indeed, nay be limited to a single
remark; and it should simply run that Anthony Trollope has no place at all in
Victorian literature. We did not think so in England in the fifties, the sixties, and
the seventies, in the heyday of Victorian romance; and I do not think we ought
to pass the judgment now. I shall have to put our friend Anthony in a very moderate
and prosaic rank. But in view of the enormous popularity he once enjoyed, of the
space he filled for a whole generation, I cannot altogether omit him from these
studies of the Victorian writers.

Harrison devotes twenty-five pages to Trollope. He thinks that
Trollope's »reputation may perhaps partially revive, and (that) some of
his best works may be read in the next century». In conclusion he wonders
»why our new youth persists in filling its stomach with the poorest trash
that is 'new' — i.e. published in 1895, whilst it will not look at a book
that is 'old' — i.e. published in 1865, though both are equally unknown
to the young reader». In the middle of his essay Harrison himself has
given a solution of this 'curious problem':

If there are fashions, habits, and tastes which the rising generation is certain
to despise, it is such as were current in the youth of their own parents about thirty
or forty years before them. The collars, the bonnets, the furniture, the etiquette,
the books of that age always seem to the young to be the last word of all that is
awkward and »bad form», although in two or three generations these very modes
regain a certain quaint charm. And for the moment poor Anthony represents to
the emancipated youth of our time all that was »banal» and prosy some thirty
years ago.

This solution may describe a regular phenomenon (although Saintsbury did not think so), but no doubt the reaction against 'Victorianism',
with all its restraints and fixed conceptions, was stronger than the
usual revolt of young generations. We can trace the reaction in decadentism and the new romanticism (cf. above, pp. 46-7), and Harrison describes
it, somewhat unmercifully, in the apparent predilections of the youth of
the 'nineties:

The taste of our youth sets hard for a new heaven, or at least a new earth, and
if not that, it may be a new hell. Novels or poems without conundrums, without
psychologic problems, with no sexual theorems to solve, with no unique idiosyncrasies to fathom, without anything unnatural, or sickening, without hospital nasti-
nesses — are all, we are assured, unworthy of the notice of the youth of either sex
who are really up to date. In the style of the new pornographic and clinical school
of art, the sayings and doings of wholesome men and women who live in drawing-
rooms and regularly dress before dinner are »beastly rot», and fit for no one but
children and old maids.

Walter Crotch, in the number of *The Dickensian* already referred to (cf. note 60), tells us that »Dickens's decline coincided with the rise of the Decadents»; so did the decline of Trollope. According to Crotch the decline of Dickens's popularity meant that »his novels went, not unread by the public, but unnoticed by the litterateurs»; Rantavaara[64] mentions two new editions of his works published in the 'nineties. But during the fifteen years of the neglect of Trollope after 1886, not one of his most famous books, the Barsetshire novels, were republished. If »the contemporaries of Hardy, Gissing, and Meredith clung to their Dickens, Thackeray, and Trollope» (cf. note 57), they must have had recourse to old editions at least of Trollope for a considerable time.

When Crotch says that Dickens was not noticed by the *littérateurs* this must be taken to mean that the journals were indifferent to him. But Crotch says further: »Mr. Shaw, I am informed by one of his friends, almost regretted the passing of the period, because, as he put it, before Dickens became fashionable again, praise of him was a certain indication of genuine literary capacity.» Such praise then must have occurred in speech or just as hints in articles on other subjects. Similarly Trollope could hardly be neglected in such an article for instance as 'Novels of Adventure and Manners' in the *Quarterly Review*, Vol. 179, 1894. An indication that his merits were discussed in private during this period may be found in an article called 'From a Reader's Note-book' in *The Academy*, Jan.—June 1897. »It is impossible», the reader writes, »to agree with those who try to persuade us that the oblivion which has so rapidly overtaken much of Anthony Trollope's work is undeserved.» Although to this reader »'The Chronicles of Barsetshire' alone seem to possess vitality», the article is enough to show that Trollope was not altogether forgotten by the public.

A compiler of a 'History of English Literature' in this period could very well hesitate as to what space Trollope should be given. The difference between his reputation in these years and after the revival is clearly indicated by the space allotted to him for instance by Edmund Gosse in different editions of his *History of Modern English Literature*. In the first edition of 1897 Trollope is summarily dismissed in six lines, and so he is in the reprints of the next few years; in the tenth impression of 1923 his share is thirty-five lines or about one page, whereas Dickens and Thackeray enjoy two pages each in both editions.

According to the *English Catalogue of Books* none of Trollope's novels were republished after 1886 and before 1901 except for *Can You*

Forgive Her in 1889, *Marion Fay* in 1899, and *The Three Clerks* in 1900; thus the publishers practically took no notice of his novels for fifteen years. Then we find from the same Catalogue 4 of his novels republished in 1901, 10 from 1903 to 1905, and 10 again in the single year 1906. There is a definite interest and one looks for an explanation.

* * *

According to Crotch[65] the return to Dickens »dates from the year 1900, about which time references to him and to his works begin again to appear in the papers», and this return was »much more due to events than to any literary influences». Still, Crotch mentions only one event, the Boer War, which »was the end of British Imperialism; the end of the doctrine of the inevitable, and the first reawakening in England of admiration for manful qualities of resistance against odds». During the two and a half years that this war lasted »the Dickens *renaissance* took shape and form». As other causes Crotch mentions the literary influence of Bernard Shaw and Kipling. As the return to Trollope dates from about the same time, it is only natural to ask if the new interest in him, too, could not be regarded as due, in some measure, to the Boer War.

The South African War is by Crotch said to have had »an immense effect upon the mind of England; for it changed altogether the material and fatalistic view which we were beginning to take of all problems, both human and political». This wants some elucidation. As has been said, Kipling had contributed very much to make Imperialism a popular sentiment, and although he may have »loved facts but hated and feared reality»[66], the causes of British Imperialism were real and serious enough. The most serious was, perhaps, the formation of the German Empire in 1870; a strong British Empire was intended to outbalance this new power.[67] But British Imperialism had many a time been felt by the late Victorians to be a glittering show, a poor counterpoise to the efficiency of the German armies, factories, schools, and universities, which England could not rival even in 1897. When the Boer War started, it was at first a surprise to the English that the Boers dared to wage war at all against the powerful Britain; when the resistance had lasted over two years, the insular self-confidence had worn down very much indeed.[68] It became evident that public school education was not enough to ensure British superiority. And Kipling, the apostle of patriotism, discipline, loyalty, and efficiency, was ready to satirize the old presumption that battles could be 'won on the playing-fields of Eton'.[69]

The change of British sentiments effected by the Boer War, then, amounted to a sobering down, a revaluation of old standards, and this was also reflected in literature; decadentism was killed as has already been mentioned (p. 47), and the superciliousness towards the Great Victorian Novelists was beginning to abate. These events combined with a new factor to give the Victorian writers another chance with the public.

This factor was the new reading public that had arisen on account of the Education Act of 1870. The new readers had to be catered for with literature that was within their reach, a fact which must be regarded as a direct invitation for the publishers to return to the old novelists who were less 'difficult' than the modern ones. In consequence »the publishers of the early twentieth century began issuing whole series of cheaply reprinted classics».[70]

The result of the first tentative reissues of four Trollope novels in 1901 did not encourage the publishers to new experiments with his books in the next year. But now the critics had began to turn their attention to Trollope, too, as to other Victorians. The change of the public mind at the turn of the century had diminished the interest in the consciously artistic writers, and something had to be provided instead. The return to the old novelists was also encouraged by the fact that the last two decades of the nineteenth century had been poorer in fiction than the earlier period.[71]

As early as 1895 Harrison makes up his mind that contemporary literature »has infinite romantic resources, and an army of skilful novelists — and yet it has no single living writer worthy to be named beside the great romancers of the nineteenth century». »For the first time during this whole century now ending, English literature can count no living novelist whom the world, and not merely the esoteric circle of cultured Englishmen, consents to stamp with the mark of accepted fame.» Harrison goes on to comment on the »inevitable result of uniformity in education and discipline in mental training»; millions can write well but everybody is afraid of letting himself go — for fear of sneers and fastidious criticism — and originality is killed.[72] — In full agreement with Harrison, Elton (II, 370) writes: »The old geniality or hopefulness, which we have seen in the great novelists, gave way, in the strongest novelists of the new age, to a pessimistic or ironical spirit, 'noble' enough indeed in its own fashion, but an impossible thing for the world to live upon.»

The world at large wanted hopefulness, cheerfulness, and entertainment from literature, which was another inducement to return to the
Victorian novelists. The publishers may have thought that the old
writers were now to be considered essentially for the sake of the new
reading public, but to criticism the actual segregation of the readers
was somewhat inconvenient. The critics beginning to take new notice of
those novelists seemed inclined to apply the same standards to old novels
as to new ones, and found it hard work to give Trollope the recognition
they mostly wanted to give him. In consequence their reviews were
somewhat confused.

Harrison's essay on Trollope foreshadowed the interest awakening
in 1901; it was remembered and appreciated by later critics, e.g. Leslie
Stephen in 1902. Some share in the new interest in Trollope must, perhaps,
also be attributed to Henry James's article on him in *The Century*, New
York, 1883, written already before James had read the *Autobiography*,
but republished in *Partial Portraits*, 1888; for if James thought fairly
well of a writer (and he held that Trollope was in some respects admirable
and at least in some degree a man of genius), this writer could not very
well be considered quite negligible, at least not when the cult of pure art
had passed its heyday (James's opinion was referred to e.g. by Bettany
in 1905). In an article at some length in the *Dictionary of National
Biography*[73] Dr. Richard Garnett reminded its readers in 1899 of Trollope's
earlier reputation. But everybody did not agree with J. Bryce (p. 116)
that Garnett had given Trollope his due. Garnett's statement that »he
never creates — he only depicts» is severely objected to in the *Cornhill
Magazine*, Jan.—June 1901, by G. S. Street, whose praise of Trollope
as a great realist is in its turn regarded with some reserve by F. G. Bettany
in the *Fortnightly Review* four years later.[74]

Among the early reconsiderations of Trollope W. F. Lord's essay in
the *Nineteenth Century*, Vol. 49, May 1901, deserves special attention
here for two reasons: it compares Trollope's England with conditions
at the turn of the century, and it is a marked example of the frequent
doubt of the critics whether Trollope should be regarded as an artist or
not.

His work (says Lord) is, for the present generation of readers, dead; it is not that
the work is bad: it is because the world in which Trollope lived has passed away.
All Mr. Trollope's characters live under the domination of four leading ideas: the
supremacy of the House of Commons in the government of this country, the authority of the Press, the grip of the Church on the life of the nation, and the prestige
of the marriage tie.

Lord, of course, finds that these ideas can no longer be entertained, and what he says in regard to the first of them is interesting as an exposition of the political change, though not quite accurate as to the political influence of the middle classes; Lord writes:

Mr. Trollope's young men enter Parliament, or endeavour to do so, with the idea that they are aiming at the noblest position to which an Englishman can aspire, a position where they will be called upon to discharge important duties. In effect since 1882 we have . . . (had) a House of Commons with full liberty of speech but little or no opportunity for action. — — The Franchise Bill of 1885 — — brought about the extinction of the middle classes as a political force. As M. Leclerc points out the hard workers among the nobility have regained all, and more than all, of the authority wrested from them in 1832. They now rule by merit where formerly they reigned by privilege. Thus, whereas in Mr. Trollope's novels we find an idle and uninfluential nobility existing more or less on sufferance in a land controlled by a vigorous and prolific middle class, we see to-day a picture presenting precisely these features reversed: we see an all-powerful nobility controlling a country under universal suffrage, a depressed and indifferent middle class, and a flourishing democracy acquiescent in any rule that leaves them untaxed and provides them with abundance of work.

In these circumstances why should any man, not born in the purple, endeavour to enter the House of Commons . . .? — — The brains of the middle classes to go Egypt, to South Africa — anywhere except to St. Stephen's.

As to the political leadership after the Great Reform Bill, Lord's view is at variance with Young's statement: »The bourgeois ascendancy which the thirties seemed to promise was never fully achieved.»[75] (See also above, p. 22.) — In fact, Trollope's contemporary critics do not seem to share his enthusiasm for a parliamentary career; some do not even regard such a career as very suitable either for his middle class heroes or for Trollope himself. In a review of *Phineas Finn* the *Dublin Review*, Oct. 1869, expresses its surprise at such an ambition, which, indeed, was nothing but a personal fad with the author. The *Review* writes:

Mr. Anthony Trollope wishes to be a member of Parliament. It is difficult to understand why he of all men should be smitten by such a sore temptation. — — He can hardly be supposed to have retained to this time of his life any illusions as to the magic value of the letters of M.P.[76]

However, Lord's general argument that the changed political and social conditions had killed the interest in Trollope was advanced at a point of time when so much of vast import had happened since the novelist's day — colonial wars, scientific discoveries, improvement of amenities, the death of the Queen (who must have been looked upon by the new generations as a symbol of bygone times) — that Trollope's world was beginning to be invested with the interest of history; it was losing its character of being 'merely old-fashioned'. But even if his novels are »invaluable to a student of history», they are not, in Lord's opinion, likely to »have any vogue in the immediate future».

Lord finds many faults with Trollope as a novelist; »he was not an artist, he was a photographer», he says, repeating an old slogan. Then again he finds several admirable points in him, and is even ready »to claim a very high place for Mr. Trollope as a master of plot and narrative». Still he thinks that if »we are tempted to relent, and describe him as an artist, we are at once restrained by remembering the indignation with which Mr. Trollope himself repudiated the idea that he was any more of an artist than a bootmaker». — Lord's essay is essentially negative and only seems to point at the hopelessness of any revival of Trollope at that time.

Leslie Stephen, in the *National Review*, 1901—2 (Vol. 38) pleads with the readers »to make a little effort to blunt their critical faculty» for Trollope's sake.

> Nobody (he says) will listen to such an appeal; and yet if we could learn the art of enjoying dull books, it is startling to think what vast fields of innocent enjoyment would be thrown open to us. Macaulay, we are told, found pleasure in reading and rereading the most vapid and rubbishy novels. Trollope's novels are far above that level; and though the rising generation is so brilliant that it can hardly enjoy them without a certain condescension, the condescension might be repaid.

It certainly does not seem likely that anyone would listen to such an appeal even if it came from an eminent man of letters, himself convinced of Trollope's merits. Had it not been for such phrases — and there are, in this essay, several more of the same derogatory kind though advanced in a sympathetic spirit — Stephen's review of the *Autobiography* in the same essay, the first really understanding review of this admirable book, would perhaps have converted many readers into Trollopians.

In the United States, where Trollope had also once enjoyed a great reputation, three of his novels were republished in 1901, and the *Atlantic Monthly*, 1902 (Vol. 89) rejoices at the »signs of a Trollope revival».

Bettany's essay 'In Praise of Anthony Trollope's Novels', written in 1905 and referred to above, begins by stating that »within the last two years several newspaper writers have hazarded the opinion that Anthony Trollope is in the way of regaining his popularity». (As has been mentioned ten of his novels were republished in 1903—1905 in addition to the few in 1901.) In his survey of the »expert opinion» that has »long pressed hard upon Trollope», Bettany notes as one of »two interesting exceptions to the rule» the »fastidious cosmopolite, Mr. Henry James, who thus carries on Hawthorne's tradition of American admiration of 'the most English of writers'». The other exception is Street, mentioned above on p. 54, whereas even Harrison's view is by Bettany considered to have »an air of almost patronizing superiority». Bettany cannot but blame the *Autobiography* for having largely contributed to bring about the neglect of its author; »notwithstanding which», he says, »the right tone, I hold. in which to speak of Anthony Trollope is not the apologetic but one of eulogy». Bettany's praise is really worth reading as will be set forth in Part II.

By this time one invincible obstacle appears to be common to all friends of Trollope who wanted to revive him: they did not know how to advertise him with proper effect. They were convinced of his merits, and they thought they knew what they were, but these Trollopians were — unduly — embarrassed by his drawbacks, and, with the two exceptions of Street and Bettany, they could not help conveying their embarrassment to the readers of their reviews. Although the decadent offshot of the Aesthetic Movement had disappeared, the influence of the valuable part of it was to remain permanently, making also the critics more exacting than earlier, and they could not make Trollope accommodate himself to several important rules of art.

The »tradition of American admiration» was further carried on in *The Bookman*, March—Aug. 1905, by E. W. Harter, whose essay, 'The Future of Anthony Trollope', gives some interesting details of Trollope's position then:

> In the hearts of many of the passing generation there is a warm feeling for Anthony Trollope. In many private libraries he holds an honoured place, though some of the newer public libraries find that, though they must have Thackeray, Dickens, George Eliot, Reade, and even Wilkie Collins, they can easily dispense with Trollope. — — How exactly reversed is the story of his fame from that of Jane Austen's. One enters a large book-store and is offered beautiful, dainty editions of Jane Austen. One asks for Trollope and is told that it is difficult to get some of his novels, even some of his good ones. 'It will be necessary to place your order', and 'The *Autobiography* is entirely out of print.'

Harter finds that Trollope is a »sterling artist», whose »best work is true literature», and on the whole gives him more ungrudging recognition than the other critics since the new interest in him began.

> Why, then (he asks), if these claims be true, is Trollope read comparatively so little? »The ignorant masses of educated people», as Howells calls them, are in a way

responsible. A legend that Trollope is dull; the very knowledge that he is by way of being a classic; the feeling that his cult is not ultra in any way — these matters have wrought his undoing.

The critical understanding of Trollope and the sincere belief in his merits which we meet in this essay — and it could almost equally well have been written for English readers — seems to make Harter an early predecessor of Sadleir. We know now how truly Harter prophesies in conclusion:

> ... there is a very definite niche in the temple of fame for this artist. English letters are not so rich that such a real talent can be ignored. It is impossible to doubt that the present rather uncertain and sporadic recognition of his worth will in time spread and deepen until his true place is ungrudgingly allotted to him.

In some measure all these critics certainly helped to spread knowledge of and interest in Trollope; and in 1906 different publishers dared to reissue ten more of his novels. In the *Fortnightly Review*, July—Dec. 1906, T. H. S. Escott devotes an article to what he calls 'An Appreciation and Reminiscence' of Trollope and mentions his »present revival» as if it were taken for granted. In January 1909 Escott again composes an article on Trollope in the *Quarterly Review* probably occasioned by Messrs. Routledge's new edition of the Barsetshire series. Having referred to all the cheap reprints after 1901, Escott says: »It would therefore seem that there still exists a real and more or less general demand for Trollope's works among the classes of readers which have sprang up since he wrote. Whether he will share the immortality of his great contemporaries, Dickens and Thackeray, time will show.» After this follow three years of almost complete silence on Trollope, and then, in 1913, John Lane, the publisher of several new editions of novels by Trollope, issues Escott's large biography, one edition of which is called *Anthony Trollope, His Works, Associates and Originals*, while another simultaneous edition has the supplementary title 'His Public Services, Private Friends, and Literary Originals'.

Whatever value Escott's book may have as a source of information (the Stebbinses consider it unreliable, and Mr. Michael Sadleir, in a letter to me, further referred to on p. 63, says he thinks »Escott's documentation was very limited») it appears to me to be doubtful that it could have inspired much new interest in Trollope even if it had not been published at such an unpropitious date as one year before the outbreak of World War I. Its heaping of details and events in a rather pointless fashion makes the »narrative» dull reading. One characteristic is common to the two articles by Escott and his biography: Trollope's *Autobiography* is almost completely ignored in them. It is barely mentioned and Escott seems to take a curious pride in being able to dispense with it; apparently he hopes, by this omission, to give more prominence to his »twenty years' intimacy» with the novelist and to his quotations of Trollope's »table-talk».[77] But the vicissitudes of Trollope's reputation after his death were so intimately mixed up with his *Autobiography* that no passing over it could be of any service to a real revival of him.Still Mr. Sadleir, in the above letter, expresses as his opinion that Escott's book, though not good, »was genuinely pioneering, and had bad luck in being too early».

After Escott's first article written in 1906 the interest in Trollope seems to be flagging with the other essayists in the pre-war years at least in England. Perhaps they felt that they could say nothing that had not been said before. And apparently the publishers thought that the *Autobiography* was best forgotten. In her Trollope Bibliography Miss Irwin lists some half a dozen essays published in America in those years but only two English ones, both published in *The Times Literary Supplement*. One of them in 1909 reviews the new cheap editions of the Barsetshire Novels and repeats the old regret at Trollope's description of his mode of work in the *Autobiography*, which is regarded by the reviewer as a 'fatal admission'. With this opinion Arnold Bennett violently disagrees in a passage in the *New Age*, Sept. 23 1909. The other article in *The T. L. S.* in 1913 reviews Escott's Trollope Biography but neither the novelist nor his biographer finds favour in the eyes of the reviewer.

Historians of literature keep an eye on his reputation at this time, but Hugh Walker is the only one of them, as far as I know, who shows a real interest in him; he appreciates him with understanding in *The Literature of the Victorian Era*. Saintsbury in *The English Novel* (1913) is at pains to explain to himself as well as to the reader what should be regarded as Trollope's right place in literature because »it is a noteworthy thing, and contrary to some critical explanations, that, as his works drop out of copyright and are reprinted in cheap editions, they appear to be recovering very considerable popularity». In his little book *The Victorian Age in Literature* (1913) Chesterton calls Trollope — as one of the writers mirroring the mid-Victorian mood — 'a lesser Thackeray', and thus puts him in the shadow of one of the Great Novelists, the place usually allotted to him during his lifetime, and this seems to indicate the level to which Trollope's reputation had been brought by the efforts of the publishers, critics, and friends of Trollope before the Great War.

His significance had to be advocated in quite another way, and in other circumstances, to make a real appeal.

The beginning of the twentieth century almost to the outbreak of the War was characterized, like the Victorian age, by a belief in the future, a faith in progress, which was, however, moderated by the memory of the economic difficulties of the last quarter of the nineteenth century. Gas-light had begun to give way to electricity, and new vistas were opened by the invention and development of the motor-car and the aeroplane. But the socialism that had revived in the 'eighties was spreading vigorously in the Edwardian period, and the old Victorian trust in individual effort was further declining. The Labour Party secured a representation in Parliament in January 1906 and thus became a third party in the State; it influenced the policy of the Liberals, who during their ten years in office (1905—1915) initiated »measures of social reform on a scale beyond all precedence».[78] — The early part of the century was particularly the age of Shaw and Wells, and Samuel Butler joined them in their criticism of society with his posthumous novel *The Way of All* Flesh, published in 1903. Chesterton, H. Belloc, and some others, by Cazamian called traditionalists, were antagonistic to the audacious rationalism of Shaw and Wells. They wanted to model life on the traditions of the past, the ideal of the Middle Ages. All these brilliant writers, with their fresh views of life and its relations, were more or less in their prime in the pre-war period besides Kipling, Conrad, Galsworthy, Bennett and many others. If prose had been declining in the last two decades of the nineteenth century, the first decade of the new century marked a decided improvement in force, brilliance, and freshness, and this may have had some share in the difficulty of making the new generation see Trollope's true worth.

* * *

During the First World War the only two classes — in the words of Graves and Hodge — were the Fighting Forces and the Rest. This coherence dissolved with the Armistice, and the return to peace conditions was partly performed in a revolutionary and disillusioned spirit. The war had upset many previous ideas of class differences, behaviour, manners, propriety, and society in general. The further emancipation of women was perhaps the most conspicuous social phenomenon in the next few post-war years.. The scientific discoveries and mechanical inventions that had changed many outward aspects of life since the beginning of the century, had been stimulated by the war and enormously hastened these changes. The further development of the motor-car, the aeroplane, and wireless had gradually revolutionized all previous ideas of communication and the spreading of news. As regards popular amusement, it was the age of moving pictures and jazz-bands.

The industrial Revolution persevered in its tendency to create an impersonal society, substituting for the personal relation, master and workman, the impersonal forces, Capital and Labour.[79] With the full establishment of peace conditions class distinctions returned although they were not nearly so distinctly marked as before. The rise of the importance of the Labour Party was a salient feature of the immediate post-war period.[80]

American influence was strong in several spheres as a consequence of the decisive part the United States had played in the war towards its end. To draw further (mainly) from Graves and Hodge about a period still retained in the memory of half the people alive today: American terms were introduced into the language, for instance 'high-brow' and 'low-brow' for writers, books, and readers on different levels. The Americans influenced fashion and the conduct of women, business methods, journalism, and other things. But the French were the models in art and, to some extent, in literature. Impressionism, cubism, futurism, expressionism and similar movements in art became the fashion some ten or twenty years after they had been more or less generally known in France. The low-brow public after the war read story-magazines, Sax Rohmer's Chinese romances, some of the pseudo-scientific books by Jules Verne and Wells, the Tarzan books by the American writer Burroughs, Elinor Glyn's love stories, and P. G. Wodehouse. The high-brows were addicted to poetry, and their addiction had already begun during the war. Among the most famous high-brow writers of poetry and fiction were T. S. Eliot, James Joyce (whose famous *Ulysses* was published in 1920), D. H. Lawrence, Virginia Woolf, and Aldous Huxley; while Somerset Maugham had been prominent among the upper middle-brows ever since the beginning of the century. The most important literary periodical after the war was, and still seems to be, *The Times Literary Supplement*, first published in 1902.

It was a strange world, indeed, compared with the Victorian Age, and it is, perhaps, no wonder that the new world did not feel respect for that age. The Edwardians had criticized it; now it was being derided.

»The post-war generation of the 'twenties, at once emancipated and disillusioned», to quote Professor Basil Willey (p. 51), »found compensation
for its own aimlessness in mocking at the earnestness, the high tone, the
'moral thoughtfulness', of its grandparents.» And Lytton Strachey
»voiced better than any one else the ironical disrespect of the twentieth
century towards the Victorian age, charged with smug sentimentality
and half-voluntary purblindness».[81] It is odd to consider that Trollope,
commonly regarded as the most typical Victorian of all novelists, should
be introduced into such a world and gain recognition in competition
with the great number of modern, talented novelists, intelligent, original,
skilful, and with an immense variety of knowledge from different
spheres of life and science at their command.

A few years after the war there appeared two somewhat diverging
testimonies to the popularity of Trollope. Wilfrid L. Randell writes in the
Fortnightly Review, July—Dec. 1920:

It is not easy at first sight to find satisfactory reasons why the works of Trollope
fail to attract more than a very limited circle to-day — for in spite of some pleasing
and inexpensive reissues of the Barsetshire series his readers appear to be few.
If we freely admit that Charles Dickens was the finer artist, there yet seems not
such a great gulf between the two as to account for the immense difference in
popularity.»

(According to the *English Catalogue of Books* the last reissues of the series
had been in 1914 and 1915 with the addition, in the World's Classics
Series, of *The Warden* in 1918.) Randell considers the inadequate popularity of Trollope to be due to his lack of style and his way of putting himself
into the story.

The other testimony was to be found in Michael Sadleir's article, 'A
Guide to Anthony Trollope', in the *Nineteenth Century*, Jan.—June 1922:

It is easy in fiction to create a nine day's wonder, but hard indeed to win the
esteem of ninety years. Trollope has achieved that victory. Oblivion can now
never be his, for he has lived his bad times and survived. As must any artist worth
the name, he has suffered temporary eclipse — temporary, indeed, but so severe
as at one time to threaten permanence. He was scorned as dowdy and parochial
by the brilliant metropolitans of a succeeding generation. Only in the hearts of quiet
folk and among readers uninstructed in the genius of their own time were his books
remembered and cherished. Until, slowly and slowly, opinion has begun to change.
Indeed, Trollope is in a fair way to become once again the fashion. For a while he
will be honoured by the enthusiasm of the intellectuals. Then, when they have
turned their volatile benevolence to some other quarter, he will settle firmly in
the respect of the critical. And that will be at once fame and his deserts.

Sadleir goes on to give a summary analysis of Trollope's novels, mostly in groups. His article is pervaded by a tone of intimate familiarity with Trollope's works, a thorough understanding, and a conviction of his own competence to give the novelist his due. One feels that Trollope's reputation had at last passed into the hands of the right man.

But what had made Sadleir so confident of Trollope's future? Certainly no recent editions of his novels, for there had been none since those mentioned above, with the only addition of *John Caldigate*, reissued in 1922. While brooding on this question, I ventured to write to Mr. Sadleir himself and he kindly wrote an answer, dated Oct. 14, 1954, giving me some information on this point and some others. As recounted in the preface to his *Bibliography of XIXth Century Fiction*, Sadleir had been 'struck by the contrast between the small type one-volume reprints of Trollope and the novels of George Meredith in handsome three-volume state. If Meredith were published in this dignified and legible form, why not over the same period Trollope also?' He became 'a collector of Trollopian three-deckers' and gradually, as he read his first editions, 'an enthusiast for nearly all his work'.

It was obvious to me (Sadleir continues) that these novels were far more important in the genealogy of English fiction than the pundits of the day were willing to admit. Also — as I have no doubt was the case — a »discovery» of Trollope was imminent, and I was lucky enough to get in ahead of others and to have the use of the vital family material.

To this material, however, Sadleir had access only after he had written the above article.

One of the most important signs of the imminence of a 'dicovery' of Trollope was evidently George Saintsbury's essay 'Trollope Revisited' published in *Essays and Studies by Members of the English Association*, 1920, VI. In his *Trollope: A Commentary* Sadleir asks the reader to contrast Saintsbury's essay in his *Corrected Impressions* of 1895 (cf. above, p. 48 ff.) with 'Trollope Revisited' to find how the great critic in 1920 was 'conscious of Trollope's qualities where once he recognised only his limitations'. Saintsbury does not give any reason for his remarkable change of opinion, but says by way of apology: »A man had need to possess a curious and perhaps rather unenviable opinion of his own immutability, who thinks that any critical judgment of his is itself immutable.» But Sadleir (p. 365) thinks the change is due to the critic's increased age:

Seldom can the influence of the actual age of a critic on his opinions have been shown more clearly. The effect of personal maturity on critical judgment and the

manner in which the instinctive subversiveness of youth gives place to the more
tolerant understanding of middle age are brilliantly set forth in Havelock Ellis'
preface to his book *The New Spirit*.

Sadleir must have overlooked the fact that Saintsbury was no youth
in 1895. He was fifty, and he writes in 'Trollope Revisited' that, when
composing his *Corrected Impressions*, he had been acquainted with Trollope's novels »for an even longer period than that which has elapsed since».
It seems somewhat difficult to understand how anyone at fifty could be
charged with immaturity on account of his age. (Sadleir himself was not
even forty when his *Commentary* was published.)

But there is another kind of growth of the critic, a maturation
naturally increasing with age, but not necessarily caused by the advance
of age; this growth is admitted by Saintsbury himself, partly in his
'apology' mentioned above, but expressly in his *History of Criticism*
(II, 440—1) written almost twenty years earlier:

> Criticism is, on the one hand, an art in which there are so few manuals or trust-
> worthy short summaries — it is one which depends so much more on reading and
> knowledge than any creative art — and, above all, it is necessary to make so many
> mistakes in it before one comes right, that, probably not one single example can
> be found of a critic of importance who was not a much better critic when he left off
> than when he began.

Saintsbury himself is a striking example of the maturation of a critic
— if we are to consider the renewed and constant popularity of a writer,
i.e. the judgment of the common reader, as the supreme authority. At
fifty he had formed an opinion of Trollope, which to his puzzlement
seemed to be wrong about eighteen years later when he wrote *The
English Novel* (cf. above, p. 59), and which, after a lapse of seven years
more, he had to acknowledge to be definitely wrong because that was
now obviously the verdict of the 'supreme authority'.

I have maintained that Saintsbury's criticism of Trollope in 1895
shows the influence of the literary fashion of that time (cf. above, pp. 47-8).
This influence is evident from his enthusiastic appreciation of Walter
Pater's critical views in his *History of Criticism*, III (p. 544 ff.), published
in 1906, even if he may have, as he says, 'always held' them himself.
In 'Trollope Revisited' he does not give up his principles, but there are
different ways of adapting principles. Since the end of the previous
century a more tolerant spirit had been gaining ground in literature.
The aesthetes, surviving for instance in the 'Bloomsbury Group' (in
which Lytton Strachey was a prominent figure), were far from the only

literary authorities in the new century, and their mocking of the Victorians in the 'twenties was a phenomenon that only affected limited circles of readers. If it would have been difficult, and perhaps unimaginable, for a professional critic and literary historian who was jealous of his prestige to give Trollope due recognition in 1895, it was no longer so in 1920.

'Trollope Revisited' contains much praise although the critic's provisos are numerous. After a survey and scrutiny of Trollope's works and characters, Saintsbury gives his new opinion of the novelist's place in literature here condensed:

> I do not think that he will, by the best judges, ever be thought worthy of the very highest place among novelists or among English novelists. He is by no means only '*for* an age'; but he is to a certain lowering though not disqualifying degree '*of* an age'. Short of Austen, Scott, Thackeray and Dickens, I do not know any nineteenth century novelist whose superiority to him in some ways is not compensated by their inferiority in turning out personages and incidents of actual contemporary life.

And Saintsbury ends his essay by —

> commending Trollope, as the first step backwards, to any one who has the praise-worthy desire to free himself from the most degrading of intellectual slaveries — that of the exclusive present.

Although such careful wording could hardly make any proselytes, Saintsbury's change of opinion may have strengthened Sadleir's confidence in Trollope's future.

In a letter of 1950 from the Oxford University Press, the publishers of the World's Classics series, I was told that »after the first war the combined enthusiasm of Sir Humphrey Milford (the Publisher to the University of Oxford) and Mr. Michael Sadleir led first to the inclusion of the *Autobiography* in the series, with an introduction by Mr. Sadleir.» Thus in 1923 the once 'unfortunate' and today famous book was reprinted for the first time since 1883. For forty years it had been tabooed, and not even after the partial revival of Trollope's novels had anyone dared to republish it. But Sadleir (and no doubt Sir Humphrey Milford, too) understood its true value, and perceived that the book, after all the ado about it, could not be ignored in an attempt at making the public appreciate Trollope according to his real deserts. And in his Introduction to the new edition of 1947 (The World's Classics) Sadleir is pleased to be able to write:

> By its very intransigeance and assertive bluntness (it) has remade more than ever it unmade, has re-established more effectively than ever it disestablished,

the fame of the man who wrote it and of the long list of wise, tender, and unpretentious novels which he created.

Already in Charles Whibley's review of the edition of 1923, the book was asserted to be »among the few best autobiographies which have been written in English»[82], an opinion commonly shared ever since.[83]

In 1924 *The Claverings* was included among 'The World's Classics' with an Introduction by G. E. Street, the old Trollope enthusiast, who did not think that the critics had »quite reinstated him yet». But having referred to this edition in their aforesaid letter to me, the publishers write:

> By this time a world wide demand for Trollope was established, and our reprints followed thick and fast in no very obvious order — some of them because the kindness of the author's son, Mr. Henry Trollope, put the novels published posthumously (and thus still in copyright) at our services; others at the suggestion of individual readers.

The great number of new editions of Trollope's novels published after 1923 according to the *English Catalogue of Books* and the statements of many essays and reviews confirm that the demand became wide and was steadily increasing after that date. In addition to the new edition of the *Autobiography* (reprinted in 1924 and 1928), the increasing number of essays on Trollope and the references to him in various books helped to maintain and intensify his popularity.

As no other single individual has done so much to revive Trollope as Michael Sadleir, it might be excusable here to quote from his letter to me already referred to, his own account of the circumstances which helped him to bring about the standard work *Trollope: A Commentary*, first published in 1927 and reissued seven times by 1947:

> In 1920—21, when my children were small, I rented a little house near Stroud in the Cotswolds. Just across the deep valley through which runs the railway and the canal, in the small town of Minchinhampton, lived Anthony Trollope's son — Henry Merivale Trollope.
>
> As the idea of writing something about Trollope — biographical, bibliographical, perhaps both — took firmer hold of me, I dared to write to Henry Trollope, sending him the *Nineteenth Century* article to which you refer (as well as some bibliographical publications mentioned by Sadleir — »this was about 1924», he says). Henry Trollope responded kindly, asked me to visit him and after some delay expressed himself willing to help in any way possible the full-length biography now contemplated.

It was thus the 'vital family material' was left to his disposal.

Although there can hardly be a doubt that Sadleir's biography was the main influence in the revival of interest in Trollope, Sadleir's own

tribute to the Publisher already mentioned seems also worth quoting
from the same letter:

> The rapid establishment of Trollope as a permanent major novelist was largely
> due to the enthusiasm of the late Sir Humphrey Milford of the Oxford Press, who
> included a long list of the novels in the *World's Classics* and so assured for them
> an immense distribution.

The First World War might have been an indirect, a general cause
of the vogue of Trollope. The war was followed by disillusionment for
the next few years, but as disillusionment is nothing to live upon, it was
conquered by a yearning for a world of set values and no serious social
or political problems. Writers like Joyce and Virginia Woolf retired
into private worlds, and the common reader was disposed to retire
into Barsetshire, as is indicated by the popular writer J. B. Priestley in
the *Saturday Review*, Nov. 12, 1927:

> Barset is a capital place to end the day in because it is so different from the rest
> of the world we know. It is indeed a haven of rest. We are, it seems, all nerves
> and baffled aspirations — — and our novelists must write about us as they find us.
> (But) those people in Barset, so comfortable, so dull, so limited in their ideas, so
> rigidly fixed in their social life, are better people to read about than those clever
> fellows and bold girls who drift from studio to night-club, from Oxford to Florence,
> in the novels that pile up on our tables.

And Trollope was not only read but honoured as never before, which
we find for instance from Desmond MacCarthy's declaration in his
Portraits (1931, p. 272):

> I say without hesitation that he is held in higher estimation than George Eliot,
> and that not a few consider him a greater *novelist* than Thackeray (against this
> Trollope himself would loudly protest), though they would admit him to be very
> inferior to Thackeray as a writer.

Desmond MacCarthy's own high opinion of Trollope's work is so
much the more remarkable as he himself »was an unmistakable, though
'humanized' variation of the intellectual school of our prophets», i.e.
the 'Bloomsbury Group'.[84] His appreciation is explained by his general
view of the novel (p. 271):

> It is tenable that one of the mistakes of late nineteenth-century and early
> twentieth-century criticism has been to regard the novel as »a work of art» in the
> same sense that a sonata, a picture, or a poem is a work of art. It is extremely
> doubtful whether the aim of the novel is to make an aesthetic appeal. Passages
> in it may do so; but it aims also at satisfying our curiosity about life and engaging
> our sympathies quite as much as at satisfying the aesthetic sense.

* * *

The Second World War, with its greater horrors for the civil population
of England than those sustained during the First, sent readers to Trollope's
novels in exceptional numbers. The Publishers of the World's Classics
write in their letter previously mentioned:

There is no doubt that the greatest demand for these books was during and
after the war, and the demand still (in 1950) remains fairly high. It is difficult,
however, to disentangle the influences which caused all books to be in very much
greater demand during this period. It is clear, however, that the B.B.C. programmes
of dramatized versions of Trollope's books maintained this demand and increased
it for the particular book being dramatized at the time, as this is apparent from
our experience with other books by other authors dealt with in this manner by
the B.B.C.

The letter further discloses that »at the present moment there are thirty-
three of Trollope's books in the World's Classics». Besides, many other
publishers had reprinted his books, as they were out of copyright. That
such a number of Trollope's works should be on any publishers' list in
1950 was more than even his most devoted admirers before Sadleir
could reasonably have expected. By that year, however, the demand
for his books had passed its peak, which was probably reached during
the B.B.C. campaign.

The Listener, Dec. 28, 1944, contains an article called 'The Decline
and Rise of Anthony Trollope' by H. Oldfield Box, whose account of his
own reason, as well as that of the public, for turning to Trollope at this
time corresponds to the general sentiment voiced by Priestley in 1927.[85]
Box had found that from the beginning of the war his pleasure in reading
Trollope »was heightened by the contrast between the stormy times we
live in and the quiet solid security of Trollope's own mid-Victorian
world». When he had turned some of the novels into radio plays, »it soon
appeared that many thousands of listeners» shared his sentiments. »We
are, in fact», says Box, »at the height of a Trollope revival.» In May 1945
Elizabeth Bowen contributed to the 'campaign' with a radio play called
Anthony Trollope, A New Judgment, in which a young soldier, when
leaving for the front, chooses novels by Trollope to be his companions
in the trenches.

The enthusiasm for Trollope about this time must have been something like a craze to judge from John Wildman's short article on 'Anthony
Trollope Today' in the American journal *College English*, Apr. 1946.
According to the information Wildman had gathered for this article
from booksellers and publishers, it was »almost impossible» to buy any
of the Barsetshire novels in London, Cambridge, or Oxford: the scarcity

of Trollope's works was »the result both of the smallness of editions and of the tremendous revival of all Victorian and earlier classics, but in Trollope more than in anyone else». Owing to the paper shortage the demand could not be adequately met by the publishers. A letter from Sadleir had given Wildman to understand that the demand for Trollope was not merely a passing whim and that ordinary readers — not collectors — were willing to pay up to four times the normal prices for his books, which was more than could be accounted for by the fall in the value of money. Besides the radio interest in Trollope Wildman mentions an adaptation of *The Last Chronicle* for the stage called *Scandal at Barset* and presented in London from Oct. 5,1944 for about three months. — The immense vogue of Trollope is further attested to by Box again, who writes in *The Trollopian*, March 1946, that his revival »has now reached truly amazing proportions», and that »any of the author's fifty or so novels are eagerly seized upon». Box is »able to state with conviction that in England at any rate he is at present more widely read than any other of the great classical novelists». — In America, too, according to an article by C. J. Vincent in *Queen's Quarterly*, 1945, LII, No. 4, Trollope's novels were »being read not only by the elderly or by the discriminating few, but by the public at large, by all classes and all ages».

In 1945 Mrs. Lucy P. Stebbins and her son, Mr. Richard P. Stebbins, published in New York a book called *The Trollopes: The Chronicle of a Writing Family* — »a bitter and relentless assault on the integrity, personal character, and hitherto accepted reputation of Anthony Trollope» (Sadleir[49]) — but still the first psychological approach on a large scale to Anthony Trollope's life and letters. Another indication of the growing scholarly interest in Trollope was the start, in the same year, of *The Trollopian*, at first a semi-annual, then a quarterly journal, in 1949 rebaptized *Nineteenth-Century Fiction*, and from the beginning edited by Professor Bradford A. Booth in Los Angeles.

In October 1945 Charles Morgan, in his Introduction to a new edition of the *Autobiography* (the one used as a source in this study), concluded that Trollope was no longer a 'party-feud' as 'avowed Trollopians were ceasing to worship and anti-Trollopians to denigrate him'; his reputation was 'settling down' and he was »almost, though not quite, in his niche». Sadleir, in his comments on the book by the Stebbinses[49], expresses some doubts as to such a peaceful issue: »It will be interesting to see how, between the Scylla of gullible affection and the Charybdis of acrimonious culture, Trollope and his reputation fare.» However, the »strange amalgam of admiration for and antagonism toward Trollope himself»[86] manifested by the Stebbinses does not seem likely to do his reputation much harm, fanciful and prejudiced[87] as their biography must seem to most readers.

* * *

Looking back on this survey of Trollope's revival I find that, however much different critics and enthusiasts contributed to it, the three wars of Britain in this century seem to have been essential for calling forth the mood in which this disputed mid-Victorian novelist could best be appreciated. There is a revival after the Boer War[88], rather tentative at first as if the approaches were made with a feeling of shame because of the previous neglect, but then getting stronger till about 1906 when at least the interest of the critics seems to be abating. After World War I there is again a return to Trollope, similarly setting in with noticeable force a few years after peace but while the shock of the war is still remembered; in the 'thirties the interest begins to decrease; there are fewer articles on Trollope, and, according to the *English Catalogue of Books*, the number of republications is about one third of that of the 'twenties. By the time of World War II Trollope is, however, generally known to the reading public of all classes; the readers already turn in enormous numbers to his books before the war is ended; and then again, a few years after the war, the enthusiasm is abating. The B.B.C. programmes with Trollope themes probably intensified the readers' interest beyond the 'normal', but the response was ready and the effect more noticeable than with other old novelists appearing in the radio programmes.

»There are recurrent times in a sensible reader's life», says D. MacCarthy (p. 275), »when he may prefer Trollope's novels to almost any fiction.» The story of Trollope's reputation shows that such times have recurred in the life of the whole English nation. When the minds of people have been unsettled by the calamities of war and its consequences, when the world of the present has seemed to be tottering, the English have turned to the stable world of Trollope's novels again and again. This seems to be one of the highest tributes that can be paid to any writer.

II

The Criticism

The history of Trollope's reputation seems to show that in the end it
is the common reader that is the supreme critic, which was also the conviction of Dr. Johnson[1] and Trollope himself[2], as it is bound to be the
opinion of all writers who strive for popularity. Still for an answer as
to what has been considered the intrinsic value of his books, we must
mainly look into the criticism by his contemporaries and posterity in
articles and books.

If »only such reading-matter as is of permanent value», i.e. worth
reading for a longer period than some years after its publication, if only
such writings deserve the title of literature[3], then the history of Trollope's
reputation further shows that much of Trollope's work deserves that title.
And even if, like Lucas (pp. 200, 325), we demand that the writer worth
the name shall prove his power by keeping 'a long enough hold on intelligent readers', 'at least a century', we find that Trollope has satisfied
the condition. By Liddell's and Q. D. Leavis's classification of literature
his work should further be regarded as 'high-brow', the only group calling
for serious literary criticism, although it is of course not 'high-brow'
with the implication 'difficult'.

The purpose of this study requires that the main interest should be
focused on the question of the standards by which Trollope has been considered to possess or not to possess permanent value. Were it possible to
sound the opinions or the impressions of the common reader on these
points, that would no doubt throw some additional light on the matter, but
hardly as much as Lucas (p. 326) seems to think when writing that an
author may receive »a few letters from readers (usually far more interesting
than reviews)» and that the readers he »must respect remain hidden in the
crowd». If, as Lucas says, the reviewers (by which he apparently also
means the critics) are »largely geese», it is difficult to understand why the
average readers should be less like geese if asked to give an opinion.
The common readers seem to me to be the supreme critics only by their
unconscious mass reactions during a long period towards a certain work of
art, but those reactions say nothing of its qualities in detail, the qualities
by which the work pleases or displeases. Lucas's censure of critics seems
to be due to his view that »the pleasurableness of art remains a matter of
individual taste» (p. 303) and should not be discussed, in which he sides

with »Jeffrey's fundamental principle that taste has no laws, and is a
matter of accidental caprice».[4] Still the appeal of art has been discussed
since time immemorial irrespective of individual tastes and at least some
general views have been commonly accepted as guides. Saintsbury says
of the value of the critic's work:

> Unless the critic is utterly incompetent and bad . . . his mere contact with
> a work of art must result in something useful, in a critical datum and fact for the
> future. It is very unlikely — if he is a person of even rather more than average brains
> it is practically impossible — that the exact equation or conjunction of his tempera-
> ment, and the character of the work, will ever recur. — — That he judges under a
> certain system, even a wrong one, will not detract from the value of the result,
> save in quantity. — — And this result, in its own line and sphere, is as much a
> »thing», and a thing of interest, to the critical student of literature, as a new beetle
> to the man of science, or a new judgment of the House of Lords to the man of law.
> Nay, to such a student it has a higher interest still: it is in rank and line (*mutatis
> mutandis* again) with the work criticised, with a picture, with a sonata, as a thing
> of art itself.[5]

Leslie Stephen's view on this point seems also worthy of note: »Even the
most reckless criticism has a kind of value when it implies a genuine
(even though a mistaken) taste. So long as a man says sincerely what he
thinks, he tells us something worth knowing.»[6]

A. The Judgments by Trollope's Contemporaries

According to Kathleen Tillotson (p. 16) the beginnings of serious
criticism of novels are noticeable in the eighteen-forties although the
critics then »did not get very far in establishing critical standards».
In his *Autobiography* (p. 232 ff.) Trollope gives his own opinion of the
state of criticism in 1876, and must be taken to refer to the criticism of
fiction:

> Literary criticism in the present day has become a profession — but it has
> ceased to be an art. Its object is no longer that of proving that certain literary work
> is good and other literary work is bad, in accordance with rules which the critic
> is able to define.

Here Trollope seems to overlook the fact that what 'rules' critics had so
far defined applied to poetry and drama; and it is difficult to imagine
what earlier criticism he regards as an art if it is not in the first place
that of Johnson and Coleridge, who did not, however, criticize novels.
He is evidently mixing literary categories. After that he is both thinking
and speaking of fiction only:

English criticism at present rarely even pretends to go so far as this. It attempts, in the first place, to tell the public whether a book be or be not worth public attention; and, in the second place, so to describe the purport of the work as to enable those who have not time or inclination for reading it to feel that by a short cut they can become acquainted with its contents. Both these objects, if fairly well carried out, are salutary.

This is mainly the method of the reviewer in *The Times* where, especially in 1870 and the next few years, the articles on his novels are hardly anything but fairly long summaries of their contents. — Such guidance, Trollope continues, is at any rate better than no guidance at all. But 'real substantial criticism is costly', and »critical ability for the price we pay is not attainable. It is a faculty not peculiar to Englishmen, and when displayed is very frequently not appreciated.» Trollope seems to be ignoring the criticism of the quarterly and monthly periodicals, perhaps because they mostly dealt with whole batches of his books, several of which had been long in the market when the articles appeared; the criticism in these periodicals contains a great deal more than is even hinted at by Trollope.

Trollope does not, however, deplore so much the lack of critical ability as the dishonesty of the critic who »tells us what he does not think, actuated either by friendship or by animosity». And this, he says, is »the sin in modern English criticism of which there is most reason to complain». He probably knew what he was talking about, but as he himself has never been accused of having deviated from his own 'golden rule' »that there should be no intercourse at all between an author and his critics», we may take it for granted that his critics were not very much actuated either by friendship or animosity — not until he himself gave offence to some of them, or to those whose opinion could influence the critics, by *The Way We Live Now* and his *Autobiography*.

In his classic essay (as Mrs. Tillotson calls it), 'The Art of Fiction', first published in 1884, Henry James approaches his subject in the form of criticism of Walter Besant's pamphlet published under the same name. The want of a theoretical basis for this art up to that time is pointed out by James in the beginning of his essay:

Only a short time ago it might have been supposed that the English novel was not what the French call *discutable*. It had no air of having a theory, a conviction, a consciousness of itself behind it — of being the expression of an artistic faith, the result of choice and comparison. I do not say it was necessarily the worse for that. — — It was, however, *naïf*; and evidently if it be destined to suffer in any way for having lost its *naïveté* it has now an idea of making sure of the

corresponding advantages. During the period I have alluded to there was a comfort-
able, good-humoured feeling abroad that a novel is a novel, as a pudding is a
pudding, and that our only business with it could be to swallow it. But within a
year or two, for some reason or other, there have been signs of returning animation
— the era of discussion would appear to have been to a certain extent opened.

Still we shall find that much of the criticism by Trollope's contemporaries was guided by reasonable principles, in part, perhaps, taken over
originally from the rules for poetry and drama, in part formed by intui-
tion. At any rate this criticism can tell us something about the causes of
Trollope's appeal irrespective of, or perhaps even because of, what V.
Woolf calls »the partiality, the inevitable imperfection of contemporary
criticism».[7] To this criticism by the mid-Victorians proper we shall have
to add the views of Henry James, who was nearly thirty years Trollope's
junior, the conscious artist, who wrote his much appreciated essay on
Trollope in 1883.

                              *   *   *

> *Critics will praise a writer for a wide range, for it
> is an easy and obvious thing for them to distinguish.*[8]

Trollope's range is, indeed, considered by practically all his critics
or reviewers after it became evident that he was a writer whose interest
in contemporary society was something remarkable. In this he differed
from his great contemporaries, who mostly, when not writing tracts for the
times (like *Sybil* and *Alton Locke*), preferred a setting in the past thereby
disclaiming, as Mrs. Tillotson (p. 95) says, 'the responsibility of inter-
preting contemporary life'. It gradually dawned upon the readers that
some very ordinary aspects of this society were, in fact, Trollope's perpetual subject. And the way in which he treated his subject was felt to
be inseparable from it as good fiction requires. There is a note of pleasant
surprise in the often quoted comment made by Nathaniel Hawthorne
in a letter of 1860 to Fields, the Boston publisher:

Have you ever read the novels of Anthony Trollope? They precisely suit my
taste, — solid and substantial, written on the strength of beef and through the
inspiration of ale, and just as real as if some giant had hewn a great lump out of
the earth and put it under a glass case, with all its inhabitants going about their
daily business, and not suspecting that they were being made a show of. And these
books are just as English as a beef-steak. Have they ever been tried in America?
It needs an English residence to make them thoroughly comprehensible; but still I
should think that human nature would give them success anywhere.[9]

A great lump out of the earth, that is to say England, or what represents England, and all its inhabitants going about their daily business — this is here found to be roughly Trollope's subject after the publication of three of his Barchester novels and some other books by him. His range, implied in the subject, is found to be determined by human nature to such a degree as to secure his novels universal appeal. Trollope himself later 'came across this piece of criticism' and his comment on it shows how genuinely he rejoiced in Hawthorne's happy observations:

> The criticism, whether just or unjust, describes with wonderful accuracy the purport that I have ever had in view in my writing. I have always desired to 'hew out some lump of the earth', and to make men and women walk upon it just as they do walk here among us — with no more of excellence, nor with exaggerated baseness — so that my readers might recognise human beings like to themselves, and not feel themselves to be carried away among gods or demons. (*A*, 137—8.)

In focusing the interest of his novels on middle-class life he appears to have done more for his immediate success than critics in our century are quite aware of. Mrs. Tillotson (p. 83) quotes Harriet Martineau on the readers' taste towards the end of the 'thirties: »People liked high life in novels, and low life, and ancient life; and life of any rank presented by Dickens, in his peculiar artistic light . . . but it was not supposed that they would bear a presentment of the familiar life of every day. Youths and maidens in those days looked for lords and ladies in every page of a new novel.» But though »the ghost of the aristocratic novel was still walking in the eighteen-fifties»[10], it is evident that Trollope's middle-class themes were introduced at a point of time when the public was particularly ready to welcome them as a change from the fashionable novels.

At first, after the publication of *The Warden* (which was regarded as having for its special subject a topical scandal) and *Barchester Towers*, his social domain was taken to be more or less limited to the life of the clergy, »a single profession», as *The Times* writes on Aug. 13, 1857, but one in which the author »has found a less hackneyed theme» than Mrs. Gore, whose 'snob-appeal', to employ Mrs. Tillotson's term, had been the object of Thackeray's burlesque in *Punch* in 1847 under the title 'Lords and Liveries' etc. We notice, however, that Mrs. Gore's book, *The Two Aristocracies*, reviewed together with *Barchester Towers* in *The Times* under 'New Novels', is still given the precedence in order and at least as much attention as Trollope's novel. Although the reviewer does not look upon the people of *The Warden* and *Barchester Towers* as a social class but a single profession, to which in general it is »bad policy for a novelist to confine his attention», »the subject is so fresh», in the opinion of the reviewer, »and the representation so vivid, that the contracted limits of the story are forgotten, and we are left to wonder that more has not long ago been made of such promising materials». But as, after these two books, Trollope was seen to take a great interest in people of other professions, too, the critics at last concluded that contemporary middle-class was, in fact, the sphere in which he constantly sought his themes. The *National Review*, reviewing *Orley Farm* in 1863, defines the people of this story in words which could be used as a general description of the people of most of his novels:

> The real interest of the story is concentrated upon well-to-do, decorous, and deservedly prosperous people, who solve, with a good deal of contentment and self-satisfaction, the difficult problem of making the most both of this world and the next.

And this is at the same time perhaps the best description, in so few words, of what has been regarded as the typical mid-Victorian middle-class (cf. above, p. 20).

The readers did welcome Trollope's books about the middle-class, but the ordinariness involved in the subject has mostly proved a veritable stumbling-block to those whose business it has been to explain the appeal of these novels. Middle-class life has probably been felt as the least inviting subject for any novelist. Arnold Bennett writes in 1909: »The best novelists do not find their material in this class. The material itself lacks interest, lacks both moral and spectacular beauty.»[11] Still Bennett appreciated Trollope. As we shall see, Trollope's contemporaries did not usually find the middle-class, the philistines proper, of their own period in the least more interesting *per se*, and this can also be inferred from the caustic passage just quoted about *Orley Farm*.

Bennett is »convinced that only a supreme artist could now (in 1909) handle successfully the material represented by the class in question».[12] The mid-Victorians were no doubt less spoilt with clever and eminent artists than Mr. Bennett, but the critics who appreciated Trollope mostly also understood that his ordinary subject required extraordinary skill. Contemplating his characters the *North British Review*, 1863 (XL, 375—6), writes:

> It does not in the least degree diminish — it rather increases — the skill which was required for their creation; but perhaps it may help to account for our familiarity with them, when they have been created, that they are not, as we have said extra ordinary people. Some of them have a little more wit than is common; but they are not stronger, abler, braver, richer in imagination, or more tender in sensibility than a courteous novelist must suppose the generality of his readers to be.

Here the Review touches upon a vital point in Trollope's appeal: by making his characters thus unpretentious Trollope makes them congenial to his readers (as he said he wanted to, see above, p. 75); and the surest aid for this purpose was obviously to choose the characters out of the very class that numbered the majority of his readers.

This appeal, however, to be genuine, further demanded that the author should appear to be one with his public, and there is no mistaking the fact that the reviewer quoted is himself under this impression. The article in the *North British Review* discusses nine of Trollope's novels, but the reviewer »cannot help thinking it a happy accident that Mr. Trollope should have written books at all», because »the whole tone and habit of mind implied in these novels is that of a man of activity and business, rather than of a man of letters». But »the great charm» of his novels, the reviewer continues, seems to lie in the fact that »while we read them we are made to share, in the easiest way, the experience of a man who, in going through his own daily business, has been brought in contact with an immense variety of people», a man who »shares the thoughts and feelings of the majority of educated Englishmen». (*NBR*, 370.) This is, in fact, the secret of his success (we must take the reviewer to mean), the explanation of his superb ability to represent ordinary life in all its details, a »point in which he resembles if he does not even rival the great writer» — Thackeray:

> There is no other male writer that we remember, who has seized so successfully the true character of the petty intrigues of society, of family feuds, of household discomforts and household pleasures, of small malignities and daily kindnesses. He seldom attempts, with success, to penetrate deeper than other people to the ultimate springs of all the good and evil ... But the surface world with which he does deal, the characters which come within his range, the manners, affections, sympathies, of ordinary people, the common activities and occupations, the accidents and trivialities of life, these things are represented with marvellous truth and minuteness of detail, and at the same time with a certain sobriety of tone which is singularly characteristic of English society. (*NBR*, 371.)

But are these things worth representing 'with marvellous truth'? we might ask ourselves, a question that some critics have by now been asking themselves for a hundred years. The answer at the end of this article at any rate is, not very convincingly, in the affirmative: »His novels will not raise our minds very far above the weary trivialities of common life; but ... if we can be amused with a picture of common life — as all people with any healthy curiosity of mind must be — he paints it for us, of the present generation, with an almost unrivalled delicacy and discernment. No novels are more pleasant than the best of Mr. Trollope's.»

However, as other critics have found, this is not the right question to ask when we are contemplating Trollope's range. The *North British Review* admirably explains why Trollope could awaken the interest of the common reader, amuse him, and make him familiar with his characters by gratifying, as James expressed it[13], 'the taste for emotions of recognition', but the *Review* seems to take it too much for granted that a general 'picture of common life' denotes his range, aim, and appeal. Within this picture of middle-class life were to be found the varieties of people, mostly distinguished by their professions, that went to create the social tension and human interest of Trollope's stories, and these varieties, much more than the stories themselves with their 'accidents and trivial realities of life', seem to form the proper exponents of his range — besides the individual character-delineation which will be considered later together with plot and story.

As has already been mentioned, clerical life as treated in *The Warden* and *Barchester Towers* was found to be a fresh and promising subject. Trollope returned to it again and again, and there is no denying that in the opinion of both his contemporaries and posterity it was his best choice. To this Flaubert would have said: »One is not at all free to write this or that. One does not choose one's subject. That is what the public and the critics do not understand. The secret of masterpieces lies in the concordance between the subject and the temperament of the author.»[14] Trollope himself says that he 'conceived the story' (see above, p. 17), but whatever term we prefer, the subject was found to be congenial to him; the *Edinburgh Review*, 1877 (Vol. 146, p. 464) for instance writes of *The Warden* and *Barchester Towers* as really forming one story:

He was doubly fortunate in the choice of his subject, for it not only appealed strongly to the fancy of his readers, but proved to be particularly suited to his talents.

By the 'subject', however, the *Edinburgh*, like most other critics when treating these books, does not refer so much to the 'story' as to the clergy represented (»It is the people, and especially the clerical personages, who give the character to the story.»[15]); and these personages have been much appreciated in the other Barsetshire novels, too.

The greatest wonder to most of the critics was that Trollope could write of the lights and shadows of clerical life as if he had first-hand knowledge of it; in fact, he was believed to draw from experience. The impression of real knowledge was, perhaps, heightened by the fact that the subject had not been treated from the exclusively worldly point of view before. *The Warden* might have reminded many of his readers of the novels of Charlotte Yonge, but *Barchester Towers* must have already opened their eyes to the wide difference.[16] And even *The Warden* manifested a sufficiently worldly view to be striking at least to a clergyman; the Rev. James Pycroft, who was a writer, too, is reported to have said of it to William Longman, the publisher: »Here at least you are breaking new ground. The domestic economy of the Church, as it is sketched here, is absolutely virgin soil.»[17]

The *North British Review* (in the article of 1864 already referred to) found that Trollope knew how to use the 'glaring badge of the cloth' as the external of his 'sketches of human nature', and forms an exception in not being impressed by his 'knowledge' of clergymen and their ways (p. 376). But even such a serious critic as J. Herbert Stack, writing in the *Fortnightly Review*, 1869, shares the popular assumption:

He knows more, we think, of English parson life than any man in England. He has somehow got behind the clerical waistcoat, and can count its throbs. . . . an able, observant novelist like Mr. Trollope, knowing the clergy by heart . . . (V, 197—8).

In Henry James we find another example of what Cazamian means when writing (p. 1210): »As to the accuracy and immediacy of his (Trollope's) reproductive talent, he has deceived competent judges.» Having not yet read the *Autobiography*, James also assumes that Trollope wrote even his first two clerical novels from real knowledge:

Trollope had lived long enough in the world to learn a good deal about it; and his maturity of feeling and evidently large knowledge of English life were for much in the effect produced by the two clerical tales. — — What he had picked up, to begin with, was a comprehensive, various impression of the clergy of the Church of England and the manners and feelings that prevail in cathedral towns.[18]

This assumption explains in part James's low opinion of Trollope's imagination (to which I shall revert later), but it is really a high tribute to Trollope's powers as there is no reason to disbelieve his own repudiation of any special knowledge of the clerical order:

I have often been asked in what period of my early life I had lived so long in a cathedral city as to have become intimate with the ways of a Close. I never lived in any cathedral city — except London, never knew anything of any Close, and at that time had enjoyed no peculiar intimacy with any clergyman. My archdeacon, who has been said to be life-like . . . was, I think, the simple result of my moral consciousness. It was such as that, in my opinion, that an archdeacon should be,

... and lo! and archdeacon was produced, who has been declared by competent authorities to be a real archdeacon to the very ground. I have felt the compliment to be very great. ... — but in writing about clergymen generally, I had to pick up as I went whatever I might know or pretend to know about them. (*A*, 95—6.)

This is a good illustration of Liddell's rule (p. 39) that »what is important to an artist is not his experience but his range», because (in the words of Lord David Cecil quoted by Liddell) »only some aspects of his experience fertilize his imagination». What little Trollope saw of clergymen in his early years — for instance his mother's father, the Vicar of Heckfield (A, 36), who died when Anthony was nine, the masters of Harrow School, and the Vicar of Harrow — must have formed his bent, been enough to 'fertilize his imagination'. When the critics attributed his lifelike descriptions to experience, they made themselves liable to the same abuse of the word as, according to Liddell, is common to »contemporary writings about artists», too, writings in which experience means only external experience.

Trollope's power of describing young girls in love was a cause of almost equal wonder to his public. »Love is the master passion of every novelist», as a reviewer wrote in *The Times* in 1862, but the subject could be handled in different ways. The moral point of view in those times of propriety and prudery was of course of great importance in any discussion of this passion, and I shall revert to it again later. Trollope's success in this was, however, largely attributed to his ability to draw just the sort of girl that the majority of the readers, or at least the readers feeling social responsibility, seemed to prefer to any other. In fact, it seems probable — although I have not seen it suggested by anybody else — that his concentrating rather on the girl than on the passion was the only way, in this period, of avoiding giving offence and still preserving the interest; at least this appears in part to account for his success.

Blackwood's, Sept., 1867 (Vol. CII), in an article on 'Novels' seems to express the proper Victorian sentiments on Trollope's girls. Having very thoroughly condemned the decline of the traditional morality of the English novel, a change to be noticed perhaps since Jane Eyre made her »protest» against convention and carried on by »Miss Braddon and Miss Thomas and a host of other writers», the reviewer writes:

It is good to turn aside from these feverish productions ... Though they seem to flourish side by side, and though the public, ... seems to throw itself with more apparent eagerness upon the hectic than upon the wholesome, still we cannot but

hope that Mr Anthony Trollope has in reality a larger mass of readers than Miss
Braddon . . . In Mr Trollope's books there are no women who throw their glorious
hair over the breast of any chance companion; indeed, the red-haired young woman,
exuberant in flesh and blood, and panting for sensation, is unknown in them.
— — To him her hair is clearly a secondary matter. He takes, strange to say, a
great deal more trouble to show us what was passing through her mind. And it is
true that he does reveal this with an amount of variety which has pointed many
a gentle joke against him. His knowledge of the thoughts that go through a girl's
mind when she is in the full tide of her individual romance is almost uncanny in its
minuteness. How did he find it all out? — — It is not he who makes us ashamed of
our girls. He gives us their thoughts in detail, and adds a hundred little touches
which we recognise as absolute truth; but we like the young women all the better,
not the worse, for his intuitions. They are like the honest English girls we know.

It was felt, in fact, to be somewhat against the order of nature that a
man of Trollope's age should be able to penetrate into the minds of such
females with such a sure touch, making them at the same time very
charming creatures indeed. We remember that he was already forty when
the first of the Barsetshire novels was published, and there were no signs
of diminishing insight into the maiden heart with his advancing years.
Most critics (the one writing in the Spectator, 1883 — probably C. H.
Hutton — is one exception) are unanimous in praising him for this ability,
even if some, like those of the National Review, 1863, and the Fortnightly,
1869 (J. Herbert Stack), think it is ability wasted upon a worthless
subject, or in a worthless way. The Edinburgh, 1877, seems to voice the
general sentiment on this power in a writer of Trollope's age and sex,
and we know the article to be attributed to Henry Reeve, the editor:

Here we have a middle-aged or elderly gentleman worming himself into the
hearts and confidences of young ladies, and identifying himself with the innermost
workings of their minds; and a very remarkable phenomenon it is. If manifold
theoretical experience and an assumption of ready sympathy could make a trustworthy guide and confidant in love-affairs, Mr. Trollope might stand father con-
fessor to the spinsterhood of feminine England. (P. 462.)

This reminds us of Richardson who was fifty when he published Pamela
although he had already practised compiling love-letters for country girls
in his boyhood.

After Barchester Towers it was soon noticed that the interest of
Trollope's novels began to centre, as James says, »more or less upon a
simple maiden in her flower». This is simply stating that the subject was
to Trollope of first importance. He writes in his Autobiography (p. 201):
»It is admitted that a novel can hardly be made interesting or successful
without love». But as has been said, he really takes a greater interest

in the girl than in the passion. Henry James gives by far the most exhaustive and admiring analysis of the girl in Trollope's novels and her appeal:

Trollope settled down steadily to the English girl; he took possession of her, and turned her inside out. He never made her the subject of heartless satire . . .; he bestowed upon her the most serious, the most patient, the most tender, the most copious consideration. He is evidently always more or less in love with her, . . . But, as I have said, if he was a lover, he was a paternal lover . . . He has presented the British maiden under innumerable names, in every station and in every emergency of life, and with every combination of moral and physical qualities. — — Trollope's heroines have a strong family likeness, but it is a wonder how finely he discriminates between them. — — They are so affectionate. Mary Thorne, Lucy Robarts, Adela Gauntlet, Lily Dale, Nora Rowley, Grace Crawley, have a kind of clinging tenderness, a passive sweetness, which is quite in the old English tradition. Trollope's genius is not the genius of Shakespeare, but his heroines have something of the fragrance of Imogen and Desdemona.[19]

This piece of criticism, very elucidative as it is in regard to Trollope's powers, is at the same time good evidence of the fact that his contemporaries were inclined to contemplate his girls in bulk. They are, indeed, looked upon by several critics more as a 'subject' than as 'characters', no doubt because there soon appeared so many of them but also because of the subjugated position allotted to woman in Trollope's fictitious society and in life, too, even at the end of Trollope's period. It is evident that most of his critics were rather pleased with the 'affectionate', 'clinging' type of girl that he himself preferred and was so skilful in drawing.

One periodical, however, the *North British Review*, 1864, pays some special attention to Trollope's young men, too, as a subject:

There are a class of people in England, even more numerous than clergymen, and even more like one another. There are young men in the world, now-a-days, which to judge from the novels of the last generation, was not formerly the case. In the old times, when there still were heroes, no one thought of bestowing on a young man who was born to make love, and be strong and handsome, and meet with difficulties, and be helped out of them, any superfluous character or interest. Mr. Trollope has abandoned the old tradition.

Here he is found to be surpassed by Thackeray. »But nowhere», the reviewer continues, »has his talent been more successfully employed than in describing the characteristic features of young Englishmen. Peregrine Orme, Johnnie Eames, Charley Tudor, and half-a-dozen more, are portraits of a kind that nobody before Mr. Trollope has succeeded in drawing.» (P. 377.) Still, on the next page, the reviewer says that »his

girls are even better than the boys». — The fact is that Trollope himself
is much more interested in girls as a subject; however truly he may have
drawn young men, he has not been able to make them attractive, or even
very interesting (with a few exceptions), because of his principle not to
make his people too excellent or too base; and his unheroic type of young
man seldom calls forth much comment from the critics. But it was always
safe to make girls loveable, and not only safe but, as Reeve says, »the
best excuse for their becoming objects of those imprudent passions that
are the framework of his stories».[20]

A group of six Trollopian novels have been distinguished as 'political'
on account of their setting in a society of politicians and their circles.
Politics are part of his theme in some other novels, too, especially *Ralph
the Heir*, in which he made use of his own electioneering experiences.
But as has already been indicated (p. 55), Trollope's own enthusiasm
for a political career was not understood by his contemporaries, nor did
politics as the subject of his novels awaken their interest to any large
extent. One passage from the *Dublin Review*, 1872, XIX, 399, seems
to sum up fairly well the general sentiment:

> He is evidently very fond of politics, and has mastered every detail of the
> mechanism of government. But he leaves the impression that his taste is for the
> near horizons in politics; that he knows the wire-pulling and the *personnel* . . .
> better than the large interests. The politics in his works are small, and the politicians
> either cold, viewy, and doctrinaire, like Plantagenet Palliser, or cunning, fussy,
> and shallow, like Phineas Finn.

As the politics presented in these books apparently left the average
reader cold, he looked perhaps for the human interest in the stories, and
can be imagined to have asked himself, as the *Contemporary Review*, 1869
(XII, 143), did in regard to *Phineas Finn:* »Can it be worth while to keep
up all this immense and splendid apparatus of modern society to grow
such poor cabbages as these?»[21] Henry James's verdict is very short:
»His political novels are distinctly dull, and I confess I have not been
able to read them.»[22]

Even when the criticism is less condemnatory than in these quotations,
or the articles indicating the failure of *The Prime Minister*, it shows that
the political novel was at least regarded as belonging to the borderland
of Trollope's range. It is questionable whether politics can be considered
ever to have belonged to the proper range of any novelist, including
Disraeli, the inventor of this species of novels.[23] Otherwise Trollope's
political novels could be chosen to illustrate Liddell's rule (p. 43) that

»the novelist's range cannot, voluntarily, be extended» to include for instance 'material gathered after early middle life'. When Reeve recommends the novels as »both pleasant and profitable reading for the foreigner who desires an insight into our political institutions»[24], he is unintentionally satirical and, in fact, puts them beyond the pale of fiction.

Escott in his biography of Trollope writes (pp. 270—71) that those British readers 'who cared for the political novel' were still in Trollope's period under the spell of Disraeli's early novels. The popularity of Disraeli as a public character in the 'seventies no doubt helped to maintain the enthusiasm for these novels, which were written, as Professor W. L. Burn points out in the *Nineteenth Century*, March, 1948, »in a period when politics were far more lively and exciting than they were between the 'fifties and the 'seventies». These external circumstances apparently combined to lessen Trollope's chances of interesting his readers in this theme.

Reviewing *Orley Farm* on Dec. 26, 1862, *The Times* expresses its astonishment at the sudden interest in law displayed by »all our novelists», and Trollope is said to follow »the fashion of his tribe» when he »comes to us berobed and bewigged» to tell this story. Reeve in 1877[25] observes that »Law is a fertile source of inspiration to Mr. Trollope as to most habitual novel-writers». Some critics had by then censured him for insufficient knowledge of the subject and for his moral opinions of the legal profession, but Reeve points out[26] that »it is his habit to deprecate criticism by pleading that his novelist's law is good enough for the novelist's purpose».

The charge of ignorance of the subject was justified, as especially the expert examination of the crime and prosecution of Lady Mason in *Orley Farm* has proved in our century.[27] But it seems that we should here be concerned with the question: To what extent, in the opinion of his contemporaries, did Trollope's inaccuracy affect his novels from a literary point of view? To the *North British Review* it is at any rate so objectionable that, out of about seven pages devoted to the discussion of *Orley Farm*, the Review gives nearly six to the exclusive condemnation of his unsupportable attack upon the morality of the legal profession, and has very little to say about the literary merit of the novel. Later literary critics seem to take little interest in the liberties taken by Trollope in legal matters — although *Orley Farm* has remained one of his famous novels — perhaps because he at least improved in *The Eustace Diamonds* having consulted an expert; and the *National Review*, Jan.—

April, 1863, discussing the former book, had already reduced the question to what was probably felt by most readers to be its right proportions:

A discriminating critic, who appears to write with professional enthusiasm, has been at the pains to tear the whole thing to pieces, and to show that in every essential particular Mr. Trollope did not know what he was talking about, that no such facts as those on which he grounds his insinuation could possibly exist, and that all but a few black sheep in the profession do precisely what Mr. Trollope says that they ought. So much good labour seems to us in a large degree wasted upon a writer with whom instruction is necessarily subsidiary to amusement, and who scarcely pretends to any but the most superficial acquaintance with the evils of which he complains.

This could almost be taken to refer to the review in *The Times*, where some of his mistakes and his wasted indignation against lawyers (»clap-trap») are also pointed out and deplored as having nearly spoilt »a good story».

By his subjects concerning law Trollope wanted to 'create the needed biting interest' (as he says in *Phineas Finn*, Ch. XXIX), the sensational element, which, according to his theory, a good novel should contain while remaining realistic (*A*, 204). But what really mattered to Trollope and his readers (critics) was the reaction of the personages concerned as human beings. As his father had been a lawyer, Trollope had in his early youth seen much at least of the behaviour of lawyers, and, in their human relations to society, his lawyers, like his clergymen, were felt to be well within his range as is indicated for instance by the *Dublin Review*, 1872, p. 425:

His lawyers, not so numerous as his clergymen, are as distinct and as memorable. Mr. Furnival . . . and Sir Thomas Underwood, are quite as admirable in their way as the Barchester people, and as the casual curates whom we find in the not actually clerical novels.

Trollope's range is further found to include people of various descrip-tions, such as sporting men, money-lenders, and election-agents, who all »will bear inspection» according to the *Dublin Review*, 1872 (p. 425). But although the *North British Review*, 1864, calls him »the novelist *par excellence* of the moment» and praises his ability to »describe his world and ours, with vivacity and grace, with a delicate appreciation of the niceties of character and manners in plain straightforward English» resulting in »a picture of society, wonderfully real and true» (pp. 370—71), the opinion of the *Review* that Trollope not only appeared to be, but was genuinely, one with the public (cf. above, p. 77) could not but diminish his merit as an artist in the eye of this critic as well as of some

others who more or less shared this opinion. The *Review* regards him as
rather an ordinary man, his observations of life as nothing out of the
common, and his way of drawing characters from different spheres of
life as nothing remarkable, nothing that could not, perhaps, be done by
anybody with some talent and an eye for how easy it all really is, because
»in so complex a state of society as ours» every man is usually »better
known to his dearest friends by the things that are outward and conventional than by his own intimate nature».

A wonderfully lifelike picture may therefore be produced by a skilful combination of features that are merely external; and if to such features of this kind as are
supposed to be peculiar to the individual, one or two strongly-marked class-
characteristics can be added, the result will be a portrait as recognisable to most
readers as their own familiar acquaintances. (P. 376.)

This seems equal to saying that Trollope's personages are what E. M.
Forster calls 'flat' characters, such as can be summed up in one single
phrase because they display only two or three facets, and are unalterable
because not changed by circumstances. In fact, the reviewer says in another passage (p. 384) that Trollope »has not enabled us to form a conception of what they (the parsons) are out of the four corners of Barchester
Towers». The only exception from this 'flatness', in the opinion of the
reviewer, is Thady in Trollope's early novel *The Macdermots of Ballycloran*
(1847), and it is evident that the reviewer is not really satisfied with 'flat'
characters. Forster, who prefers the 'round' ones, too, finds at any rate
that »a novel that is at all complex often requires flat people as well as
round»[28], and the usefulness of 'flat' characters is thought by Muir to be
even greater than Forster admits.[29] However, by 1864, when the article
of the *North British Review* appeared, Trollope had not yet reached the
summit of his power and hardly even thought of his *Last Chronicle*.
This reviewer may consequently be more easily excused than later critics
for practically identifying Trollope's range with his power of observation
and his experience of life as seen by the physical eye.

Contemporary opinion of the width of Trollope's range necessarily
refers to his knowledge and may be summed up in the words of the
Spectator, Oct. 27, 1883: »The great characteristic of all his novels is
knowledge of the world.» His faithful admirer the *Dublin Review* sees
in it an asset which, combined with the novelist's tact and moderation,
makes him practically unique. In 1872 the *Review* writes (pp. 397—8):

His keen and extensive knowledge of the world, of society in its widest and also
in its narrowest meaning, puts him out of the reach of ignorant imitators. Even

Mr. Thackeray was easier of imitation than Mr. Trollope is, because he occasionally fell into exaggeration, and anything which is overdone lends itself to the coarse attempts of the copyist. Nothing is so difficult to imitate as moderation, as the exquisite justness of vision which sees everything as it is, and the correctness of touch which presents it in its exact proportions; the accurate line on which a given mind will travel under given circumstances, and the good taste which will never purchase effect at the price of distortion.

Several other critics were also inclined to applaude the accuracy of his detail as a literary merit by itself:

... an appreciation of minutiae which enables him always to assign to his characters of every class their fitting costume, language and mode of mind. (*National Review*, 1858, VII, 428.)

... these things are represented with marvellous truth and minuteness of detail. (*North British Review*, 1864, cf. above, p. 77.)

In the good-humoured but acute truthfulness which constitutes the subtle attraction of Mr. Trollope's writings, even in the case of those readers who are not aware that what they are instinctively pleased with in fiction is its truth, ... (*Dublin Review*, 1869, XII, 364.)

Even when apparently wishing to censure Trollope for his painstaking exactness, *The Times*, Aug. 26, 1869, though with less fervour than the *Dublin Review*, admits the force of his fidelity to facts. In an unfavourable review of *He Knew He Was Right* the paper writes:

His writings have no aesthetic purpose; ... he looks at human nature as a man looks out of a window, painting exactly what he sees, up to the exact square of a pane. And the fact that he takes no trouble to devise plot or incident, but rather to avoid them, shows the strengbth of his pen. — — Mr. Trollope, by sheer fidelity of rendering, carries us with him ...

The article ends, however, in a wish »that he would give us something beyond a mere piece of realism». — Again, on Aug. 24, 1875, *The Times* praises the force of *The Way We Live Now* mostly on account of its faithful rendering of reality:

»The Way We Live Now» is only too faithful a portraiture of the manners and customs of the English at the latter part of this 19th century. For all its exactitude, however, it is neither a caricature nor a photograph; it is a likeness of the face which society wears to-day. — — Mr. Trollope's hand has not lost its cunning, nor his mind its habit of just observation.[30]

The purpose of this novel obviously demanded a certain exactitude, but at bottom Trollope's purpose was the same in all his novels, which accounts for his struggle for accuracy.

To some critics his accuracy was bound to suggest the idea of photography, which is mentioned in the last quotation. We find it used both for depreciation and appreciation:

Mr. Trollope, it has been truly said, is a mere photographer; he manipulates with admirable skill, he groups his sitters in the most favourable attitudes, he contrives an endless series of interesting positions; but he never attains to the dignity of an artist. He has a quick eye for external characteristics, and he paints exclusively from without. (*National Review*, 1863, p. 32.)

In 'The Three Clerks' we have a faithful photograph of the embryo stage of official existence with the young gentlemen of the upper middle class, who are run for prizes in harness of red tape. (*Edinburgh Review*, 1877.)

(Similarly Leslie Stephen praises Fielding about the same time when writing, »His scenery is as realistic as a photograph.»[31])

But the contempt of mere photography displayed by the *National Review* is nothing but dissatisfaction with external portraiture, with 'flat' characters, with rearrangement of the material; while, according to Liddell (p. 33), novelists, who have not liked to be called photographers, »have generally meant that they were not . . . merely turning a gaping lens uncritically upon life, and producing an uninspired copy of unselected material». The modern photographer, however, is an artist, and selects his material. Like him, Liddell maintains, the novelist should select, should »carefully compose» his picture. In support of this view Liddell quotes James's preface to *The Spoils of Poynton:* »Life has no direct sense whatever for the subject, and is capable . . . of nothing but splendid waste.» But in 'The Art of Fiction' (pp. 16—7) James says:

Selection will take care of itself . . . In proportion as in what she (Fiction) offers us we see life *without* rearrangement do we feel that we are touching the truth; in proportion as we see it with rearrangement do we feel that we are being put off with a substitute, a compromise and convention. — — Art is essentially selection, but it is selection whose main care is to be typical, to be inclusive.

To the *North British Review*, 1864, Trollope's fiction gave the impression of life just because of his non-selective method (i.e. it appears to the critic to be non-selective):

It is not merely that the incidents are such as occur, and the characters such as may be met with every day. The atmosphere also is that of real life. (P. 371.)

But the realist in fiction is careless about plot. His sole object is to describe men's lives as they really are; and real life is fragmentary and unmethodical. (P. 372.)

And contrary to the *National Review* James finds in Trollope no re-arrangement; he attributes Trollope's success to the fact that into his mirror the public, at first especially, grew very fond of looking — for it saw itself reflected in all the most credible and supposable ways, with that curiosity that people feel to know how they look when they are represented, »just as they are», by a painter who does not desire to put them into an attitude, to drape them for an effect, to arrange his lights and his accessories.[32]

It was, however, inevitable that Trollope should frequently be charged with commonplaceness because of his 'object to describe men's lives as they really are'. The critics generally felt like James that art is 'essentially selection', or like Hardy that »a story must be worth the telling», and that »a good deal of life is not worth any such thing».[33] And even when his reputation had reached its summit, some of his contemporaries thought that even in his best books he depicted life that was in part not worth depicting. J. Herbert Stack writes in the *Fortnightly Review*, 1869, V, 196:

He has a true artist's idea of tone, of colour, of harmony . . . is fidelity itself in expressing English life; is never guilty of caricature. Why then are many of his stories, with all their merits, not enduring works of art? Simply, in our opinion, because his choice of subjects is utterly wrong. The genteel public of the day may demand photographs of surly-looking men and simpering women, which they call likenesses of themselves and their wives; but no amount of skill can make common-place men and common-place incidents and common-place feelings fit subjects of high or true literary art.

However, the general discussion of the matter of subject has shown that an author's work can hardly be condemned because of his particular choice. James writes: »If we pretend to respect the artist at all, we must allow him his freedom of choice. Some of the most interesting experiments of which it (art) is capable are hidden in the bosom of common things.»[34] According to V. Woolf »'The proper stuff of fiction' does not exist; everything is the proper stuff fo fiction.»[35] Even the test suggested by Mrs. Wharton does not rule out Trollope's subjects; she writes: »Any subject considered in itself must first of all respond in some way to that mysterious need of a judgment on life of which the most detached human intellect, provided it be a normal one, cannot, apparently, rid itself.»[36]

In view of Trollope's success and reputation it seems hardly necessary to point to the criticism which was exactly the reverse of Stack's opinion. Such criticism has already been quoted. But it is interesting to note that some critics even found his subjects to be unique — because they were commonplace. Hawthorne's famous comment (above p. 74) contains something to that effect. The *North British Review*, 1864 (pp. 374—5) writes:

Mr. Trollope . . . creates, or rather portrays, a character which is not the less amusing, because it is perfectly commonplace. Some female writers have possessed this peculiar subtlety in still greater perfection (but not with his maturity and knowledge of the world).

James's judgment may be said to have become classic: »His great, his inestimable merit was a complete appreciation of the usual.»[37] — Reeve's opinion, in all its triteness, seems to reflect the appreciation of the average reader:

He shows how very little need go to an entertaining story, and that the experiences of the most apparently commonplace individuals may make excellent material for the clever novelist.[38]

Further developing his objection against Trollope's subjects, Stack, in the article quoted from the *Fortnightly*, finds that too many of his characters are 'of the time' and do not show 'deep touches of the human nature of all time, which will make them live for ever as types of general humanity' like Squire Western, Parson Adams, and Parson Trulliber; and he asks, »how many of them will be referred to thirty years hence as alive?» If we may take this to mean that Trollope's books could be expected to meet with neglect at the end of the nineteenth century, we know that Stack happened to be right. But the later revival would have astonished him.

Stack, perhaps better than any other of Trollope's contemporaries, illustrates how easy it is to go astray in judging contemporary literature, in which, as Daiches says (p. 225), »the most 'objective' critic is not immune». (Cf. V. Woolf quoted above, p. 74.) Stack is not at all such a reckless blunderer as for instance Jeffrey (one of the first *Edinburgh* reviewers), who »accepted whatever seemed to a hasty observer to be the safest opinion».[39] There are others of Trollope's contemporaries who condemn him — erroneously to a great extent as we know now — and mingle less praise in their blame than Stack, but hardly any one that aims with the same seriousness at objectivity. In 1869, 'the peak year of Trollope's reputation' (cf. above, p. 30), he undertakes more or less definitely to answer the questions he asks at the beginning of his article: »What is Mr. Trollope's rank as a novelist? Not estimated by the verdict passed on his stories, hot from the press, or by the demand at Mudie's? What will be said of his books twenty or thirty years hence? Which of them will be reprinted then, and read anew, and criticised anew, by a generation yet in its perambulators?» And he proposes to himself to try Trollope's books »by the two standards — the high literature of all ages, and the human nature of all time». It is curious to note how little the standards avail if the critic has not been endowed with the necessary perspicacity.

Stack is partly right in his opinion of the period interest in Trollope's characters (cf. above, p. 50); his chief objection to them is, however, their apparent lack of depth. It is one of the commonest in criticism of Trollope, but Stack differs from most other critics in crediting him

distinctly with ability to do better if he chooses, as is best shown in
The Last Chronicle; and he even suggests a definite subject within the
clergy.

We accept (says Stack) his revelation of Crawley struggling with poverty and
shame, of Mark Robarts fighting off debt; but has he never heard of any conflict
deeper, higher, fiercer, worse? — — A new life has come into the Church. — The
Erastianised, . . . port-drinking, . . . earthy, incumbent is often succeeded by some
man who believes that he has a divine mission, . . . Now the conflict of ideas
between such a man and the parishioners accustomed to the old rector and his old
ways, is just what no newspaper or history can ever give us; but which an able,
observant novelist like Mr. Trollope, knowing the clergy by heart, could admirably
describe. Surely in this sharp almost tragic contrast there is something higher,
nobler, for a novelist than the pecuniary embarrassments of worldly parsons, or
their relations with squires, bishops, and bishops' wives.

As to the subject of young ladies in love Stack writes:

He knows English girls by heart. — — But surely English ladies suffer
occasionally other agony than doubts as to whether this or that lover is to be the
man thrown over, accepted, snubbed, encouraged, or drawn on. We do not say
a word against love in stories . . . But there are deeper chords in woman's nature
that this kind of love does not touch; and as the prose laureate of English girls of
the better class, why should not Mr. Trollope record something else beside flirtations
that end well? Lady Glencora Palliser is pretty and true gliding over thin ice with
her handsome lover . . . But suppose she had run away? Is there nothing deep,
dark, and deadly in human nature and human sin to be painted vividly so that our
souls may be purged by terror, and pity, and stronger thoughts than amusement
at unmarried jilts, married flirts, and young mothers?

Had Trollope followed Stack's advice as to the clergy, it seems that
he would have written stories much more stamped by the period than
he did of his own accord. As to Lady Glencora, James is of the opinion
that »the actual woman would have made a fool of herself to the end
with Burgo Fitzgerald.»[40] The futile wish to reform Trollope is also
apparent in other critics than Stack. *The Times,* Aug. 26, 1869 (reviewing
He Knew He Was Right), calls the wish 'hypercriticism' caused by
'the very excellence' of his works, and writes: »We cannot help wishing
that a man who can do so much would do a little more; that he would
give us something beyond a mere piece of realism . . .»

The *Dublin Review,* 1872 (p. 399) simply judges that »he is no deep
writer; he would not be at once the product and the representative of
the times if he were.» And this otherwise laudatory and conscientious
article of 38 pages ends by finding that »Mr. Trollope falls short in two
of the attributes of a great writer. They are breadth and height. His

landscapes of life are deficient in perspective; and his men and women
are deficient in soul.» His spiritual limits are suggested less harshly by
Reeve:

> If he has laboured long and successfully in his special sphere, he has learned
> where that sphere has its limits. He has seldom attempted to go beyond the powers
> he is conscious of, or to soar to a sustained flight in an atmosphere too refined for
> his pinions. (Etc. as quoted on p. 29.)

This is almost agreeing with the rule of Liddell (p. 46): »A novelist writing
absolutely in the middle of his true range will be writing his best.» The
Dublin Review and Reeve, like other critics already quoted and many
later ones, never suspected that Trollope's range extended farther into
the inner man than his most popular novels seemed to indicate. But the
discussion of 'character' will show that his contemporaries had a higher
opinion of him than can be inferred from the isolated judgments on his
spiritual level.

The critics do not mention the 'psychological approach' but that is
evidently what many of them miss in Trollope's works. His psychological
insight was more or less indirectly recognized when his characters were
contemplated as is only natural because psychology was not one of his
subjects but one of his means. In the *North American Review*, 1864
(XC, 292—8), however, his psychology is once regarded as a subject and
praised, only to be blamed, in the same article, as a means; it seems that
the reviewer cannot fix the psychological aspect steadily in his mind:

> Mr. Trollope's chief characteristic as a novelist is the microscopical power of
> his mind, the power of tracing the moral effects of minute circumstances and
> minute actions. He can give a name to the »light trifles of air» that influence women,
> and disclose those subtle springs of action, the workings of which must often
> be almost inscrutable to those who are moved by them. In this he excels even
> Thackeray . . .
> His characters are made, rather than shown by circumstances, the hands of the
> clock seeming to move the works. — — Trollope is a simple observer . . . one
> whose knowledge of men stops at their manners, or the obvious motives that
> influence individuals or artificial and social classes of men.

Which is he, the discloser of the inner man, or the painter of external
aspects? Perhaps the reviewer wants to say that he is both, and then he
cannot be said to be wrong; but one feels that he should have expressed
himself differently. — The *Dublin Review*, 1872 (p. 399), defines what
it misses thus: »He is not profound, or philosophical, or speculative in
any universal, or indeed wide sense. — — In many respects he is narrow,
with a representative narrowness.»

Psychology had been brought into English fiction by George Eliot and Meredith[41], or, in a broad sense, even by earlier authors of novels of the inner life, one of whom was Jane Austen[42]. Miss Austen's art has been appreciated in a way that tends to formulate a rule: »She shows that it is not width of vision but depth that is important.»[43] However, Miss Austen's external circumstances set the limits to her range: she *had* to work the inner life almost exclusively — as Liddell admits himself. But depth seems to have become very important to Trollope's contemporaries, too, and we have seen how they find with regret that they cannot but assign him rather a modest rank in literature because of his apparent lack in this respect. This is at least what the critics do. To the common reader his appeal was probably unaffected by the critics' concern, as Stack 'fears', the *Dublin Review* (1872) takes for granted, and James expounds with much sympathy for the reader's view.

If »pretentiousness rather than lack of scope is the enemy of great art»[44], Trollope has at least escaped that enemy, which is not denied by any of his critics. The charm of his unpretentiousness was felt from the beginning; it is explicitly and convincingly pointed out for example by *The Times* in its review of *Barchester Towers* in 1857. (Cf. also the *NBR* quoted above, p. 77.) This quality can be discovered without any subtle critical discernment and it appeals to the common reader at least as much as to the critic. Daiches (p. 119) writes: »The scale between mere craftmanship and significant art — — is a large one, and value of one kind or another can lie anywhere within its range. All we ask is that a book does not pretend to be what it is not.»[45]

According to the review in *The Times* the mass of new English fiction published annually about 1857 was of a kind that made *Barchester Towers* (and we must infer *The Warden*, too) particularly welcome to the public 'for the utter absence of pretension'. 'It is the vice of an immense number of fictions that they are novels only in form; in spirit they are sermons, political pamphlets, philosophical inquiries . . . anything but novels. And how often are we met with pretences of a different kind — one man, in fancied imitation of Dickens, overpowering us with geniality; another in foolish aping of Thackeray, indulging in tremendous cynicism . . . Who that glances over these publications does not long for a little common sense and good feeling, for amusement without the intrusion of theories, and for excitement without the ostentation of superior wisdom?' The unpretentiousness might be, as the reviewer says, a negative merit, but it determined his approach and, in some measure his range, and it certainly contributed to his appeal as was testified by James when almost all that came from Trollope's pen was available for estimation:

> As an artist he never took himself seriously; many people will say this was why he was so delightful. The people who take themselves seriously are prigs and bores; and Trollope, with his perpetual »story», which was the only thing he cared about, his strong good sense, hearty good nature, generous appreciation of life in all its varieties, responds in perfection to a certain English ideal. According to that ideal it is rather dangerous to be explicitly or consciously an artist — to have a system, a doctrine, a form. — — His honest, familiar, deliberate way of treating his readers as if he were one of them, and shared their indifference to a general view, their limitations of knowledge, their love of a comfortable ending, endeared him to many persons in England and America.[46]

Rafael Koskimies tells us that this confidential, intimate and democratic attitude on the part of the narrator towards his public is, in fact, to be regarded as one of the oldest principles in the art of fiction although it has been especially adopted by the English tradition of great novelists such as Fielding, Scott, and Dickens.[47]

In the above passage, however, James speaks more for the common reader than for himself; his own view is that fiction should be taken seriously and the novelist should regard himself as an artist as is expressly declared for example in his essay 'The Art of Fiction'. — But Trollope's unpretentiousness must be connected with, was perhaps a result of, his 'appreciation of the usual' (although James does not say so). James points out that this appreciation was not a 'merit' that was to be attributed to Trollope only; women writers had worked successfully in the same field.

> Trollope, therefore, with his eyes comfortably fixed on the familiar, the actual, was far from having invented a new category; his great distinction is that in resting there his vision took in so much of the field. And then he *felt* all daily and immediate things as well as saw them; felt them in a simple, direct, salubrious way, with their sadness, their gladness, their charm, their comicality, all their obvious and measurable meanings.[48]

James clearly accepts Trollope's unpretentious sphere of subjects, and in appreciating the fact that 'his vision took in so much of the field' James decidedly differs from all the critics who insist on 'depth'. Coming from this conscious artist, the appreciation is all the more remarkable, but it seems to be in strict accordance with his theories: 'We must grant the artist his subject, his idea, his *donnée:* our criticism is applied only to what he makes of it.'[49] After his choice 'his standard is indicated' and we can 'apply the test of execution'.[50] — 'The only obligation to which in advance we may hold a novel, without incurring the accusation of being arbitrary, is that it be interesting.' 'A novel is in its broadest definition, a direct impression of life: that, to begin with, constitutes its value, which is greater or less according to the intensity of the impression.'[51] James admires Trollope's power of exciting the impression of seen and felt life through his width of vision, and James asks no more — 'to begin with'.

As James points out, Trollope, in his writings, adapted himself to 'a certain English ideal' in his unpretentiousness. At the same time he adapted himself to what we now regard as the 'Victorian' attitude *par excellence*, and the fullest approbation of his compliance with this ideal is to be found in the article of the *Dublin Review*, 1872, already quoted many times. In pointing out his 'modernness of spirit' the *Review* praises him for his selection of subjects, and not only for what he leaves in but also for what he deliberately leaves out:

> To him the aberration of taste which welcomed the coarse attractions of sensationalism could never have seemed otherwise than a passing error; . . . The world knows where to turn for the faithful portraiture of the present which alone it loves to study, under many aspects, and with the further advantage that the omitted aspects are those which it does not greatly care to have forced upon its attention. Want, misery, the sufferings of the poor, have no place in his later works. — — The awful calamities, the smashing catastrophes, the agonizing griefs of human life, he does not deal with, or deals with in a way that surrounds them so skilfully and so naturally with the commonplace which we have always with us, that they are not tragic to our minds. (Pp. 400—401.)

This leaves no doubt as to Trollope's appeal to his 'philistine' contemporaries, but James (writing in 1883) believed that, just because he was satisfied to write for the day, he would be read by posterity, too.[52]

The conventional, moral and religous codes of the period had to be observed strictly by a writer who wanted to appeal to the average reader. One cannot but feel today that these narrow limits were a great handicap, as they were already felt to be by James when he wrote with admiration: »He accepted all the common restrictions, and found that even within the barriers there was plenty of material.»[53]

* * *

> *Analysis of a novel in terms of plot and
> character, is an invaluable test of the writer's
> specific aptitude as a novelist.*[54]

However, as Liddell also says (p. 72), plot is »only artificially separable from character» — which view had already been expressed by James in 'The Art of Fiction' (p. 13) — and this is particularly true of the Trollopian novel because there is usually very little of a plot to separate in it as he recognized himself when writing:

> I have never troubled myself about the construction of plots ... I am not sure that the construction of a perfect plot has been at any period within my power. But the novelist has other aims than the elucidation of his plots. He desires to make his readers so intimately acquainted with his characters that the creatures of his brain should be to them speaking, moving, living, human creatures. (*A*, 209.)

In other words, Trollope took such a great interest in his characters that he thought the plot needed no special attention on his part, and would perhaps take care of itself once the characters were conceived. He went so far as to declare openly: »When I sit down to write a novel I do not at all know, and I do not very much care, how it is to end.» (*A*, 228.) And although he thought the plots of such a writer as Wilkie Collins wonderful in their way, Trollope could not himself appreciate his novels: »I can never lose the taste of the construction ... Such work gives me no pleasure. I am, however, quite prepared to acknowledge that the want of pleasure comes from fault of my intellect.» (Ibid.) Thus we find Trollope by his idiosyncrasy immune to Collins's influence in plot-construction while Dickens was not.[55]

Trollope's carelessness about plot was evident to anyone (cf. e.g. the *NBR*, quoted above, p. 88), but the reason of this carelessness is best expressed by James:

> If he had taken sides on the droll, bemuddled opposition between novels of character and novels of plot, I can imagine him to have said (except that he never expressed himself in epigrams[56]), that he preferred the former class, inasmuch as character in itself is plot, while plot is by no means character.[57]

In his negligent attitude towards plot Trollope went farther than the other Great Novelists although their tendency was the same. Edith Wharton (p. 131) writes: »The novel, in the hands of English-speaking writers, has always tended, as it rose in value, to turn to pictures of character and manners, however much blent with dramatic episodes, or entangled in what used to be vaguely known as a plot.» Cecil says of the

Early Victorian Novelists (p. 7): »The main outline of their novels is the same. Their stories consist of a large variety of character and incident clustering round the figure of a hero, bound together loosely or less loosely by an intrigue and ending with wedding bells.»

Still, Trollope was fully convinced that a novel should tell a story. James finds that 'his perpetual »story» was the only thing he cared about', but is at a loss how to define it because 'as a general thing he has no great story to tell'. »The thing», says James, »is not so much a story as a picture; if we hesitate to call it a picture it is because the idea of composition is not the controlling one.»[58] His 'perpetual story' is, however, the story of the perpetual feuds going on in life, especially in mid-Victorian life. »It is in these feuds that the real interest of the novel is intended to lie», the *North British Review*, 1864 (p. 385), writes of *Barchester Towers*, but this applies to most of Trollope's novels. This appeal is, the Review believes, nothing less than »the universal interest in every species of conflict between men» and this is what makes 'his characters in action' so interesting, too, in spite of his deficiencies as a constructor of plots (*NBR*, 378). The 'social feuds' or 'conflicts between men' depicted by Trollope cannot be called 'pictures' in the proper sense of the word, the sense in which James uses it (Cf. MacCarthy, quoted above, p. 67); but 'social pictures' (employed for example by Reeve) seems to be a suitable metaphor with its implication of 'scenes from the stage of life'. — As has already been mentioned (above p. 76), middle-class society has not been felt to be a very exciting subject; but this is hardly true of its social feuds, which are probably more exciting than those of the other classes and the social strifes of the mid-Victorians were probably more interesting than those of other periods in the history of England (cf. above, p. 23).

If social feuds, social relations, and manners are to be made the chief interest of a novel, it seems that the construction of plot, or even the composition of a story[59], may very well be of secondary importance to the writer, while he is likely to concentrate upon character, especially character in relation to society. Trollope is, in fact, a good representative of one kind of novelist defined by Mrs. Wharton (p. 145), »the novelist to whom his subject first presents itself in terms of character, either individual or social», and has the advantage of such a writer »that he can quietly watch his people or his group going about their business, and let the form of his tale grow out of what they are, out of their idiosyncrasies, their humours and their prejudices, instead of fitting a situation onto

them before he really knows them, either personally or collectively».
Indeed, Mrs. Wharton's general definition reminds us of the criticism
on Trollope by Hawthorne (above p. 74) and James, who writes:

> We care what happens to people only in proportion as we know what people
> are. Trollope's great apprehension of the real, which was what made him so interest-
> ing, came to him through his desire to satisfy us on this point — to tell us what
> certain people were and what they did in consequence of being so. That is the
> purpose of each of his tales; and if these things produce an illusion it comes from
> the gradual abundance of his testimony as to the temper, the tone, the passions,
> the habits, the moral nature, of a certain number of contemporary Britons.[60]

Yet it is somewhat remarkable that James nowhere in his essay says a
word of the social strife, which is, as has been mentioned, the real
interest of Trollope's stories and the main impetus to the actions and
thoughts of his characters.[61]

Social feuds were what Trollope saw going on in the life about him,
and he perceived that most of his contemporaries were very much
engaged in them. Naturally his characters, to be 'human beings like to his
readers', had to be engaged in such feuds, too. But he could not conceive
of a novel without a moral purpose:

> A writer of stories must please, or he will be nothing. And he must teach whether
> he wish to teach or no. How shall he teach lessons of virtue and at the same time
> make himself a delight to his readers? — — The novelist, if he have a conscience,
> must preach his sermons with the same purpose as the clergyman, and must have
> his own system of ethics. (He must try to) make virtue alluring and vice ugly,
> while he charms his readers instead of wearing them. (*A*, 200.)

A passage from his *Thackeray* (p. 203) will make his meaning quite clear:
»Without the lesson, the amusement will not be there. There are novels
which certainly can teach nothing; but then neither can they amuse any
one.» These ideas were not put down until twenty odd years after the
conception of *The Warden*, but his work shows that they were more or
less clear in his mind when he set himself to do the same as Defoe,
Fielding, and Thackeray had done — 'to reveal society to itself' through
character.[62]

A moral outlook certainly appealed to the Victorians but at bottom
they were probably like humanity at large in not liking the novelist to
point his moral too openly, which Trollope was quite sure of when
writing that the first duty of a novelist was to please. In his *Thackeray*
(p. 202) he writes: »The palpable and overt dose the child rejects; but
that which is cunningly insinuated by the aid of jam and honey is

accepted unconsciously and goes on upon its curative mission. So it is
with the novel.» This wording no doubt is horrible, but the principle
is sound all the same, and he managed admirably to put it in practice.
In fact, although his contemporaries notice the general 'wholesomeness'
and moral purity of his tone, they are unaware of any moral purpose in
his stories. The *National Review*, 1858, contemplating the first three
Barsetshire novels and *The Three Clerks*, classes him among the novelists
to whose books 'a retributive justice is essential' but who write 'purely
to amuse'. Still the moral view of *The Warden* is conspicuous enough,
at least to James who writes: »It is simply the history of an old man's
conscience.» And he finds that »a motive more delicate, more slender, as
well as charming could scarcely be conceived».[63]

In another passage James writes: »He must have had a great taste for
the moral question; he evidently believed that this is the basis of the
interest of fiction.»[64] It seems to have been the basis of it to a great many
of his contemporaries. The criticism of *Orley Farm* is a case in point.
The Times, Dec. 26, 1862, is tempted to pronounce the novel his best so
far, and calls it »the old story of Rebekah, who defrauds her eldest son
of his birthright in order to confer it on the younger». By the *Cornhill
Magazine*, 1862 (VI, 702—4), the novel is believed to make readers »happy
for a few hours, and, if read aright, to make them better for the rest of
their days — a book not only stirring their interest, but enlarging their
sympathies by its pictures of life». The reviewer finds, however, that
in his book Trollope makes a misplaced apology to his readers for having
asked their sympathy for a sinning woman, Lady Mason, the principal
character. But he admits the existence of the prejudice and finds in it an
excuse for his own wish to expatiate on the morality of the story:

> We expected that certain critics would raise the old foolish cry about making
> guilt interesting; and our expectations have not been deceived. But the guilt is *not*
> made interesting; it is the sinner we pity, not the sin we absolve. Never for a single
> instant is the reader's moral judgment in suspense. The author permits himself no
> sophistication as to the nature of the sin. Not one of the characters — not even the
> sinner herself — exhibits the least oscillation on this point. But nevertheless the
> sinner is loveable as a woman ... We do not murmur at her punishment, but we
> feel with her, feel for her. There is no false glare of melodramatic interest, there is
> none of the prurient curiosity awakened by celebrated criminals.

There is no denying the fact that the moral question is regarded as
the basis of the interest of *Orley Farm* in this piece of criticism as well as
in the review of *The Times* where the author of the modern version of
that strange oriental story' is said to deal »not with mere manners, but

with the very heart of humanity». This is granting the novel — the successful main story in it — the proper distinction of literature as Daiches and
Lucas have recently defined it; it is finding that the novel produces, in
the terms of the former, 'insights' along with the pleasure of 'recognition', that it possesses, in the terms of the latter, 'influence value' besides
'pleasure value'.

As *The Small House* was just then serialising in the *Cornhill*, the
Magazine had a special reason to favour Trollope, but considering in
addition the favourable reviews of *The Times* and others, it is surprising
to find how different an opinion the *National Review*, 1863, gives of the
novel apart from the reviewer's moral satisfaction with it. An attack
by M. Forgues in the *Revue des Deux Mondes* on »the affected severity of
our social code, the delicacy of our taste, and the boasted prudery of our
literature» gives the *Review* occasion to point to *Orley Farm* as »perhaps
the most satisfactory answer that can be given to so disagreeable an
imputation». »Here», the reviewer exclaims, »it may fairly be said, is the
precise standard of English taste, sentiment, and conviction. Writer and
readers alike look at the performance from a strictly moral point of view:
there is a general air of purity, innocence, and cheerfulness.» As the French
journal renewed the attack on the same grounds — by holding up some
poor and less moral novelists as representative of England[65] — Trollope
thus gained the additional importance of being looked upon as an up-
holder of the moral tradition in which the nation took its pride. But the
National Review has hardly anything at all to say of the main story in
Orley Farm and its principal character because of the abundance of reasons
to blame the novel, and perhaps because the main story had been so much
praised by others before.

Trollope's moral views were regarded with universal respect when they
were applied to such pathetic stories as that of Mr. Harding, Lady Mason,
Mr. Crawley, Lady Ongar, and Lady Laura Kennedy, to mention a few
in the crowd. But the philistine morality of his domestic scenes and love-
stories sometimes provoked comments of boredom, or even downright
condemnation like the main part of the article in the *National Review*.
Selecting the description of the Christmas party at Noningsby as a suitable
illustration of the essence of Trollope, the *Review* quotes him and comments upon the passage in a way which supplies an example of what
devastating representations could be given of his novels by those who
were disposed to do so. An extract must suffice:

»— — Had any one told her (Miss Madeline Staveley) in the morning that she would that day have rapped Mr. Graham's knuckles with a kitchen-spoon, she would not have believed that person. But it is so that hearts are lost and won.»

All the point in this sort of scene depends on the innocence of the performers; and it is because Mr. Trollope can manufacture passages of the kind in any quantity required, that he has made himself the favourite writer of the day. The people on whose behalf he interests one are thoroughly sterling, warmhearted and excellent. Every body would be glad to spend Christmas at Noningsby, to go for a walk on Sunday afternoon with the good-natured old judge, to have a chat with Lady Staveley, and to receive a rap on the knuckles from Miss Madeline. What every body would be glad to do, every body likes to read about, and hence a universal popularity without either an exciting plot or forcible writing, or the least pretence at real thoughtfulness, to support it. (P. 31.)

The conclusion of the reviewer that 'such delineations are but very low art and may degrade the tastes' seems plausible enough after such a representation. — To this may be contrasted the opinion of *The Times*, which holds that Trollope deserves high praise for these pictures of domestic life, too (»He has drawn nothing more attractive . . .»); the reviewer looks upon this part of the book as being on a different level from the main story but equally successful, if not better, of its kind.

The criticism of *Orley Farm*, besides displaying the predominance of the moral interest of the period, is an early and admirable example of the antithesis of the two principal attitudes towards Trollope which are noticeable in the mass of criticism on him during the hundred years here considered: satisfaction with, or at least tolerance of, his 'Victorianism' or philistinism on the one hand, and dissatisfaction with, or intolerance of it on the other. The gradual changes of fashion (cf. above, pp. 29, 40) had its undeniable share in this antithesis, but it must always also been due in part to the irreconcilable differences of temperaments in readers and critics.[66] Individual taste was more likely to influence contemporary opinion of Trollope than of other writers because his contemporaries were bound to identify themselves with his characters more closely than with the characters of the other novelists who were given to exaggerations in one way or another and set their tales mostly in the past. This is why his immediate success was greatly determined by the measure in which he could make his characters like the ideas his readers had of themselves.

Exuberant evidence of the popularity of his characters because he gratified this desire is given in the passage quoted above on page 28 from the *National Review*, 1863: »More than a million people habitually read Mr. Trollope, and they do so because the personages in his stories correspond to something in themselves . . .» (but we have seen what the reviewer himself thought of Trollope's and his readers' standards in the review of *Orley Farm*). This is simply saying that he appealed to popular taste, but there are popular tastes and popular tastes (cf. above, pp. 80—81, the quotation from *Blackwood's*). The *Dublin Review*, 1872, (p. 426), admits his appeal to the sound sort of popular taste with a tone of good-humoured resignation when 'contemplating the long line of his social novels'. And we have seen James's evidence of the same appeal (above, p. 94).

The remarkable thing evinced by this popularity is the force of the appeal of his commonplace characters to such a large host of readers. It was far from enough that he made them like his average contemporaries. The secret of this force is found to be in Trollope's attitude to his personages, his approach to his subject, and in my opinion the *Dublin Review*, 1872, (pp. 394—6) gives the best contemporary presentation of his power as a painter of character, and the first forcible appreciation of the grand impression of the bulk of his personages suggesting a world (though the reviewer does not speak of the suggestion in actual words), and not to quote the passage at some length would be to disregard the deposition of a principal witness of Trollope's appeal to his con- temporaries:

He is in one sense the most serious of writers . . . His seriousness consists in his air and tone of absolute belief in the personages and the circumstances of his own creation. — —. In this he is absolutely and pleasantly opposed to Mr. Thackeray. He never talks about having played out a play and shutting up the puppets, . . . he would not on any account acknowledge them to be puppets, but wishes them to be believed in with faith and recognized with knowledge like his own. — — There are no characters in fiction so real, as persons, to the world, as the creations of Mr. Trollope. We talk as familiarly, and perhaps more frequently, of some of Mr. Dickens's bright, fantastic fancies . . . But we talk only of a few . . . We quote them when exceptions, oddities, vagaries are in question . . . But Mr. Trollope has given life, and speech, and motion to scores of portraits, has set them to walk abroad and continue, and to have their names on men's lips when actual every-day affairs and incidents of life are talked of, to rise up in one's memory in one's silent cogitations, to suggest themselves as matters of fact, the readiest, handiest, most suitable of comparisons, and illustrations. They come from all sides of his many- sided pictures of life . . . He avoids all exaggerations, in either good or evil, with such care and success, that sometimes one is almost provoked with him, especially in his later works, for his perfect, undeviating reasonableness; but his people, life- size and life-like, are all thoroughly real to his readers, as he forces his readers to feel they are to himself. — — He is more than the painter, more than the sculptor of his people; he is the biographer of them all. He does not only imagine Archdeacon

Grantly and Johnny Eames, and put them into certain stories to play their parts in certain incidents, as is mostly the whole utility and destiny of fictitious persons in novels; he looks at them and into them, he turns them about; observes them, lives with them; knows them so thoroughly well and intimately, that he makes us know them almost as fully, and in quite a separate way, from the actual set of circumstances in which he exhibits them. The Arabins and the Thornes, the Greshams, the Crawleys, and the De Courcys are still in Barsetshire, the Last Chronicle notwithstanding, and Crosbie and Johnny Eames are also no doubt to be found at their respective offices, not quite a quarter of a mile from Charing Cross.

One almost suspects that Trollope was inspired by this praise to write in his *Autobiography* (p. 209) the passage about the novelist's only way of making his characters 'living, human creatures' to his readers:

This he can never do unless he know those fictitious personages himself, and he can never know them unless he can live with them in the full reality of established intimacy. They must be with him as he lies down to sleep, and as he wakes from his dreams. He must learn to hate them and to love them. He must argue with them, quarrel with them, forgive them, and even submit to them.

Even the *National Review*, 1863, had noticed with approval his great zest, as to which he compares favourably with the yawning Thackeray:

Mr. Trollope has no touch of this affectation; he does his very best: he believes in the piece, he detests the villains, admires the heroes, and can scarcely refrain from caressing his pet heroine when she crosses his path. If he comes for a few moments on the stage, it is only to bustle about, to adjust the ropes, to hurry the scene-shifters, and assure the beholders that no pains are being spared for their entertainment. (P. 37.)

We find that even the intrusion of the author himself into the novel is tolerated when it is found to be a result of his own enthusiasm for the story. In fact, intrusions by authors were common practice in the old novel, e.g. in Thackeray's books, and 'contemporary objectors were rare', says Mrs. Tillotson (p. 252) mentioning one objection made by G. H. Lewes in 1850.

But in 1858 the *National Review* (VII, 425) resents one kind of intrusion that most of Trollope's critics have found offensive, at least in the form in which it occurs in *Barchester Towers*. James writes of it in *Partial Portraits* (p. 116):

He took a suicidal satisfaction in reminding the reader that the story he was telling was only after all, a make-believe. — — In describing the wooing of Eleanor Bold by Mr. Arabin he has occasion to say that the lady might have acted in a much more direct and natural way than the way he attributed to her. But if she had, he adds, »where would have been my novel»? The last chapter of the same story begins with the remark, »The end of a novel, like the end of a children's dinner party, must be made up of sweetmeats and sugar-plums». These little slaps at credulity (we might give many more specimens) are very discouraging, . . . inexplicable . . . deliberately inartistic . . . It is impossible to imagine what a novelist takes himself to be unless he regards himself as a historian and his narrative as history.

Although James thinks that Trollope had endeared himself to the readers by his unpretentiousness and lack of seriousness (see above, p. 94), his own principle is that fiction »must take itself seriously for the public to take it so» as he writes in 'The Art of Fiction'. He condemnes the 'apologetic attitude' as a remnant of »the old superstition about fiction being 'wicked'», which demands that a story should »more or less admit that it is only a joke». He looks upon Trollope's admission »that the events he narrates have not really happened» as »a terrible crime», and »it shocks me», he says, »every whit as much in Trollope as it would have shocked me in Gibbon and Macaulay». Then he ought to have been shocked by Thackeray, too, whose attitude, however, is defended by Mrs. Tillotson: »Believing in truth, he can afford to admit that what he writes is fiction. And the illusion is not thereby broken.» But Trollope's greater seriousness of tone in general is no doubt the cause of James's particular indignation with his lapses. It is evident that Trollope in such cases oversteps the bounds of that measure of objectivity which cannot be violated without damage to the illusion even if we admit, in the words of Koskimies (p. 121), that *diese Grenze sehr dehnbar ist und eine eigentliche Norm nicht aufgestellt werden kann.*

As has been noted above (pp. 84—5) Trollope's eagerness to come forward personally in his novels to attack the legal profession was resented mainly because of his ignorance of legal matters, not so much because of his intrusion *per se*. Having discussed these attacks, the *National Review,* 1863, writes that »it would be easy to multiply instances of the same sort of unsubstantial complaint thrown in without any real conviction, as a sort of sentimental garnishing to a matter-of-fact narrative», and argues against his idea that, in the words of the article, »the present race of country gentlemen are a sad falling away from the traditional benevolence of their race». Various digressions into such subjects as the civil service, competitive examinations, etc. in *The Three Clerks* are mildly disapproved of by the same *Review* in 1858 and regarded as somewhat irritating deviations from the story although the author is thought to display »a sound common sense» in them.

Trollope's occasional vulgar characters are strongly disapproved of by the *National Review* in its article on *Orley Farm*:

He drops every now and then with suspicious ease into a society which is simply repulsive in its stupid coarseness; and as he has not the extravagant fun that Dickens pours over low life ... these parts of Mr. Trollope's writings are singularly tedious and unattractive.

Other critics are usually much more lenient in their disapprobation of his vulgarity, which for example the *North American Review*, 1871 (contemplating *Ralph the Heir*), attributes to an inheritance from his mother. James simply says that he »is by no means destitute of a certain saving grace of coarseness».[67]

Now and then some of the critics discover that his vulgar characters appear in his underplots,,or even for the sake of these underplots, which are naturally regarded as digressions and often condemned. But according to Sadleir (pp. 169—70), Longman's reader in his report, Dec. 8, 1856, of *Barchester Towers* condemned even the 'chief actors' of the book, among whom he counted the Signora Neroni, for their utter low-mindedness and vulgarity. The manuscript was altered but not, or not materially, as to the Signora, and although *The Times* does not mention her at all in its review of the book, the *National Review*, 1858, gives an opinion of her which agrees with that of Longman's reader and may therefore be regarded as fairly representative of what Sadleir calls »the squeamish 'fifties». The reviewer writes:

> She is an intrusion upon the stage, utterly out of harmony with the scenes and persons round her, and we cannot but think with the nature of her sex. It is a pity that such a person should have been allowed to force herself on the reader's acquaintance, or the eminently respectable society of the cathedral city.

James's opinion is in accordance with what is thought in our century: »The idea of transporting the Signora Vesey-Neroni into a cathedral-town was an inspiration.»[68]

Most of all, the critics deplore the digressions in *The Last Chronicle of Barset*; the underplots or parallel stories are here, too, found to concern less refined people. Stack of the *Fortnightly*, 1869 (pp. 191—2), asks pathetically, »Why intrude those sketches of comedy and farce — very fair, as they go — into what might have been a very finished story — an enduring piece of English art?» The *Dublin Review*, 1883 (p. 327), like other critics, is annoyed by suddenly being taken, in this book, into 'exceedingly vulgar and low-minded' company. Stack writes, »it seems that, with nothing but a knife, we could make his 'Last Chronicle' one-half shorter and fifty-fold better worth preservation». This is what other critics and some publishers wanted to do, too, and they wanted to do so

with several of his other novels, but any suggestions to cut them down
were indignantly refused by the author. The three-volume system is by
Reeve declared to have been 'Mr. Trollope's bane', and he mentions this
novel as an illustration.[69] *The Last Chronicle* was, incidentally, published
in two volumes but this of course does not alter the gist of the statement.
If, as Quiller-Couch says, »the expensive and artificial vogue of the three-
volume-novel did wonders for Trollope in one generation, to kill him
for another», at any rate his contemporaries did not think the demand
for regulation length did any wonders for the artistic structure of his
books.

Trollope's choice of peculiar names — such as Dr. Pessimist Anticant,
Mr. Sentiment, Mr. Neversay Die, Mr. Stickatit, and (for physicians)
Mr. Rerechild and Mr. Fillgrave (the list could be made very long) — is
censured by the *National Review*, 1858, and James, and both find that
they spoil the illusion. The former hopes, however, because *Doctor
Thorne* contains very little of 'this species of nicknaming', that »Mr.
Trollope has become ashamed of it, as of a trick which belongs of right
to the lowest order of farcical absurdities» (p. 431). It is less frequent in
his later books but he could not bring himself to give it up entirely. »It
would be better to go back to Bunyan at once», says James.[70] Of Mr.
Quiverful, who appears first in *The Warden* as a poor clergyman with
many children, James observes that, »it matters little so long as he is not
brought to the front. But,» he continues, »in *Barchester Towers* . . . Mr.
Quiverful becomes, as a candidate for Mr. Harding's vacant place, an
important element, and the reader is made proportionately unhappy
by the primitive character of this satiric note.» To me, however, he does
not seem to become very important; Trollope clearly intends him to
appear somewhat ludicrous as a passive adjunct in the struggle for
mastery between Mrs. Proudie and Mr. Slope.

In his monograph on *Thackeray* Trollope seems to answer two of the
objections made to himself, the one as to names, and the other as to
vulgarity:

Vanity Fair is especially declared by the author to be a »novel without a
hero» . . . But Captain Dobbin does become the hero, and is deficient. Why was he
called Dobbin, except to make him ridiculous? Why is he so shamefully ugly, so shy,
so awkward? Why was he the son of a grocer? Thackeray in so depicting him was
determined to run counter to the recognised taste of novel readers. (P. 93.)

As is seen from this, Trollope took the same view as James that an
important character should not be given a ridiculous name, and we find

that he himself put his theory into practice fairly well. — Most of his contemporary critics do not seem to object to his 'funny' names *per se*.

Trollope writes further (loc.cit.) that a novel should contain both the virtuous and the vicious, the dignified and the undignified but that »here, in this novel, the vicious and the absurd, have been made to be of more importance than the good and the noble». And he finds (p. 98) that though readers 'complain of pages which are defiled with that which is low, yet the absurd, the ludicrous, and even the evil, leave more impression behind them than the grand, the beautiful, or even the good'. This was already his conviction when writing *Barchester Towers* where we find the following lines (Ch. LI): »The sorrows of our heroes and heroines, they are your delight, oh public! their sorrows, or their sins, or their absurdities; not their virtues, good sense, and consequent rewards.» In other words, he had a feeling that whether or not the novelist did his duty to give the undignified a subordinate place, it would 'leave more impression behind it' than the dignified. He also believed of the novel that it must please, or as he writes in *Thackeray* (p. 191): »Its only excuse is to be found in the amusement it affords.» Consequently absurdities, the undignified, became an important, even if subordinate, element in his work, and he put it in even when readers felt it was not wanted; and he was not discriminating enough to avoid the distasteful vulgarism of which he was in some cases justly accused.

Still, his sense of humour, even when resulting in comedy and farce, was frequently praised, mostly perhaps as displayed in *Barchester Towers*. The *Dublin Review*, 1869 (XII, 363), probably expresses the average opinion of what was appreciated in his less exuberant work: »His quiet humour plays a part in his pictures of domestic life like that of light reading in serious study; it comes in, and brightens up things and persons, blending pleasantly with business.»

Love is the constant ingredient in all Trollope's stories in accordance with his opinion that »a novel can hardly be made interesting or successful without love», »because the passion is one which interests or has interested all» (*A*, 201—2). James, perhaps, expresses best what the novels no doubt appeared to be like to many of Trollope's readers:

His story is always primarily a love-story, and a love-story constructed on an inveterate system. There is a young lady who has two lovers, or a young man who has two sweethearts; we are treated to the innumerable forms in which this predicament may present itself and the consequences, sometimes pathetic, sometimes grotesque, which spring from such false situations.[71]

The situations may be somewhat 'false', but they are usual in comedy. Yet the 'plot' was good enough as handled by Trollope for we may take Reeve to voice the general sentiment when writing:

> When we embrace, in a comprehensive retrospect, the long series of his works, it is curious to observe how ingeniously he has contrived to vary that very common-place and unoriginal idea. Time after time in his practical experience it has been as fruitful of interest and fresh situations as if it had never been handled before.[72]

Still, the too long hesitations of the girl, or sometimes the young man, were censured by some critics, for example the *Dublin Review*, 1872 (p. 401):

> He is apt to make persons to whom such calculating sagacity could hardly come naturally, balance the *to be or not to be,* of everything too calmly and too long. Numerous instances of this imputation of almost impossible cautiousness and self-restraint, this mental seesaw, present themselves on examination of his later novels; and it is remarkable that he most frequently represents their exercise precisely in that class of human affairs in which impulse is supposed most generally and legitimately to act, that is to say, in love affairs.

To this could be answered that several of Trollope's stories with much 'shilly-shally' about match-making are not really love-stories; they are social pictures like the main part of *Ralph the Heir*, which the *Review* mentions as an example illustrating what it complains of. The question of marriage in them is not only a question of love; it is a question which involves several social and moral aspects. The *Review* could further have been reminded of the observation made in its article on *Phineas Finn* in 1869 (XII, 370) that 'Mr. Trollope knows how to distinguish with amazing subtlety love-making from love'.

On the other hand the public did not want to put up with social pictures when it expected 'a real love-story' as *Blackwood's* writes in May 1870, protesting against *The Vicar of Bullhampton*.

> We decline to believe (says the reviewer) that a history of how Miss or Mr Somebody managed to get married is at all the same thing. It is hard for us to say a word against a writer from whom we have received so much amusement; but we must entreat him to consider his ways — to take thought and mend — to go back upon his original canons, and to free us of the Mary Lowthers.

The interest of this book, too, is, as James finds, »essentially a moral, a social interest».[73]

If the love element in Trollope's later books was thus found to be receding, as must be assumed to the particular regret of the public at large, his critics were at any rate not aware of any prearrangement, of any didactic purpose in his novels. The digressions already mentioned (p. 104) and occasional preachings on the subject of marriage were things apart from the story. Though noticing the moral and social interest of the novel last mentioned, James says in so many words that »it would be difficult to state the idea of this slow but excellent story».

However, Trollope does not look upon the love-theme only as a means to gain popularity. He expressly declares that it is his desire to 'teach wholesome lessons in regard to love' (A, 202). He considers the subject to be very serious and the novelist's influence and responsibility to be very great in this matter particularly.

> I regard him (he says) who can put himself into close communion with young people year after year without making some attempt to do them good, as a very sorry fellow indeed. — — The novelist creeps in closer than the schoolmaster, closer than the father, closer almost than the mother. He is the chosen guide, the tutor whom the young pupil chooses for herself. She retires with him, suspecting no lesson, safe against rebuke, throwing herself head and heart into the narration . . . and there she is taught, — how she shall learn to love; how she shall receive the lover when he comes; how far she should advance to meet the joy; why she should be reticent, and not throw herself at once into this new delight. — — The young man . . . too will there learn either to speak the truth, or to lie; . . . lessons either of real manliness, or of that affected apishness . . . which too many professors of the craft give out as their dearest precepts.[74]

Such theories expressed thus outspokenly a few years before his death (in *Thackeray* in 1879) and confirmed after it (in the *Autobiography*) must needs affect his reputation. However sound, they must strike his readers as extremely commonplace, philistine, and unbelievably naive for any one with any pretensions to be a writer at all.

Still the comments on the way he put his theories into practice, as far as they were noticed, are here of a greater interest. *The Times* reviewer of *Orley Farm* in 1862 characterizes the Noningsby episodes very much as the result of such ideas as Trollope entertained and the praise seems to be sincere:

> There are the prettiest love scenes, in which all the gentlemen and all the ladies act with a correctness that is truly laudable. The way in which they make love to each other without ever getting off the rails is a miracle of art. Especially do we admire the formulas which he has invented for persons who make proposals of marriage. It used to be said . . . that in the performance of this interesting ceremony people are very much guided by novels as their book of fashion. — — And we must give his formulas the double praise of being sufficiently varied and of having no nonsense in them.

Reeve of the *Edinburgh* (1877, p. 470) contemplates Trollope's »pet doctrine of the propriety of matrimony in almost any conceivable circumstances when the lovers are young», which he finds to be 'in-culcated more uncompromisingly' than elsewhere in *The Bertrams* where the author exclaims: »Ah! young ladies, sweet young ladies, dear embryo mothers of our England as it will be, think not overmuch of your lovers' incomes. He that is true and honest will not have to beg his bread, neither his nor yours.» Reeve calls him an 'earnest preacher' but finds the doctrine so questionable that he thinks it »might make careful mothers hesitate as to putting these pleasant stories of his 'into the hands of young people'». *The Times* reviewer and Reeve are clearly mid-Victorians proper. Stack objects to the routine of Trollope's handling of the theme (see above, p. 91). The *Dublin Review*, 1883 (XL, 332—3) objects to his doctrine mostly, it appears, to get an opportunity to speak for Catholicism:

> The one good goal held out alike to girl and man, as much in Trollope's novels as in any tale of fairy prince and princess familiar to us from the nursery, is simply to marry and live happy for ever after. That there even exists a higher phase of life Trollope ignores; indeed, we fear, might have denied. — —

These comments on his attitude and opinions seem, however, to weigh light as a feather against the evidences of the charm emanating especially from his earlier love-stories. The fact that they were 'pure and healthy' was important not only because of the moral code of the period but because their charm was found to be inherent in this pureness (cf. above, p. 80; and p. 101, the *National Review* on 'the innocence of the per-formers'). In spite of its ideas about 'a higher phase of life', the *Dublin Review*, 1883, like others, falls under this charm as radiating for instance from *The Small House at Allington*, of which the *Review* (pp. 325—6) writes: »The interest of the book lies in Lily's deep love for a worthless fellow. — — The power with which the deep purity of her love is drawn is so great . . . Lily Dale's is a perfect picture of a woman's perfect love.» No higher praise could be conferred on any love-stories than Reeve's verdict upon Trollope's that they show the author's power of 'time after time' treating the theme (and even the same variation of it) 'as if it had never been handled before'. But as has been mentioned (above p. 80), the interest is really focused rather on the girl than on the story (Lily Dale's story is rather an exception in exciting about as much interest as her character); the success of Trollope's love-stories is found by the critics, more or less clearly, to be due to his power of representing the English girl in love, the 'simple maiden in her flower'. »There is art», says Stack[75], »in Trollope's not introducing us to the girl (Grace Crawley) until she is loved». And Stack points out what an important artistic

contribution Grace Crawley's love-story is to the effect of the mainly
tragic *Last Chronicle*. But it is not the main plot of this book, just as the
love-story in many other Trollopian books is more or less what the
Dublin Review, 1883, finds it to be, 'a mere episode'. James's sweeping
statement that 'his story is always primarily a love-story' must be
modified by substituting 'often' for 'always'. Love is an important part
of life, everything, young people may feel, but Trollope knows it is only
a part. »He tells», the *Dublin Review*, 1883 (p. 318), writes, »more than one
story, the main interest of which centres in the doings and sufferings of
those well advanced in life.»

The comedy and the love-stories in Trollope's novels aimed at securing
the popularity without which he thought the novelist worked in vain.
Very often the emotional appeal of his work is also noted and commented
on as a thing apart whether found in the love-stories, the social interest
in marriage, or other sides of human intercourse described by him. It is
found that »he is not a sentimentalist like Mr. Dickens»[76], and we note
that Trollope himself finds that the pathos of Dickens is not human, but
'stagey and melodramatic' (*A*, 221). Still »there is», as the *Dublin Review*
writes in 1872 (p. 401),

no lack of healthy emotions, or of unhealthy emotions, in Mr. Trollope's novels;
he apportions them as they are apportioned, in fact, to human beings; but there
is an absence of demonstrativeness, a quietude, perfectly in keeping with the
standard of good breeding.

The pathos of some of his stories, or parts of them, is, in fact, looked upon
as raising him far above his ordinary level. *The Last Chronicle* is un-
animously put first for this quality; »*The Warden* comes next», says Stack,
but the 'humanizing pathos' of Lady Mason's story in *Orley Farm*
seems to be more admired by others, for instance the *Cornhill*. »In a
hundred places in Trollope», says James[77], »the extremity of pathos is
reached by the homeliest means. He often achieved a conspicuous intensity of the tragical.» But James differs from other contemporary critics[78]
in appreciating also *He Knew He Was Right* for the pathos of the suspicious husband who gradually grows mad. In this novel, says James,
Trollope »has not sacrificed to conventional optimism; he has not been
afraid of a misery which should be too much like life». (James praises
him for 'the same courage' in the history of Mr. Crawley and in that of
Lady Mason.) But, as Trollope writes in the *Autobiography* (p. 280),
'the unfortunate man' failed to evoke the intended sympathy, and the
reason is given by the *Dublin Review* (p. 425) thus:

Mr. Trollope does not adorn the man with qualities to inspire interest before his calamity overtakes him, and so he fails to evoke compassion after it has done so. Nobody can care whether Louis Trevelyan is mad or sane, for he is an ill-tempered snob from the beginning, and his wife is detestable.

»A modern reader», says Sadleir (p. 393), »must inevitably find the unhappy, haunted creature rather pathetic than repellent». »This was not», he adds, »the only occasion upon which Trollope showed himself in advance of the taste of the time». It is rather remarkable that Sadleir ignores James's appreciation of this character; in fact, he does not refer to James's essay on Trollope at all, which, I think would be the only fair thing for him to do after his peevish account of James's early (1866) condemnation of *The Belton Estate*. — The pathetic situation of such a subordinate character as Lady Scatcherd in *Doctor Thorne* is justly appreciated by the *National Review*, 1858 (p. 433): »There is much truth and pathos in the picture of her desolate solitude of spirit, when left absolutely alone to bear 'the burden of an honour whereunto she was not born'» having been the hard-working wife of a stone-mason before he was knighted.

The pathetic is often conspicuous in his dispensation of poetic justice, and the story of Lady Mason is a case in point. Whatever aesthetic rules Trollope may have violated, he felt like Liddell (p. 107) that 'wanton cruelty on the part of an author towards his characters is shocking', and was found to regard even the wicked with so much sympathy as to make them pathetic when punished. The fairness with which he administers poetic justice is perceived by the *North British Review*, 1864, perhaps with more acuteness than by other contemporary critics. Contemplating the fate of Mr. Crosbie, who jilts Lily Dale and »sells himself to marry an Earl's daughter» in *The Small House*, and Alaric Tudor in *The Three Clerks*, »who speculates with his ward's money», the reviewer writes (p. 395):

They do very contemptible things, but they are not irredeemably bad; and when they have smarted under such cutting, yet restrained scourgings, as no dispenser of poetic justice knows better than Mr. Trollope how to administer, we are glad to think that they may take their places once more among mankind, and are not driven for ever beyond the pale. — — Mr. Trollope shows nowhere so much of what Dr. Arnold called »moral thoughtfulness», as in the kind of retribution with which he visits such delinquents as Crosbie and Alaric Tudor.

His way of dispensing rewards and punishments is noted by the same reviewer for another characteristic, which would, perhaps, have struck him even more if he had been able to read Trollope's avowal in the *Autobiography* that his purpose was to teach moral lessons.

.There is, indeed (the reviewer writes), no very broad and palpable system of rewards and punishments in his long series of novels, any more than in the world which they are intended to represent. The good apprentice does not always become Lord Mayor; nor is the idle one sent to the gallows. (He may hang his hero, or heroine, the reviewer points out, as when he leaves Lily Dale unmarried.) But although there is no hint of any kind of connexion between good and evil in themselves, and good and evil fortune, bad actions produce their moral consequence as they do in the world.

The reviewer goes on to speak of Crosbie's retribution quoting a passage which he calls 'a picture of social degradation'. The *Dublin Review*, 1883 (p. 325), shows a keener sense for the artistic quality:

The description of Crosbie and his feelings is a masterpiece in fiction. We see the innermost workings of his nature, his weak worldliness and repeated vacillation and even, in his better moments, his own contempt for himself, painted to the life.

But Trollope could also desist from passing judgment as is found by the *Pall Mall Gazette*, Jan. 20, 1881, in its review of *Dr. Wortle's School*, one of his last novels, in which »a very delicate question is discussed in the spirit of genial common-sense that characterizes Mr. Trollope's philosophy». Trollope is here found to balance morality and charity and, while keeping them 'alike wholesome', to leave the question of right or wrong open in the given case. »Probably», says the reviewer, »most readers will endorse the view of Mr. Puddicombe, and 'love him (the doctor) the better for what he did, though they dare not say that in morals he was strictly correct'.» We might add that the poetic justice administered in this story indicates at any rate once more that Trollope is against social prejudice.

It seems that most of Trollope's contemporary critics might well have agreed to James's conclusion:

Trollope will remain one of the most trustworthy, though not one of the most eloquent, of writers who have helped the heart of man to know itself. — — His natural rightness and purity are so real that the good things he projects must be real. A race is fortunate when it has a good deal of the sort of imagination — of imaginative feeling — that had fallen to the share of Anthony Trollope; and in this possession our English race is not poor.[79]

This conclusion of James's article seems to form a kind of summing-up of Trollope's significance. Anyhow, it must be interpreted as genuine praise for James says in 'The Art of Fiction' (p. 21): »There is one point at which the moral sense and the artistic sense lie very near together; that is in the light of the very obvious truth that the deepest quality of art will always be the quality of the mind of the producer. No good novel will ever proceed from a superficial mind.»

8 — *Rafael Helling*

As was noted earlier (p. 102), a whole world seems to be suggested by
the enthusiastic description of the mass of Trollope's characters in one
passage of the *Dublin Review*, 1872. This is evidently in some measure the
impression of Reeve, too, who in the *Edinburgh*, 1877 (p. 458), observes
that Trollope »is rather an artist of the Rubens stamp, who dashes off
broad yet telling effects on long stretches of canvas; and . . . carries his
leading figures through an assorted succession of works». But the strongest
and most elaborate contemporary evidence of such an impression is given
by the *Dublin Review*, 1883 (pp. 323—4):

> Trollope must have felt no small confidence in his power to sustain the reader's
> interest in his characters, and also an assurance that the previous stories had been
> read, to have adopted the plan of carrying a history of fiction, through book after
> book. Not but that each story is complete in itself; yet to fully enjoy the succeeding
> ones, those novels which came before ought to have been read. — — The Barsetshire
> series is very like real life. We are set down in a country town, and at once make the
> acquaintance and become interested in our neighbours. Time goes on; and now
> and again a group which has been made prominent in one story disappears in the
> next . . . Our favourites and our real friends, however, stay on, only we see more
> now of one and then of another of them. For example: Eleanor Warden (sic) is
> the heroine of »The Warden», and again, as . . . Mrs. Bold, of »Barchester Towers».
> She then becomes Mrs. Arabin; and for the future plays a subordinate part in the
> history of Barchester. — — If we look back at our own lives for the last five and
> twenty years, is not this very much what we have actually experienced?

We note that this reviewer is contemplating 'The Chronicles of Barsetshire', published by Chapman and Hall as a separate series in eight
volumes already in 1879, four years before this article; we note further
that this observation of the continuity and totality of the 'Chronicles'
is made in distinct terms only after the novels had been brought out as
such a series through the efforts of the author himself. Whether aware
of the separately published series or not, James also notices Trollope's
»practice of carrying certain actors from one story to another — a practice
(James continues) which he may be said to have inherited from Thackeray,
as Thackeray may be said to have borrowed it from Balzac».[80] But he
appears to belittle the difficulty of portraying society in this way when
writing: »It is a great mistake, however, to speak of it as an artifice
which would not naturally occur to a writer proposing to himself to make
a general portrait of a society»; just as he seems to find the construction
of a society an easy thing to do for a writer with a mind for such things:
»He has to construct that society . . . Trollope constructed a great many
things — a clergy, an aristocracy, a middle-class, an administrative class,

a little replica of the political world.» This fact James finds worthy of no further comment. 'The historian of fine consciences', as Conrad calls James[81], shows little interest in these aspects of Trollope's genius and work.

But the *Dublin Review* in the passage last quoted voices an opinion that came to be shared by several prominent critics of the twentieth century. In spite of 'the partiality, the inevitable imperfection of contemporary criticism' (to cite V. Woolf's phrase once more), the writer of this article, evidently finding his author worthy of a more careful study than other contemporary critics found him, appears to have sensed much of the novelist's real appeal, his lasting quality, and to have sensed more of it than even many later critics. And already in 1872 the same *Review* gave, as we have seen from several quotations, a remarkably profound and enthusiastic appreciation of Trollope especially as a painter of society.

When pointing to the society of Barsetshire with its changing generations the *Dublin Review* evidently has the notion that by the construction of this society Trollope enhances our interest in his characters and their lives although the passage begins by putting the matter the other way round, by wondering that the author thinks our interest in his characters is strong enough to be sustained through a number of books, through a lifetime in the society of Barsetshire. Indeed, Trollope did not 'plan' his 'Barsetshire series' at all, it just grew, as we find from his preface to 'The Chronicles', but I shall revert to this point later. For the moment it is enough to establish the fact that Trollope is thought to have essentially increased our interest in his characters by the 'method' here referred to because it makes them more life-like to us, more like our real acquaintances than ordinary fictitious characters; in other words, because it increases our pleasure of recognition.

But long before this pleasure-value of Trollope's 'artifice' was analysed in words, it must have been felt by his readers if there was any such value. »All values are vain, unless we can feel, as well as see, their value», to quote Lucas (p. 261). In *Blackwood's*, 1867 (CII, 276—8), we find a critic's expression of such feelings:

> There is nobody living who has added so many pleasant people to our acquaintance, or given us so many neighbourly interests out of our own immediate circle. — — Yet we would chide our beloved novelist for his 'Last Chronicle'. *We* did not ask that this chronicle should be the last. We were in no hurry to be done with our friends. And there are certain things which he has done without consulting us against which we greatly demur. To kill Mrs Proudie was murder, or manslaughter at the least. — — As for old Mr Harding, our grief for his loss is yet too fresh to permit us to speak of him. We should like to go to Barchester . . .

This is the earliest example I have found of a veritable nostalgia for Trollope's fictitious world, of which the Barsetshire series was felt to present the nucleus just as it was commonly regarded as representing his best work. His other novels were often more or less impatiently brushed away by the critics with a longing reminder of the Barsetshire novels, as is done for instance by *The Times*, Aug. 26, 1869, when writing in its review of *He Knew He Was Right:* »The Barsetshire series show us his high merit; and they are so equal, so perfect in themselves, and so necessary to each other, that we wish for nothing else than they can give us.» Reeve expresses the feeling thus:

The novel (*Barchester Towers*) has fallen into its place in the sequence which had made us so thoroughly at home in the mixed society of Barsetshire. — — (In the later books) we are delighted to renew our former acquaintanceship or intimacies; to remark how our friends are looking, and whether they have greatly changed since we saw them last. — — We have always a pleasant home-feeling when we meet the Luftons or the Greshams in a crush. For they bring back the memory of pleasant days, and charm us with their allusions to happy old times.[82]

As has been mentioned in Part I, the nostalgia of our century for this world may be explained by the wars and the feeling of social insecurity. From the passages quoted above — to which may be added the one quoted on pp. 102—3 from the *Dublin Review*, 1872 — it is evident that Trollope's contemporaries already found in his novels not only the means of an escape which every story provides but a distinct country, to which they longed to go, a dreamland at once remote and near and real; and all the better for not being quite identical with the real world, for leaving so many aspects out of the picture as the *Dublin Review*, 1872, points out though somewhat incorrectly calling Trollope's fiction »a faithful portraiture of the present» (see above, p. 95).

> *The test of the novel is that it should be a l i v e. No subject in itself, however fruitful, appears to be able to keep a novel alive; only the characters in it can.*[83]

Trollope expresses the same conviction when writing that the novelist's chief aim is to make his characters to his readers »speaking, moving, living, human creatures». And in human nature he sees the novelist's supreme guide although he believes that the common reader is the supreme critic (cf. above, p. 71). When writing of Dickens's popularity, »Such evidence of popular appreciation should go for very much, almost for everything, in criticism on the work of a novelist', the 'almost' is put in reluctantly, or with some doubt, because »the primary object of a novelist is to please; and this man's novels have been found to be more pleasant than those of any other writer». (*A*, 221.) But to Trollope Dickens is an exception in being able to 'dispense with human nature', and because, in Trollope's opinion, his characters 'are not human beings', Trollope is rather unhappy about being compelled to find the 'collected world of readers' wrong in preferring Dickens to Thackeray. Trollope does not try to deny the contradiction between his own principles in this case, but we must take him to mean that, even if the primary object of the novelist is to please, he should please by keeping his characters within the bounds of human nature. In other words, he seems to declare that he has an artistic principle, the realist's principle, from which he does not want to deviate even if the common reader, the supreme critic, should declare him to be wrong. In his opinion Thackeray stands as the first novelist because »his knowledge of human nature was supreme, and his characters stand out as human beings, with a force and truth which has not, I think, been within the reach of any other English novelist in any period» (*A*, 217).

Human nature is regarded by Trollope as the novelist's particular guide in dialogue: 'Knowledge of human nature will tell him with accuracy what men and women would say in this or that position'. And this knowledge he will acquire by listening and observing. (*A*, 216.) But for the sake of artistic delicacy and effect Trollope does not want the novelist to follow 'nature' uncompromisingly: »The novel-writer must so steer between absolute accuracy of language — which would give to his conversation an air of pedantry, and the slovenly inaccuracy of ordinary talkers, which . . . would offend . . . — as to produce upon the ear of his readers a sense of reality» (*A*, 215). In *Thackeray*, Ch. IX, he expounds the same theory with the characteristic addition that the realistic writer (by 'the realistic' he means 'that which shall seem real') »has to maintain varying distances in accordance with the position, mode of life, and education of the speakers». In other words, the dialogue, to have the appearance of naturally spoken language, should also reveal the position of the personages to society at large.

Before these theories of Trollope's had been published in print, several critics had found occasion to praise his dialogues. The *Dublin Review*, 1869 (p. 369), for instance, called them 'natural' and 'characteristic'; and Henry Reeve gave it as his opinion that Trollope's realism had, in fact, helped to make him unique in them:

Mr Trollope has had a multiplicity of imitators, but no successful rivals in his particular line. Realism slightly idealised is his guiding law; yet imagination must play no insignificant part in it. — — Take the pains to examine those dialogues by Mr. Trollope which occupy so large a space in his works. Select a single one of them almost at random, and you will pronounce it a piece of faithful reporting and a creditable effort of the memory. To all appearance there is really very little in it; no brilliant bits of epigram or stinging repartees; very possibly not a single line that is pointed enough to be worth the quoting. Yet — — when we have come to the end of the book . . . we shall find that it is the undefinable qualities of that talk which have given us so hearty an interest in the speakers.[84]

If human nature (somewhat modified) taught Trollope how to make his characters speak, he was also well aware of the fact that human nature — particularly the natural inclinations of his readers — demanded that the novelist should strive for a 'pellucid' and 'harmonious' style in general simply in order to be read and not rejected: »Let him have all other possible gifts — imagination, observation, erudition, and industry, — they will avail him nothing for his purpose, unless he can put forth his work in pleasant words» (*A*, 210).

This means style in the narrow sense of language, which James censures in Trollope while admiring its effects and thus creates the ambiguity that Morris Roberts, in his Introduction, xiii, to *The Art of Fiction*, finds characteristic in James's criticism, an ambiguity which is due to the fact that James does not regard subject and style as separable things.

Trollope is not (James writes) what is called a colourist; still less is he a poet he is seated on the back of heavy-footed prose. But his account of those sentiments which the poets are supposed to have made their own is apt to be as touching as demonstrations more lyrical. There is something wonderfully vivid in the state of mind of the unfortunate Harry Gilmore (in *The Vicar of Bullhampton*). . .; and his history, which has no more pretensions to style than if it were cut out of yesterday's newspaper, lodges itself in the imagination in all sorts of classic company.[85]

If his 'heavy-footed prose' could produce such an effect, the *Dublin Review*, 1872 (p. 398) seems indeed to be right in regarding his style to be »in harmony with the purport and nature of his novels» and we can hardly wish for anything better.

It seems, however, rather useless to pay much attention to Trollope's style in a narrow sense of the word because what matters in his story or portraiture is its cumulative effect, or as James says, »the gradual abundance of his testimony», »the slow and somewhat clumsy accumulation of small illustrations».[86] Most of his contemporaries find his language admirable, clear, masculine, and so on, as a means of conveying his meaning, and *Blackwood's*, 1862 (p. 372), sees in it a reflection of his own enthusiasm: »His style of writing is brisk and flowing, assuring us that the author enjoys the work he is engaged in, and fully believes in his own creations»; while James, as we have seen, regards Trollope's style as journalistic, but finds at the same time that his work had decidedly those qualities which, as Daiches would say, distinguish 'literature' from 'journalism'.[87] To W. H. Pollock's high opinion of Trollope's style, expressed in 1883, I shall revert later.

In fact, though James in the passage last quoted speaks of 'style' in its narrow sense, he has simultaneously in mind the comprehensive meaning given to the word, for instance, by Mrs. Wharton, who defines style as »the way in which they (the incidents, but the definition should apply to the characters as well) are represented, not only in the narrower sense of the language, but also, and rather, as they are grasped and coloured by their medium, the narrator's mind, and given back in his words». She continues (p. 24): »It is the quality of the medium which gives these incidents their quality; style, in this sense, is the most personal ingredient in the combination of things out of which any work of art is made. — — Style in this definition is discipline.» Daiches's (p. 34) definition also seems helpful: »Style then — to employ this term for that use of language which distinguishes art from mere communication — is a handling of words in such a way as to produce both recognition *and* insight.» And although in his criticism James prefers such conceptions as the novelist's sensibility and angle of vision[88], style in this comprehensive sense is, no doubt, what James praises in Trollope when contemplating 'the impression of life' in his books:

> It is a marvel by what homely arts, by what imperturbable button-holding persistence, he contrives to excite this impression. Take, for example, such a work as *The Vicar of Bullhampton*. It would be difficult to state the idea of this slow but excellent story, which is a capital example of interest produced by the quietest conceivable means. — — If the interest is gradual it is extreme and constant, and it comes altogether from excellent portraiture. — — There is something masterly in the large-fisted grip with which, in work of this kind, Trollope handles his brush.[89]

In this comprehensive sense 'style' must be taken to imply, among other conceptions, tone and atmosphere, but, as the moral aspects and the 'seriousness' of Trollope have already been treated, I think only Stack's and James's notions of Trollope as an artist in this respect are worthy of further notice. Stack writes:

> In one respect Mr. Trollope deserves praise that even Dickens and Thackeray do not deserve. Many of his stories are more true throughout to that unity of design,

that harmony of tone and colour, which are essential to works of art. — — He has
a true artist's idea of tone, of colour, of harmony; his pictures are one; are seldom
out of drawing; he never strains after effect; he is fidelity itself in expressing English
life; is never guilty of caricature.[90]

The praise is so much the more noteworthy as Stack is annoyed at
Trollope's digressions and his 'utterly wrong' choice of subjects (see
above, p. 89).

James thinks that Trollope's »fund of acquaintance with his own
country — and indeed with the world at large — was apparently inexhaustible» because of his travels 'all over the globe' and his work at the
Post-Office. This makes James compare Trollope's »tone of allusion to
many lands and many things — — with that narrow vision of humanity
which accompanies the strenuous, serious work lately offered to us in
such abundance by the votaries of art for art who sit so long at their
desks in Parisian *quatrièmes*». Trollope is »so occasional, so accidental,
so full of the echoes of voices that are not the voice of the muse», while the
French »are nothing if not concentrated and sedentary», but still
»Trollope's realism is as instinctive, as inveterate as theirs», and »I think»,
says James, »he tells us, on the whole, more about life than the 'naturalists'
in our sister republic» because »his perception of character was naturally
more just and liberal» than theirs. This advantage, however, Trollope
shares with English writers in general, James concludes. Whatever their
inferiority in other respects to the French, »they have been more at home
in the moral world; as people say to-day they know their way about
conscience».[91]

An appreciation of the quality of the novelist's mind seems to be
implied in all criticism on fiction, but more, perhaps, in the evaluation
of imagination than other aspects. Something of the writer's imaginative
power will certainly be seen from the work, but it may also lead to false
conclusions, as is evident from the criticism on Trollope before his *Autobiography* was published or read.

In the concluding passage of James's article (above p. 150) we find
a reserve expressed in the words: »the sort of imagination — of imaginative
feeling — that had fallen to the share of Anthony Trollope». Earlier in
the article (p. 102) James says:

The striking thing to the critic was that his robust and patient mind had no
particular bias, his imagination no light of its own. He saw things neither pictorially
and grotesquely like Dickens; nor with that combined disposition to satire and to
literary form which gives such »body», as they say of wine, to the manner of

Thackeray; nor with anything of the philosophic, the transcendental cast . . . which we associate with the name of George Eliot. Trollope had his elements of fancy, of satire, of irony; but these qualities were not very highly developed, and he walked mainly by the light of his good sense, his clear, direct vision of the things that lay nearest, and his great natural kindness.

The statement that »his imagination had no light of its own» has later been taken as depreciation, but if the reader contemplates the whole passage quoted, he will probably feel that the statement is meant as an explanation of James's earlier declaration that Trollope's »great, his inestimable merit was a complete appreciation of the usual». At least James's intention appears to be only to explain. Even if James had once in his youth, when twenty-three years of age, written that *The Belton Estate* was a 'stupid book, without a single idea', and even if he »was to become one of the typical minds of the aesthetic period» as Sadleir writes (p. 392), James's article of 1883 seems to be a sincere attempt to understand and interpret the essence of Trollope. His opinion of 'the votaries of art for art' quoted above does not show any great awe of such 'aesthetic' writers as Flaubert and Daudet. But to my mind much in this article goes to show that James was puzzled. Trollope's means were so simple, the effects of many of his novels so great; you could put your finger on some points of great merit, but then you would discover the absence of so much that you had expected — »as a general thing he has no great story to tell»; »not even much description» (of the kind cultivated by the French realists); »leaving so many corners unvisited, so many topics untouched»; 'no more pretentions to style than a newspaper' — and as to his imagination, could he be really said to have much of it as compared to his great contemporaries? It would not tally with his 'appreciation of the usual' if he had, James seems to have thought.

Still James does grant him a certain kind of imagination in another passage of his article (apart from the conclusion quoted on p. 113); having described how Trollope could write even 'on the tumbling ocean in his small sea-chamber', James writes:

Trollope has been accused of being deficient in imagination, but in the face of such a fact as that the charge will scarcely seem just. The power to shut one's eyes, one's ears (to say noting of another sense), upon the scenery of a pitching Cunarder and open them upon the loves and sorrows of Lily Dale or the conjugal embarrassments of Lady Glencora Palliser, is certainly a faculty which could take to itself wings. The imagination that Trollope possessed he had at least thoroughly at his command. I speak of all this in order to explain (in part) why it was that, with his extraordinary gift, there was always in him a certain infusion of the common. He abused his gift, overworked it, rode his horse too hard. (P. 99.)

James evidently thinks that much imagination was not really needed to produce Trollope's work and, curiously enough, he calls Trollope's power of drawing character an 'instinctive perception':

> The source of his success in describing the life that lay nearest to him, and describing it without any of those artistic perversions that come, as we have said, from a powerful imagination, . . . the essence of this love of reality was his extreme interest in character. This is the fine and admirable quality in Trollope . . . If he was in any degree a man of genius (and I hold that he was), it was in virtue of this happy, instinctive perception of human varieties. — — He never attempted to take the so-called scientific view . . . He had no airs of being able to tell you *why* people in a given situation would conduct themselves in a particular way; it was enough for him that he felt their feelings and struck the right note, because he had, as it were, a good ear. If he was a knowing psychologist he was so by grace; he was just and true without apparatus and without effort. He must have had a great taste for the moral question; he evidently believed that this is the basis of the interest of fiction. (Pp. 104—5.)

It seems as if James thought that if you did not take yourself seriously, if you did not prove by some turns of expression that you knew the psychological explanations of what your characters did, no matter how life-like you made them by your 'instinct', then 'imagination' was too fine a word to be employed to denote your 'quality'. It also seems that, as James felt the impetus to Trollope's interest in character to be 'a great taste for the moral question', this 'taste' was perhaps something, too, that the critic could legitimately speak of instead of 'imagination' in Trollope's works. Again, like some other critics (cf. above, pp. 79 and 86 ff.), James also attributes Trollope's power of characterization to some mystic 'knowledge':

> He knew about bishops, archdeacons, prebendaries, precentors, and about their wives and daughters; he knew what these dignitaries say to each other when they are collected together, aloof from secular ears. He even knew what sort of talk goes on between a bishop and a bishop's lady when the august couple are enshrouded in the privacy of the episcopical bedroom. This knowledge, somehow, was rare and precious. No one, as yet, had been bold enough to snatch the illuminating torch from the very summit of the altar. Trollope enlarged his field very speedily . . . But he always retained traces of his early divination of the clergy. (P. 112.)

Still we find that James, long before Cecil and Liddell, knew that the artist's range, the work of his imagination, is more important than external experience (cf. above, p. 80). In 'The Art of Fiction' (pp. 10—11) he very thoroughly expounds the relation between the writer's knowledge of facts and the subject as represented in his work. »When the mind is imaginative», he says, »— much more when it happens to be that of a man of genius — it takes to itself the faintest hints of life, it converts the very pulses of the air into revelations.» Such a mind has »the power to guess the unseen from the seen», it belongs to an individual of »the people on whom nothing is lost». James illustrates what he means by telling how an English lady-novelist »had been congratulated on her peculiar opportunities» to learn »the nature and life of the French Protestant youth» of which she had given so true an impression in one of her tales, whereas her opportunities had consisted in a glimpse of some young Protestants »seated at a table round a finished meal». But her admirers had asked her »where she had learned so much about this recondite being». As we know Trollope had been asked similar questions as to his clergy. Comparing what James writes of the lady-novelist to his passage about Trollope's clergy, written only about a year earlier and so carefully avoiding the word 'imagination', one cannot help thinking that, in spite of the many good things he said of Trollope, James was prejudiced against him in some measure. After all he could hardly have been the conscious artist he was, if he had not been. James's criticism is a very good illustration of the fact that, even with the best intentions to adopt a liberal view of art, the 'aesthetes' were unable to acknowledge the full merit of an unconscious artist.

On the other hand James's criticism in general abounds in such expressions as 'direct impression or perception of life', 'felt life', 'the artist's prime sensibility, which is the soil out of which his subjects spring', 'vision of life'[92], 'the »taste» of the poet is . . . his active sense of life'[93]; and he has been thought to mean in these cases that a novelist selects and composes his slice of life, creates, as Morris Roberts expresses it, »a new value and a new importance», that, in short, »The artist's imagination is a life-giving faculty».[94] His calling Trollope's power of drawing character 'instinctive perception', 'rare knowledge', or even 'divination' also seems to require an interpretation, but if, fundamentally, James does not mean 'imagination' by these terms, it seems difficult to understand what he means.

Twenty years earlier the *National Review* called Trollope's characters 'public property' and wrote about »the prolific imagination which has called them into existence». The following appreciations also supply interesting contrasts to James's over-subtle distinctions:

There is no fair use of the word in which it can be said that the inventor of so many characters is destitute of imagination. (*North British Review*, 1864, p. 391.)
»How do you know what we women say to another when we get alone?» asked

a lady. Trollope's answer is not recorded; but had he answered truly, perhaps he would have said he did not *know*, he only *imagined*; and being gifted with a true imagination, we have a satisfactory result. (*Dublin Review*, 1883, pp. 329—30.)

In several passages, however, James admits that Trollope could give to his work what James calls in other writings 'a sense of *felt life*'; and if, as Daiches says (p. 133), a 'creative imagination alone' can give it to fiction, it seems reasonable to conclude that the most important critics (including James, but excluding Stack) among Trollope's contemporaries acknowledged in words or in thought that he had all the imagination he wanted for his work, and that this work demanded no little amount of it. Daiches (pp. 133—4) supplies a passage which appears to contain the very standard by which Trollope's imagination can be aptly measured:

Novels, if they are good novels . . . are all, in the last analysis, expressions of the author's excitement about life, about experience. The literary imagination is bound up with that excitement and cannot exist without it. That combination of recognition and insight, which we have claimed as the unique effect of imaginative literature, comes with liveliness and a sense of life. The artist . . . must first be fascinated by experience, and his interpretation must communicate that fascination.

This is what Trollope's interpretation communicates as was found by his contemporaries, especially the *Dublin Review* and Henry James. »All human doings», says James, »deeply interested him, human life, to his mind, was a perpetual story».[95]

In point of the impression of life (see above, p. 119) James might be said to give Trollope the highest praise that was possible for him to give. The impression of life is to James the impression, not of an arbitrarily invented world as might be represented in romance nor of a world represented by naturalism, but of the actual, the real, which he found in Trollope. Speaking 'from his own taste' he says: »The air of reality (solidity of specification) seems to me to be the supreme virtue of a novel — the merit on which all its other merits (including that consciously moral pupose of which Mr. Besant speaks) helplessly and submissively depend.»[96]

* * *

The article on Trollope in the *Dublin Review*, April, 1883, is written before the publication of the *Autobiography*, and its view of his level and public may partly therefore be regarded as a fairly unprejudiced appreciation of him; it seems to be an accurate general description of his literary position during the main part of his career:

Whilst Trollope's books are light and pleasant reading to the careless and unintelligent devourer of novels, who is sure to be entertained by them, they are of serious value to the student of human nature. The story runs amusingly along, and can easily be mastered by the general reader. But beyond this wide circle he appealed to real critics by revelations of life, and touches of fine humour and keen knowledge of men and women, which may have been overlooked by the many. He was fortunate in pleasing at the same time both the popular and the critical taste, and those who have unfairly designated him »the Tupper of fiction», must either have ignored or have been simply unable to appreciate the more subtle side of his genius. (P. 331.)

If he was 'fortunate in pleasing' the tastes of many, it is, as we know, equally true that he was unfortunate in displeasing the tastes of some critics, of which the *National Review*, 1863, and Stack of the *Fortnightly*, 1869, have been quoted as the most prominent examples even if Stack's displeasure is mixed with much admiration. As has been said, the voices of displeasure increased towards the end of Trollope's life, and it is interesting to note for instance that, although *The Times* in 1875 (Aug. 24) declares *The Way We Live Now* to be »one of Mr. Trollope's very best stories» and commends it warmly, the same newspaper writes two years later (Aug. 10, 1877) that in this novel Trollope »sinks below his ordinary level and grows dull over a disagreeable theme». It seems that the reviewer in the latter article was influenced by the opinion of others, by a growing prejudice against Trollope for the reasons outlined in Part I. But apart from the prejudice mostly due to the change of literary fashion, the unfavourable opinions must be largely attributed to the idiosyncrasies of the critics as has been mentioned earlier (p. 101). »Nothing», says James in 'The Art of Fiction' (p. 15), »will ever take the place of the good old fashion of 'liking' a work of art or not liking it: the most improved criticism will not abolish that primitive, that ultimate taste». Lucas (pp. 202—3) gives a number of examples of »irreconciliable differences in readers' temperaments» in their appreciation of Jane Austen irrespective of 'period or fashion'. It would be easy to make a fairly extensive list of examples of voluble personal disgust at what Trollope's admirers (James included) regard as the best in him — his characters. In these instances his characters are simply considered disagreeable or contemptible although the criticism is usually softened by humour. *The Times*, Aug. 26, 1869, gives him clearly to understand (in its review of *He Knew He Was Right*) that he would be more popular if he made his characters better than people are in life, if he gave them more 'strength and individuality of mind and character' — which goes to show that popularity was after all not found to be his highest aim (cf. above, p. 117). This reviewer, like some others, regrets it, but if it had been, Trollope would probably not be read today.

In the criticism of the next few years after the publication of the *Autobiography*, during his oblivion, and at the beginning of his revival, it is difficult to say in what degree opinions were swayed by personal bias, but the article in the *Westminster Review*, 1885 (see above, p. 43), is composed by a critic whose personal taste is more anti-Trollopian than that of any other critic I have read. The article was likely to be all the more pernicious as it invokes national pride in its protest against Trollope's portrayal of English character and manners at a point of time when English imperialism was approaching its hey-day.

Neither critics nor common readers can be told what they 'ought to like', but in every attempt to understand Trollope's appeal, like that of any artist, it is necessary to remember that, »Appreciation is more likely to be of use than depreciation»[97]; you have to be one with the man you are to judge to be able to comprehend him. For various reasons set forth in Part I, Trollope's immediate posterity could not feel at one with him and failed to see his worth.

B. Trollope in the Eyes of Posterity

Some Comments on An Autobiography

A short survey of the first reception of Trollope's *Autobiography* has already been given (pp. 41—2), but some comments seem to deserve further notice.

The Times reviews the book hot from the press in two articles, on Aug. 12 and 13, 1883, and begins the first by stating that, »In this extremely frank autobiography of Anthony Trollope there is more of the sensational than in any of his novels» greatly because to his acquaintances »the revelations of his early struggles and miseries will come as a surprise», which remind the reviewer of »the almost identical experiences of Dickens». The reviewer finds that Trollope has been »absolutely unreserved» in these disclosures, and that »the fulness of his self-analysis, with the candid opinions he expresses as to his novels, give some such personal charm to the narrative as has immortalized Boswell's 'Life of Johnson'». Henry Reeve has it (if he is, as seems likely, the author of the article on the book in the *Edinburgh*, Jan. 1884) that »since Jean-Jacques Rousseau wrote his 'Confessions' there have been few more interesting self-revelations than the autobiography of Anthony Trollope» although the interest is »chiefly literary». Still Trollope declares himself:

It will not, I trust, be supposed by any reader that I have intended in this so-called autobiography to give a record of my inner life. No man ever did so truly — and no man ever will. Rousseau probably attempted it, but who doubts but that Rousseau has confessed in much the thoughts and convictions rather than the facts of his life? (*A*, 317—8.)

The interest in the book was so much the keener as before its publication it was lamented that of his life 'few particulars seem to be forthcoming' although 'every newspaper of any standing' had a notice or an article on Trollope 'within a week of his death'.[1] Now, posthumously, and whether he intended it or no, Trollope revealed more of his inner life than the sentimental readers cared to know — those readers who liked to think that a writer was a more or less sublime being — and more prosaic facts about his life and work than could be contemplated with equanimity at a period when the demands to keep up appearances still induced so much insincerity. Still the article of *The Times* is complimentary like those of several journals (mentioned above, pp. 41—2) and quite different from its leading article in December 1882 on his death.

Reeve, however, more so perhaps than other reviewers, pays more attention to the meritorious sides of Trollope's method of work reported in his book than those which were regarded as derogatory to an artist. »Few men», he says, »who have given free reins to the imagination have looked more closely to pounds, shillings, and pence. But . . . he could idealize by sheer strength of the imagination.» And Reeve considers Trollope's description of his conception of the story of *The Warden* as »extraordinary» or even almost »incredible, were it not substantiated by facts. That power of crystallizing characters in the brain, so that imagination shall do the work of knowledge and observation, is really one of the inexplicable developments of the higher genius.» No doubt the majority of the critics would have been more pleased if they had been able to discover for themselves this power of Trollope's imagination which no one had surmised and which even James had been inclined to attribute to 'knowledge'. Reeve also notices that Trollope had 'lived' with his characters: »They clung to him as he had clung to them; and yet they never haunted him. They never cost him sleepless nights, and consequently idle and feverish days, as David Copperfield and others of his familiars

did with Dickens.» These two important points, power of imagining live
characters, especially clergymen, without the living models critics had
previously thought he had known, and the habit or need to 'live' with
these characters went unnoticed or were deliberately ignored by
Trollope's detractors because of the other things he had written (cf. above,
p. 41).

Trollope wrote, »I have never fancied myself to be a man of genius»
(*A*, 117), and Reeve remonstrates against his notion that he will not be
thought one because of the commercial 'appliances' in regard to his
literary contracts:

> We certainly should never maintain for a moment that such appliances are
> beneath a man of genius. (But) they are beyond the power and reach of most
> literary men who are anything more than mere plodders and drudges. We know
> that Scott worked very much as Trollope did . . . But cases of this kind are al-
> together exceptional; and Scott was as strong of constitution as Trollope.

Contrary to these two writers Dickens and Thackeray were 'paralysed'
for days or weeks and unable to write for want of inspiration. »The truth
is», says Reeve, »that Trollope is one of the very few examples of a man
of talent or genius, call it which we will, who had fairly got the spirit
of inspiration in leading strings.» This may seem the obvious inference
to be drawn from some passages in the *Autobiography* and this was the
impression the average reader was likely to get from the book. Judging
from his novels James had written similarly that, »the imagination that
Trollope possessed he had at least thoroughly at his command». The slight
implied in these words and the whole passage where they occur (above
p. 121) evidently indicates that an imagination that is not of the highest
order betrays its quality by being summonable at any moment. Still if
like James we find that human life to Trollope's mind was 'a perpetual
story', the opinion that he had his imagination at his command, or that
he had got the spirit of inspiration in leading strings, seems a natural
conclusion. 'The usual' would perhaps not greatly interest a writer who
was dependent on divine moments of inspiration. I shall presently revert
to the question once more.

Like so many other critics earlier and later, up to this very day, Reeve
thinks Trollope could have written better if he had not hastened his work
although he had anticipated the critics' comments on the »great evil of
rapid production» and expressed his belief as to his own production that
»the work which has been done quickest has been done best» (*A*, 161).
But while taking exception to Trollope's »arbitrary and peremptory

laws of work», Reeve approves heartily of most of his literary theories although he cannot help noting the obvious fact that Trollope himself failed to practise what he preached for the benefit of novices when he wrote so much superfluous matter, which Reeve, however, takes to be explained by the »imperative necessity» to supply the number of pages demanded by the publishers and the circulating libraries.

It is a remarkable fact that though the question of money is very prominent in all Trollope's novels, it was not resented by the critics as too vulgar a theme to be constantly brought under the reader's notice. The *North American Review*, 1864, in its article on *The Small House* even praises his skill in introducing it: »(Another) strong point is his power of depicting the different forms of the Anglo-Saxon tender passion, — the love of property.» Though not attaching much special attention to the question, the criticism generally approves of it as of a problem naturally inherent in the daily life that Trollope depicts. But the reaction was different when people read of his own faith in the importance of money in such direct words as: »I have said before how entirely I fail to reach the altitude of those who think that a man devoted to letters should be indifferent to the pecuniary results for which work is generally done. An easy income has always been regarded by me as a great blessing.» (*A*, 156.) And the other things he confessed to have loved did not make him appear much more etherial: »But though the money has been sweet, the respect, the friendships, and the mode of life which has been achieved, have been much sweeter. I prefer the society of distinguished people.» (*A*, 156—7.) Contemplating in its review of the *Autobiography* Trollope's »somewhat mundane ideal of life», the *Spectator*, Oct. 27, 1883, writes:

> Strangely enough, Mr. Trollope could create characters, and did create characters, who, if they had written down their own ideals, would have painted something which seems to us infinitely higher than such an ideal as this.

Plantagenet Palliser, Harding, Crawley, and Arabin are mentioned as examples of such characters. This does not seem to be a bad verdict upon Trollope's artistic ability, but, in view of the professed moral purpose of his writings, the 'ideals' owned to in the *Autobiography* — »the rules by which I have lived», »the causes which have instigated me to work» (*A*, 157), i.e. gain of money, fame etc. — would naturally influence the criticism of his work, too. At any rate the *Spectator* writes further:

> Mr. Trollope was thoroughly in earnest in wishing to teach a high morality by his tales . . . (but) what he understood as a high morality was a morality of a very limited kind, and involved little more for men and women in general than insisting

that girls should be modest and loving, and that men should be honest and diligent, and should know their own minds. For the most part, Mr. Trollope is content with showing up the meanness of cowardice and dishonesty, and the misery of marrying without love, and he owes it rather to the force of his imagination than to his personal ideal of what life should be, if he takes us into a finer and rarer atmosphere of spiritual feeling.

Sadleir is undoubtedly right in pointing out how offensive the book must be to the aesthetes (see above, p. 41), which he regards as the reason why it damaged Trollope's reputation. It does not, however, seem fair to attribute the reaction against it only to the aesthetes; like Batho and Dobrée (p. 289) we could also say that the book »did some harm to his reputation among the sentimental by its exceedingly unsentimental account of his habits of work», and, perhaps we should add, by his 'mundane ideal' of life, or, better, the way he expressed this 'ideal'. Sadleir has it that the book represented 'the convictions and assumptions of a vanished age, of mid-Victorianism', but it can hardly be maintained that it was especially characteristic of a mid-Victorian writer to 'go out of his way to deny his literary caste' as Sadleir says Trollope did. If he 'flouted every artistic prejudice' of the aesthetes, he was perhaps even more disappointing to the 'sentimental', to whom Dickens had recently appealed with such overwhelming success and who have probably always formed the majority of the great mass of readers. The common reader reads for his own pleasure and prefers the creditable side of human nature, which he likes to find in his authors, too. »The novelist should be a humanist», says Liddell; »we should ask if his 'writing self' is a good and valuable self».[2] From his novels Trollope's 'writing self' had been approved of by the majority of critics and readers; his *Autobiography* made them think they had made a mistake.

In Part I it has been shown how the bitterness provoked by the *Autobiography* came to get the upper hand among the critics and how the result of the condemnation influenced even Julian Hawthorne, son of Nathaniel, the great admirer of Trollope. But one cannot help feeling that Trollope deliberately overstates his mundane motives. He touches several times upon the question of writing for money and says for instance:

I confess that my first object in taking to literature as a profession was that which is common to the barrister when he goes to the Bar, and to the baker when he sets up his oven. I wished to make an income on which I and those belonging to me might live in comfort. (*A*, 107.)

He had seen his mother help her family out of economic misery by her diligent pen, so he knew money could be made in that way. He also writes:

There are those who think that the man who works with his imagination should allow himself to wait till — inspiration moves him. When I have heard such doctrine preached, I have hardly been able to repress my scorn. What the author wants, like the shoemaker, is health and a habit of industry.» (*A*, 118.)

Such passages unnecessarily lay stress on external motives and the view of simple craftsmanship. The assumption of the Stebbinses that he wrote the *Autobiography* »in bitterness of spirit», to defy the unfavourable criticism of *The Way We Live Now* (cf. above, p. 32), seems to be right in regard to these passages; at least he seems to have set himself to defy the aesthetes in them. But many passages in the book go to show how seriously he really looked upon the novelist's vocation as was perceived for instance by the *Westminster Review*, Jan.—April 1884:

Trollope held a sort of medium position between Johnson and Macaulay. He certainly wrote *con amore*, but he doggedly set himself to write. In Trollope's books, especially his earlier ones, there is abundant evidence of 'touches and retouches' and that 'pursuit of unattainable perfection' which was alien to Johnson.[3]

Sadleir offers an explanation of the reason why Trollope came to write a book that »in its extreme of shy defiance, distorted the perspective even of its author's finest qualities»:

In his heart he was at once vain and a little ashamed of his quantity and methodicality of output — vain, in that by sheer labour he had trained invention to perpetual wakefulness and his pen to write at any moment and at a uniform rate of speed . . . To subdue the vanity, he mocked himself more loudly than his critics mocked; to stifle shame, he over-emphasised the very tendency which embarrassed him. (P. 349 ff.)

In defence of Trollope's working-method Sadleir points out that it was 'originally forced on him by circumstances'. From the *Autobiography* we find that Trollope had trained himself to write three hours a day early in the morning and, according to a 'diary', so many pages a week. He was ready to write during those hours because, when not otherwise busy, he had been perpetually thinking of his characters and their fates.

I think it is possible for most sentimental people to forgive an author for owning up that he likes being paid for his work and perhaps even that he works methodically; these two things do not by themselves seem to prevent him from being an artist. But if he says like Trollope that he certainly believes in the cobbler's wax on his chair 'much more than the inspiration' (*A*, 119), sentimental readers and others, too, are unlikely to think him an artist and they cannot very well be blamed. On this point, however, Trollope did not speak the truth. He was, in fact, not ready to write at any moment. He wrote in the morning often day after day,

but there were breaks between, even weeks, when he had no opportunity
to write at all[4], and sometimes the breaks were caused by 'idleness'
(*A*, 116). Trollope like other writers suffered from 'the agonies of composition' but these agonies were not suffered at his desk, or only very
little there; as Sadleir says (p. 354) »what he wrote was the result of
days, weeks, months and years of searching thought».

Whatever his motive was in writing as he did of inspiration in his
Autobiography, three years after he had written the book he had an essay
published in *Good Words*, 1879, XX, which entirely refutes any idea that
he could write, or rather compose, at any time he chose, that he had 'got
the spirit of inspiration in leading strings', and had his imagination
'thoroughly at his command'. The article was then called 'A Walk in the
Wood', and this »rather fanciful title», as the *London Society* writes in
September 1883 (just before the *Autobiography* was published), »probably
diverted the attention of many who would have enjoyed such a literary
confession». It seems to have escaped even Sadleir when writing *A
Commentary*. The same number of this magazine contains a somewhat
abbreviated reprint of the article under the new heading 'A Famous
Novelist's Modes of Work', with such suggestive subsection titles as
'The Art of Thinking', 'The Brain-Worker and Noises', 'Tricksy Ariel',
and 'The Agonies of Composition'. »Alas», Trollope exclaims in the last
section, »when all external things are propitious, when the very heavens
have lent their aid, it is so often that it is impossible! How often is one
prompted to fling oneself down in despair.» But an article of this kind,
even if it had been more noticed, had little chance to be remembered and
believed in the shadow of the sensational *Autobiography*, although even
this book contains passages which prove that Trollope, like other artists,
was dependent on what is generally meant by inspiration. There might
be objections to regarding rapid writing as an ideal for authors, but what
made it possible for Trollope to write quickly and well was nothing but
inspiration as is evident from his account of his richest periods of work:

> When my work has been quicker done . . . the rapidity has been achieved by hot
> pressure, not in the conception, but in the telling of the story. I have trebled my
> usual average, and have done so in circumstances which have enabled me to give
> up all my thoughts for the time to the book I have been writing. This has generally
> been done at some quiet spot among the mountains . . . And I am sure that the
> work so done has had in it the best truth and the highest spirit that I have been
> able to produce. At such times I have been able to imbue myself thoroughly with the
> characters I have had in hand. I have wandered alone among the rocks and woods,
> crying at their grief, laughing at their absurdities, and thoroughly enjoying their

joy. I have been impregnated with my own creations till it has been my only
excitement to sit with the pen in my hand, and drive my team before me at as quick
a pace as I could make them travel. (A, 161—2.)

This goes to illustrate the view of Mrs. Wharton (p. 20): »Many people
assume that the artist receives, at the outset of his career, the mysterious
sealed orders known as 'Inspiration', and has only to let that sovereign
impulse carry him where it will. Inspiration does indeed come at the outset
to every creator, but it comes most often as an infant, helpless, stumbling,
inarticulate, to be taught and guided.» Trollope's habit of perpetually
'living' with his characters was his way of making this 'infant' grow,
and this method is also recognized by Mrs. Wharton (p. 18) as the
natural one for a novelist to use: »Every subject, to yield and to retain its
full flavour, should be long carried in the mind, brooded upon, and fed
with all the impressions and emotions which nourish its creator.»

The *Autobiography* did very much to make its author out to be a mere
craftsman, and it succeeded in part, in the eyes of a considerable part of
his immediate posterity. »Because», as Sadleir says, »there had never been
a literary autobiography of its kind before, its unfamiliarity jarred
readers into unfavourable judgment, not so much of the writer, as of his
work.»[5] As has been mentioned before (pp. 65—6), the book is now highly
appreciated. I shall have to touch upon some of the criticism of the
Autobiography again but, besides discussing some of the principal comments on it, this chapter has shown, I hope, why Trollope's worst
representation of himself must be refuted.

In Oblivion

Although Henry James's admirable article on Trollope, first published
in 1883, had no chance at that time against the bitterness created by the
Autobiography and against the other adverse circumstances referred to in
Part I, it probably helped (as has been stated on p. 54) to retain some
morsel of respect for Trollope with the critics. As James became better
known as the conscious artist he was — at the end of the 'nineties and
especially through his great novels of 1902—1904 — his opinion of
Trollope was taken more notice of and forms today an important part of
the criticism that has remained the nucleus of the evaluation of the
novelist.

In his adverse article quoted above (p. 48) Saintsbury speaks of
Trollope's 'comparative oblivion' in 1895, and Miss Mary Irwin in her

Trollope bibliography, lists some American and English periodicals, besides
a few books from about 1890 and the next few years, where Trollope is
discussed, or more often only mentioned, which shows that the oblivion
was not really quite complete. It might perhaps be suggested that, of all
the detractors of Trollope, Saintsbury, being an erudite critic[6], did him
the best service by this time, or so Trollope would probably have thought
himself, for he held that »if any critic wanted to spite us, he could better
do it by holding his tongue than by speaking evil of us».[7] After all, the
things Saintsbury said against Trollope do not seem to carry much
conviction. They are, it seems, too sweeping, too often repeated by
earlier critics, especially detractors, to have any damaging effect: 'No
genius', 'every-day', 'commonplace', 'not infrequently vulgar'. James's
statement that Trollope's 'great, his inestimable merit was a complete
appreciation of the usual' was bound by its sheer originality to have more
weight with those who cared about the critics' opinions. Perhaps we should
not attach too much importance to Arnold Bennett's weekly articles, but
he cannot very well be considered a bad judge of style, and he strongly
condemned Saintsbury's: »Professor Sainstbury may be as loudly positive
as he likes — his style is always quietly whispering: 'Don't listen.'»[8]
But although Bennett did not like James's novels, he thought 'he writes
like an angel and is a fine critic of impeccable taste'.[9] The difference was,
of course, in Trollope's favour.[10]

Especially in stating that Trollope's career constituted 'a warning'
Saintsbury was strangely rash for a critic of his rank. He seems to have
followed what appeared to him the sanction of popular opinion more than
any conviction of his own (cf. above, p. 64). In 1895 Harrison, too, is
well aware of the prevailing attitude towards Trollope: »It is the fashion
with the present generation to assert that he is never anything but
commonplace»; but he has formed an opinion of his own strong enough
to assert against this fashion: »This is the judgment of a perverted
taste.»[11] And as has already been mentioned, Harrison prophesies that
Trollope's reputation will revive.

A middle position between Saintsbury and Harrison is taken by
Herbert Paul, who, in an article called 'The Apotheosis of the Novel under
Queen Victoria' in the *Nineteenth Century* for May 1897, devotes three
pages to the discussion of Trollope and declares: »It is to be feared that his
books are dead. But it is a pity.» More anxiously, perhaps, than other
critics during the oblivion of Trollope Paul is wondering at the cause of
the remarkable change in his popularity:

Trollope was in his lifetime more popular than any of his contemporaries. Twenty years ago it would hardly have been an exaggeration to say that half of the novels on the railway bookstalls were his. Now his books are never seen there, and seldom anywhere else. Why was he popular? Why has he ceased to be so?

To these questions Paul himself gives an answer which, even if not accepted by any other critic I have come across, is at any rate an indication of a need to explain an oblivion which was more or less consciously felt to be unnatural and unmerited:

His popularity was due partly to his cleverness, liveliness, and high spirits, but partly also to his never overtaxing the brains of his readers, if, indeed, he can be said to have taxed them at all. The change in the position of his books produced, and produced so rapidly, by the death of the author may, I think, be thus explained. He stimulated the 'taste for which he catered. He created the demand which he supplied.

This is another way of saying that he did not satisfy the demand of all ages, the demand for universality; but the censure seems to go beyond that. To be considered to have 'created the demand which he supplied, would be the highest praise, no doubt, for a business man. For a serious novelist such 'praise' must be regarded as a severe condemnation, as simply classing his novels among non-serious literature. Still Paul does not seem to regard his 'explanation' as quite so condemning if we are to judge from his thinking it 'a pity' that Trollope's books were 'dead' and some other expressions indicating approval. It is, however, interesting to note that something like Paul's idea had been expressed more than thirty years earlier by the *National Review* in regard to the domestic scenes in *Orley Farm:* »What every body would be glad to do, every body likes to read about . . . Such delinations are, to say the truth, but very low art; and while they do not corrupt the morals, they may degrade the tastes, and foster the weaknesses of those for whose edification they are contrived.» In other words, they might work like drugs, create undesirable demands. If to Paul the demands were not exactly undesirable, we must take him to mean that they were at least artificial because the public seemed to be content to leave the supplier in oblivion.

The most important article on Trollope in the 'nineties is, of course, Harrison's, whose general opinion of Trollope's work may be regarded as condensed in his words: »It is not high art — but it is art. In his very best work he has risen above commonplace.» The details of his criticism are mainly repetitions of what earlier critics had said. In regard to Trollope's style I think Harrison makes his most felicitous and original remark:

As a rule his language is conspicuous for its ease, simplicity, and unity of tone. This was one good result of his enormous rapidity of execution. His books are read from cover to cover, as if they were spoken in one sitting by an *improvisatore*[12] in one and the same mood, who never hesitated an instant for a word, and who never failed to seize the word he wanted. — — It is a mastery which conceals itself, and appears to the reader the easiest thing in the world.

For the last sentence and when speaking of »the melodious ripple of these fluent and pellucid words» Harrison seems, however, to be indebted to Trollope's own reflections on what a good style should be like (*A*, 210 ff.). Pollock, too, had written of the concealed art in Trollope's style (see below, p. 149), but the idea does not seem to have occurred to Trollope's contemporaries generally. It is of course true that in his works we are never, as Harrison says, »bored by fine writing that fails to 'come off'», but the bias that prevented Trollope from attempting such writing was not appreciated by the fashion of the 'nineties, whereas we have seen (above p. 93) his unpretentiousness welcomed in 1857 by *The Times*, whose reviewer is so pleased with (Mrs. Gore's and) Trollope's »stories of modern life, told without any attempt at fine writing, without striving after climaxes and points, and without any design of alluring the reader by some flowery path to the precipice of some vulgar moral». Harrison further calls attention to the merits of the conversations and letters in Trollope: »In absolute realism of spoken words Trollope has hardly any equal.» »His letters, especially his young ladies' letters, are singularly real, life-like, and characteristic.» But the new generation must have been rather discouraged when reading such statements as:

And yet, although he hardly ever rises into eloquence, wit, brilliancy, or sinks into any form of talk either unnaturally tall, or unnaturally low, — still, the conversations are just sufficiently pointed, humorous, or characteristic, to amuse the reader and develop the speaker's character.

This is almost equal to saying that he is 'not so dull after all'. Trollope's merits could have been presented in a better way. Similarly, as Harrison knew himself, his pointing at the pureness of Trollope's young ladies was not likely to win any proselytes among the readers of the 'nineties, but it is illuminating in regard to Trollope's reputation, and underlines what has been found to be one of his lasting merits, his representation of the Victorian ideal of the English girl:

It was his boast that he had never written a line which a pure woman could not read without a blush. This is no doubt one of the grounds on which he is so often denounced as *passé*. In nothing does Anthony Trollope delight more than when he unveils to us the secret thoughts of a noble-hearted maiden. In nothing is he more successful; nowhere is he more subtle, more true, more interesting. In this fine gift, he surpasses all his contemporaries, and almost all other English novelists.

It must be admitted that they are »young ladies», nurtured in the conventional refinement of the last generation, high-bred, and trained in the jealous sensitiveness of what was thought to be »maiden modesty» thirty or forty years ago. That is their misfortune to-day; it is now rather silly to be a »young lady» at all, and the old-fashioned »maiden modesty» of their mothers and grandmothers is become positively ridiculous.

When expressing his admiration of Trollope's power of representing genuinely things and people he could not really have known by experience, Harrison pays a fine tribute to the novelist's imagination but with a reserve which pulls down about as much as his praise builds up: »He did all this with a perfectly sure and subtle touch, which was often, it is true, somewhat tame, and is never perhaps of any very great brilliance, but which was almost faultlessly true, never extravagant, never unreal.» And when he says that it is almost unbelievable that such a man as Trollope could do such imaginative work, he is sure to deter all sentimental readers from Trollope's books:

However much you might like his bluff, hearty, resonant personality, you would have said he was the last man to have any delicate sympathy with bishops, dukes, or young ladies. That such a colossus of blood and bone should spend his mornings, before we were out of bed, in analysing the hypersensitive conscience of an arch-deacon, the secret confidences whispered between a prudent mamma and a love-lorn young lady, or the subtle meanderings of Marie Goesler's heart — this was a real psychologic problem.

In fact, Harrison is the only critic, as far as I know, who thinks Trollope's constitution damaged his work: »There can be no doubt that this constitutional vehemence of his, this hypertrophy of blood and muscle, injured his work and dimmed his reputation.[13] Much of his work he ought to have burnt.» And the way he speaks of the *Autobiography* makes one feel that he secretly wants Trollope to remain forgotten for ever: »When, in his *Autobiography*, he let the public into the story of his method . . . and all the little secrets of his factory, the public felt some disgust and was almost inclined to think it had been cheated out of its £ 70 000.» Harrison's only comment on this is that »Trollope was no fraud, nor even a mere tradesman», which seems to be rather a poor encouragement.

In the light of Trollope's reputation today, it is interesting to find that Harrison thinks »the permanent survival may be limited to the *Barchester* cycle, with *Orley Farm* and the two *Phineas Finns*». Even this would not sound so bad, but then he must needs add: »In any case,

his books will hereafter bear a certain historical interest.» Harrison gives
the tone of the average criticism on Trollope for the beginnings of the
revival when so much of the critics' efforts was spent in attempts to
overcome the prejudice against him (cf. above, p. 57). There were a few
exceptions, but it seems that the criticism of the new century will be
best surveyed if we take the nineteen-twenties as a new starting-point
and glance back when necessary.

The New Judgment

When after the First World War the minds of people began to settle
enough for a renewed interest in literature, when Trollope's books began
to be republished in increasing numbers, and especially after Sadleir
had pointed out, most effectively in his famous *Commentary*, the claims
that Trollope must be considered to have to a permanent high rank in
English literature, critics generally became again concerned about
expounding the literary points in his works as, in 1922, Sadleir had prophesied they would (see above, p. 62). The prophecy may, in fact, be said
to have come more than true for, as has been set forth in Part I, Trollope
has been honoured by the interest of critics and, above all, by the reading
public, much more than either Sadleir or anyone else could foresee then.
Even A. Edward Newton, the American enthusiast, was hardly bold
enough when he wrote in 1920:

> Nothing is more seductive and dangerous than prophecy, but . . . I venture to
> say that, Dickens and Thackeray aside, Trollope will outlive all the other novelists
> of his time . . . And if it be Trollope's fate to outlast all but the greatest of his
> contemporaries, it will be due to the simplicity and lack of effort with which he
> tells his tale. There is no straining after effect, — his characters are real live men
> and women, without a trace of caricature or exaggeration. His humour is delicious
> and his plots are sufficient, although he has told us that he never takes any care
> with them.[14]

Although Newton's faith in Trollope is thus strong, the reasons given for
it are simple enough and not coloured by any high-strung admiration.
In his *Commentary* (p. 365) Sadleir, however, finds it well to warn against
exaggerated enthusiasm:

> Time and the evolution of opinion which it brings, have given to Trollopians
> a second chance. May it be taken soberly and without exaggeration. Though period
> prejudice destroyed him, the prejudice of another period must not be allowed to
> overstress his resurrection. Trollope deserves graver consideration than as a mere
> escapist (in the edition of 1927: bed-book) author, and at the same time a judgment

more stringent than would be passed by a new-found enthusiasm for his Victorianism.

Among the reasons why Sadleir wrote this warning might have been such an exclamation as: »How little is the humanity of Trollope known. In literature the two great Victorians were Thackeray and Dickens; but greater than these was Anthony Trollope.» This is to be found in *The Significance of Anthony Trollope* by Spencer van B. Nichols, another of the American enthusiasts. A review of the booklet in *The T. L. S.*, Oct. 15, 1925 (two years before *A Commentary* was published), begins: »To such men as Mr. Nichols (and, be it noted, they are rather American than English) is really due the credit for the revival of Trollope.» But though the review is sarcastic enough towards 'the Trollopian faith' thus displayed, the booklet, with its map of Barsetshire and first detailed classification of Trollope's novels, is found to be valuable not only by this reviewer but by Sadleir himself.

By his warning in the *Commentary* Sadleir shows that he no longer thought it likely, as he had thought in 1922, that Trollope would soon be simply shelved as one of the classics. His essay of 1922 ends in a suggestion that 'the very greatness of the author' springs from his 'Englishry':

He is intensely English, with the quiet humour, the shy sympathy masquerading as indifference, the delicate sense of kindliness and toleration, the occasional irritability, that mark a man or a book as English. But if to these qualities he owes his place in our proud heritage of literature, to them also he owes the tarrying of due recognition, for they and the artists that possess them are of all qualities and of all artists the most difficult to impress upon the sceptical outsider, seeing that their very beauty and profundity and power lie in their elusiveness.

The logical inference to be drawn from this passage is that the common English reader, or at any rate the average English critic, had for a long time proved to be a 'sceptical outsider' in regard to typically English qualities, for Sadleir means, of course, that 'due recognition' had been tarrying in Trollope's own country, but setting aside the peculiarity of such a suggestion, it is evident that to Sadleir Trollope's 'Englishry' is a very fine thing, in fact, indefinable. In spite of the warning against exaggeration in *A Commentary* Sadleir repeats on the next page his opinion from 1922 as to Trollope's elusiveness: »for even granted characterisation, Trollope's quality remains intangible, baffles resolution.» This may not be an exaggeration by itself, in fact, it can hardly be because »in the last resort the ground of our delight in excellent literature baffles analysis by common sense», as R. A. Scott-James (p. 384) has found out, but the opinion thus expressed suggests peculiar, unfathomable depths in the very man who of all the famous writers of his day had been pronounced the most philistine and least mysterious. At all events Sadleir himself appears to be one of the critics of the twentieth century who most seriously ask themselves wherein Trollope's lasting qualities are to be found.

In the nineteen-twenties a few literary historians and critics still gave Trollope dubious credit as a novelist, denying him genius outright and wondering at the continued reputation of the 'uninspired Englishman' (W. L. Phelps, Prof. at Yale, in *The Advance of the English Novel*, 1927), granting him a 'fine secondary talent which was not genius' (Rowland Grey in the *Cornhill Magazine*, 1926), calling him 'a secondary genius of real merit' (John Macy in *The Story of the World's Literature*, 1925, reprinted in 1953 in the U.S.A.), or finding him readable even if 'lacking in good taste and intellectual elevation' (Robert Aitken in *Chamber's Cyclopaedia of English Literature*, III, London, 1927). But since only those critics who have been at pains to find some explanation for the enormous appeal Trollope has made to the English-speaking world can possibly contribute to our appreciation of Trollope, it seems that we must turn to these critics taking for granted that more profundity is to be ascribed to him than is supplied by such clichés. It appears that a scrutiny of these explanations may be well started by bearing in mind Sadleir's impression of the elusiveness of Trollope's art, which he further emphasized thus (p. 366):

> The initial obstacle to a sober-minded definition of the Trollopian novel is that it provides rather a sensual than an intellectual experience. A smell, a pain or a sound is not more difficult to describe than the effect — at once soothing and exciting — produced on the reader's mind by the leisurely, nonchalant commentaries on English social life which carry his name on their title-pages.

It might seem that Sadleir, with such a high opinion of Trollope's work, could not very well be blamed for underrating it. But it is interesting, and perhaps useful, to note at the outset that even his *Commentary*, 'intended to be laudatory' as Paul Elmer More says, displeased this true admirer of Trollope because of »that recurrent note of apology which so frequently annoys me in those who profess themselves to be Trollopians» (*The Demon of the Absolute*, 1929). Indeed, even after the revival became a commonly accepted fact very few critics have been able to speak of him without this note of apology which has persistently clung to the criticism of him ever since the eighteen-nineties. But this more or less hidden scepticism might be taken as additional evidence of the special elusiveness of the appeal Trollope's work makes to his many readers.

As has been mentioned (pp. 91—3) criticism on the art of the novel, especially in England, was not regarded as very much developed at the end of Trollope's life. It is a commonplace that the novel still defies definition and rule however much it may have become technically perfected, and perhaps it will always do so by nature. This may account for the fact that criticism on fiction does not seem to have progressed noticeably even by now. If critics judge for example Balzac differently in 1950 than in 1900 (which Curtius, p. 117, finds to be such a remarkable thing), it is not necessarily evidence of better critical equipment in the latter year. Still this equipment has probably improved by the discoveries in this century within psychology, to which Lucas attaches so much importance, and no doubt within other fields of research, too, especially sociology. But the order of precedence of various authors and its changes, which Curtius finds the most interesting *in dem Felde der literarischen Kritik*[15] and which has fascinated many other critics, Saintsbury among them, to me seems rather unprofitable for the understanding of an author's appeal although it is, no doubt, indispensable to a literary historian.

The nineteen-twenties seem to have been fairly rich in attempts at finding the best critical approaches to fiction. Among the theorists at that time we find Lubbock, Forster, Mrs. Wharton, and Scott-James. Having adopted for his purposes M. Abel Chevalley's 'definition' of the novel, *une fiction en prose d'une certain étendue*, E. M. Forster expresses the difficulties in this way (p. 25): »How (then) are we to attack the novel — that spongy tract, those fictions in prose of a certain extent which extend so indeterminately? Not with any elaborate apparatus. Principles and systems may suit other forms of art, but they cannot be applicable here.» Curtius, writing in 1949, gives as it were a final definition of the nebulous thing: *Der Roman ist eine literarische Gattung ohne bindende Formtradition. Er is elastisch wie Gummi. Er kann sich jeder Materie und jeder Epoche anpassen.*[16] Such a thing might seem to offer unlimited possibilities of discussion, ever fascinating though, perhaps, unsolvable problems. However, Mrs. Tillotson, writing in 1954, finds English criticism of fiction rather poor. »One reason», she says, »for the comparative poverty of criticism of novels and the lack of dignity which Virginia Woolf ascribed to fiction is the difficulty of detaching the novel as art from the novel as pastime», which Collingwood has also discussed using different

terms in his *Principles of Art* (1938). But in James Mrs. Tillotson sees,
as it were, a pioneer in English criticism although his essays are restricted
in scope: »James was asking the right questions; his criticism must be the
chief source of any future aesthetic of the novel — as it is already of the
critical system of Mr. Percy Lubbock in his *Craft of Fiction.*»[17] No doubt
James did ask the right questions, but I think he did his most important
pioneering by emphasizing the demand that the novel should be 'perfectly
free' from rules subject to the only condition that 'it be interesting'.
The grant of this freedom has, of course, counteracted prejudice, even
the particularly strong prejudice that Trollope helped to direct at himself.

The revival, the common acceptance of Trollope as a great writer,
considerably alters the attitude of the whole set of critics. After that they
need no longer be afraid of mistaking him for an author of whose future
'life' there may be some doubt. The republication in 1923 of the *Autobiography* must have already been felt as a kind of social sanction of Trollope's
ideas of novel-writing and life in general. All at once he is found, by his
contempt of humbug, to be really very much opposed at least to the
insincerity of his age for which, especially in the 'twenties, 'Victorian' is
a term of critical abuse. There may also be some truth in the cynical statement of Walpole (writing in 1928) that, »The point is no longer whether
you write novels for money, but whether you get money for the novels
that you write».[18] From now on Trollope's work can be scrutinized without
snobbish misgivings in the full light of the *Autobiography*, which before
republication had been obtainable only second-hand, and in the
consciousness of the spectacular wonder of his growing popularity.

* * *

One of the obvious objections made against Trollope had been that he
wrote too quickly and too much. The objection will probably always be
made. It is therefore curious to note that, after the general change of
opinion in Trollope's favour, the very quantity of his novels is regarded
by serious critics with indulgence, or even as a merit. In his essay of 1920
'Trollope Revisited' Saintsbury writes:

> Trollope may claim to be, in the fullest Emersonian sense, a 'representative
> man' of professional writers of novels. Excluding Dickens and Balzac and Dumas
> père, I can think of none among English and French novelists except George Sand
> who can fairly be set against him at all. Now the prolific and professional novelist,
> if not the most precious, has been undoubtedly the most characteristic growth of
> the last three generations. So the 'highest browed' student of literature need not
> disdain a study of such a type.

Undisguised praise on this point we find in another professor, Sir Arthur Quiller-Couch, whose article on Trollope was first published in 1924:

His bulk is part of his quality; it can no more be separated from the man than can Falstaff's belly from Falstaff.[19]

The very mass of Trollope commands a real respect; its prodigious quantity is felt to be a quality, as one searches in it and finds that — good or bad, better or very much worse — there is not a dishonest inch in the whole.[20]

The view that an author worthy of the name should produce a substantial mass of books is, of course, shared by popular authors such as Priestley who writes, »Knocking off a novel or two is not being a novelist»[21], or Somerset Maugham who says something to the same effect in at least one of his books. James (whose own sequence of books became considerable) had already noted in his article on Trollope: »Abundance, certainly, is in itself a great merit; almost all great writers have been abundant.» »But», he adds, »Trollope's fertility was gross, importunate.» James's view is, as we must expect from him, that Trollope 'sacrificed quality to quantity'.

Quiller-Couch, however, writes in deliberate opposition to the fashion of his youth, to the votaries of »'art for art's sake', the *mot juste* and the rest», »the young men quite honestly and frenetically devoted to chiselling out English as though (God rest them!) in obedience to a Higher Power». At his age he finds that »time, which should bring the philosophic mind, will lead most critics who follow criticism sincerely to the happy conviction that there are no rules for the operation of genius», to which he adds:

In reading Trollope one's sense of trafficking with genius arises more and more evidently out of his large sincerity — a sincerity in bulk, so to speak; wherefore to appraise him, you must read him in bulk, taking the good with the bad, even as you must with Shakespeare.

(Quiller-Couch compares him to Shakespeare because he thinks both were more 'typically English' than probably any third author.) Nothing of this impression had presented itself to James when he wrote in his article: »As no work (of Trollope's) has higher pretensions than any other, there may be a certain unkindness in holding an individual production up to the light. 'Judge me in the lump', we can imagine the author saying; 'I have only undertaken to entertain the British public. I don't pretend that each of my novels is an organic whole'.»[22] But something of Quiller-Couch's appreciation of Trollope's abundance (which some of his contemporaries had also admired) is persistently cropping up

in the New Judgment. Walter Allen, for example, writing in 1954, finds
at least that, though one of Trollope's novels may make the impression
that its author is a 'Chronicler of small beer' as Richard Garnett had called
him, the impression made by ten is very different, »it is that of the creation
of nothing less than a world».[23] And to Allen this world is not only
Barsetshire.

Thus, since about 1920, Trollope's open boast of the quantity of
books he had written was no longer resented. Not only was his quantity
by itself found, at least by some critics, to be quality, but his boast
of it contributed to the impression of the author's sincerity, his 'un-
compromising honesty', to borrow Booth's expression from his Introduction to the American edition (1947) of the *Autobiography*. »His pride in
his accomplishment», says Booth appreciatively, »is boldly stated,
undiminished by mealymouthed subterfuge.» And a careful study of the
Autobiography revealed that his satisfaction at having produced so much
was not only due to the fact that he had earned money by his diligence.
In his review of the edition of 1923 Charles Whibley writes: »When
Trollope said that money was the real motive of his taking to literature,
he put a strain upon the truth.»[24] It was felt that his pride in his prolificness could be taken as an expression of his love of his art. »He wrote
because he liked it and because he could not help himself. His second
impulse was mercenary.» (Walpole, p. 180.) »He loved his art as his life»,
says Booth in his Introduction; »if the angels do not require novels, he
felt he would not be happy in heaven.»[25] His quantity then was more or
less distinctly felt by several critics to be imposing evidence not only
of efficiency but of a veritable obsession — an artist's obsession with his
work. Even if the typical narrator may not generally have been regarded
as *eine von einer grossen Aufgabe ganz überwältigte Persönlichkeit*, a kind
of superman, as Koskimies tells us (pp. 96—7), since Flaubert modern
criticism has been influenced by such an idea, and we know that James
(in 1884) spoke for a new generation of English novelists when terming
the novelist's calling 'a sacred office'. The suggestion that Trollope had
been forced to write by an irresistible impulse invested him with a
characteristic which has been regarded as the distinctive mark of poets
and prose writers of note.[26] Abundance is, of course, not by itself a
conclusive mark of a great writer, and Mrs. Wharton is perhaps too
definite in her view: »In all the arts abundance seems to be one of the
surest signs of vocation. It exists on the lowest scale, and, in the art of
fiction, belongs as much to the producer of 'railway novels' as to Balzac,

Thackeray or Tolstoy; yet it almost always marks the great creative artist. Whatever a man has it in him to do really well he usually keeps on doing with an indestructible persistency.»[27] Trollope's mother belongs to the multitude of abundant writers who are forgotten. Still there is some truth in Mrs. Wharton's statement, and Professor Booth, in his Introduction, applies the last sentence from her passage to Trollope.

* * *

A large space was simply indispensable for the kind of work that is Trollope's essential achievement, a picture of all mid-Victorian England in its middle-class aspects, the nucleus of which is Barsetshire. We may or may not agree with Allen in regarding Barset as 'a province only' of the whole of Trollope's work, but it seems difficult to disagree with the opinion of Mgr. Ronald Knox (writing in 1952) that the Barsetshire series is the 'single group of his works' by which he 'stands or falls'.[28] The criticism of this group must then be regarded as the touchstone of his appeal. Trollope has been much praised for the creation of his fictitious county, more by posterity than by his contemporaries, and it has often been forgotten — as it already was in 1883 by the *Dublin Review* (see above, p. 115) — that the series was created, as it were, unintentionally.

In his Introduction to the first separate set of 'The Chronicles of Barsetshire' published in 1879, the author states that »these tales were not intended to be in any sequence one to another except in regard to the two first». The reason for setting the scenes of so many tales in Barsetshire is given thus:

I had formed for myself so complete a picture of the locality, had acquired so accurate a knowledge of the cathedral town and the county in which I had placed the scene, and had become by a long-continued mental dwelling in it, so intimate with sundry of the inhabitants, that to go back to it and write about it again and again have been one of the delights of my life.

However, as he thought 'few novels written in continuation, one of another, had been successful' in earlier literature, he deliberately avoided connecting the plots and interests, which practice he thought might have tired the reader.

But now (he continues), when these are all old stories — — I have a not un-natural desire to see them together, so that my records of a little bit of England which I have myself created may be brought into one set, and that some possible future reader may be enabled to study in a complete form the Chronicles of Barset-shire.

Not until 1906 was the whole set republished, for the first time by
Bell with an introduction by Frederic Harrison, and since then repeatedly
by different publishers. Allen thinks the classification into Barsetshire
novels, political novels, and so on, might be convenient, »but it has done
its harm because, by enforcing a distinction where none really exists, it
has tended to concentrate attention on the Barchester novels at the
expense of the later books». All Trollope's work (the historical novels
apart) may make a whole in the sense that its subject is broadly speaking
contemporary England, but the classification which has singled out the
Barsetshire series must be regarded more as a consequence of than as a
reason for the public's predilection.

It took Trollope's special qualifications for the task but he had, of
course, been much helped in his creative work by the chance of his having
been born to live the fullest part of his life within the full-blown mid-
Victorian period when the conditions of middle-class England were static
enough to form the foil and material of unmistakable pictures of real
life recognizable by his contemporaries and convincing to posterity. This
lucky coincidence of qualifications and opportunity has not been very
much noticed for the advantage it gave Trollope. Priestley, however, is
fully aware of it when he expresses his regret at the impossibility of
writing in the twentieth century 'a large leisurely tale, embodying the
subdued tragi-comedy of our social life' covering 'about twenty years',
because the novelist cannot have like Trollope 'as part of his material a
settled state of society'.[21]

This brings us back to the important question of the subject. Referring
to the aesthetes of the 'nineties, Collingwood maintains (p. 71) that 'the
painfully taught lesson of the nineteenth century criticism' could be
expressed in the words: »never mind about the subject; the subject is
only a *corpus vile* on which the artist has exercised his powers, and what
concerns you is the artist's powers and the way in which he has displayed
them», whereas the 'aesthetician' today (1938) says, »the artist's powers
can be displayed only when he uses them upon a subject that is worthy of
them». As has been mentioned, James did not say exactly, 'never mind
about the subject', but something like it: 'We must grant the artist his
subject, our criticism is applied only to what he makes of it'. Still he is
anxious to add that the subject 'matters, to my sense, in the highest
degree, and if I might put up a prayer it would be that artists should
select none but the richest'.[29] His view is that we cannot prescribe to the
artist; if we do not like his subject, we don't, it is a matter of taste; but

then we must leave him alone and not criticize him at all. However, James does prescribe something to the artist when he says that, »the only obligation to which in advance we may hold a novel, without incurring the accusation of being arbitrary, is that it be interesting». We know that 'interesting' to him means everything that gives an impression of life. And in telling us that we should leave writers alone whose subjects we do not like, James virtually admits that an author can be condemned because of his subject; turning our backs upon an author is condemning him for our part. But then, of course, somebody else may not turn his back upon him. In the last resort the degree of literary excellence of a subject seems to be gaugeable from the number and qualification of the persons who do not turn their backs upon the author because of his subject.

Quite in agreement with the Jamesian view Sadleir writes in his Introduction to the »Shakespeare Head Edition» of 'The Chronicles of Barsetshire' published by Blackwell in 1929:

> The criticism most frequently made of Trollope as a novelist is that his themes and his technique are alike commonplace. As to the first, the charge is surely no charge at all but rather an irrevelance. One does not blame a gas-bracket for burning gas; it does not pretend to do anything else. Similarly, though some may prefer themes loftier than Trollope's, they express no general truth but merely their own fancy when they declare him dull and trivial. He chose his own themes, and in so doing exercised the right of any artist. If others did not like those themes he was content for them to turn away.[30]

Let us now see what Trollope's literary achievement will look like if we apply to it what Collingwood calls the view of the modern 'aesthetician', or at least what Collingwood thinks should be his view thus expounded: Literature today should be brought back into contact with its audience, and the only way of doing this is »for authors to give up the idea of 'pure literature', or literature whose interest depends not on its subject-matter, but solely on its 'technical' qualities, and write on subjects about which people want to read. This does not mean turning away from art proper to amusement or magic ... As the expression of emotion and addressed to a public, it (art) requires of the artist that he should participate in his public's emotions, and therefore in the activities with which these emotions are bound up. Writers are to-day beginning to realize that important literature cannot be written without an important subject-matter.»[31] From among the important theorists that have recently expressed themselves on the art of fiction, Lucas and Curtius may be pointed out as roughly sharing Collingwood's opinion, and the present reaction against V. Woolf's work is perhaps another confirmation of its having gained ground.

Anyhow Trollope's reputation proves that a very great number of readers, now as in his own day, approve of just that attitude on the part of the author towards his subject which Collingwood thinks is the ideal, and which was Trollope's as it is well described by Sadleir in the Introduction mentioned:

> To him the daily round, the little comedies and calamities of courtship and domesticality, the companionship and thrill of the hunting field, the gulfs which separate one class from another, the ties of sympathy which yet can bind utterly different personalities together were neither dull nor trivial. They were endlessly various, fascinating, dramatic.

This is why they absorb his readers, too. No doubt his own engrossment in his theme largely accounts for what Sadleir regards as a gift apart, meriting »the final (perhaps the crowning) tribute», viz. his power to tell a story — »and tell it so well as to take the reader right out of himself, and for a while hold him in an imaginary world, absorbed in the joys, anxieties or wanderings of imaginary people».

> The fact that he wrote of an England of eighty years ago might be expected so to influence his work that it would affect the modern reader as . . . something quaint and charming, but definitely of a vanished day. That nothing of the sort should happen is a proof of Trollope's genius, for it shows that his people are human beings . . . Not many story-tellers of any age have so divined the essential »humanness» of their fellows, have so clearly distinguished period-mannerism from fundamental impulse, that their works can be read by posterity and relished as offering recognizable portraits of human beings — of just such human beings as are known to the reader whatsoever his date and clime.

And Sadleir goes on to speak of the interest created by Trollope's »imaginary bit of England» and our neighbourly interest in his people, and we remember that his contemporaries had found pleasure in the same things. »In no series of his novels», says Sadleir, »is Trollope's amazing power of normal characterization and of creating an illusion of everyday life more evident than in that centering round the Cathedral city of Barchester.»

It is evident that a brilliant dazzling style would have been wholly unsuited to Trollope's themes, and the general opinion of his contemporaries was that his style was clear and good for its purpose. Whether independently of others or not, Harrison expresses in 1895 the idea of a concealed art in Trollope's language. Specifying 'what we must renounce in order to enjoy Trollope' Leslie Stephen writes: »We must cease to bother ourselves about art. We must not ask for exquisite polish of style. We must be content with good homespun phrases which give up all their meaning on the first reading.»[32] In fact, up to this day critics in general have not shown much interest in Trollope's style as they usually, like for instance Allen, take it simply to be 'commonplace'.

Nobody will probably ever deny that his 'good homespun phrases give up all their meaning on the first reading', only we should remember that this was what Trollope wanted them to do; and most readers do not ask for more because those phrases with their obvious meaning imply so much of the background, the culture from which they emerge, which is their special attraction to the Anglo-Saxon public. Trollope's own comparatively extensive reflections on what an ideal style should be like might, however, make a reader of his *Autobiography* and *Thackeray* wonder if he had not himself aimed at the effect of the writer who »will charm his readers, though his readers will probably not know how they have been charmed» (*A*, 212). At any rate we know that he had trained himself to write quickly and aimed at 'a good and lucid style'. »How may an author best acquire a mode of writing which shall be agreeable and easily intelligible to the reader?» he asks in the *Autobiography* (p. 163), and answers himself in this passage:

> Without much labour, no writer will achieve such a style. He has very much to learn; and, when he has learned that much, he has to acquire the habit of using what he has learned with ease. But all this must be learned and acquired, — not while he is writing that which shall please, but long before. His language must come from him as music comes from the rapid touch of the great performer's fingers; as words come from the mouth of the indignant orator; as letters fly from the fingers of the trained compositor . . . A man who thinks much of his words as he writes them will generally leave behind him work that smells of oil.

The very few critics who have found his plain language to conceal something of his ideal of style have evidently discovered one aspect of his appeal which can never strike a reader forcibly because its effect lies in its unnoticeableness. The first of these critics is probably H. W. Pollock, who as a young man had been admitted into the old Trollope's acquaintance, and whose article on him, published in *Harper's New Monthly Magazine* (New York) in 1883, does not seem to have been noticed by other critics of note (with the possible exception of Harrison) before Sadleir. Pollock writes:

> The ease with which he wrote, the uniform swing of beat of style which he always adopted, were not unapt to prevent the art of his method and the genius which underlay that art from being perceived and appreciated. It is exceptionally easy

to read any of his best-known novels, easier to read them right through without
slurring a page or line than it is to read even Scott, and by a combination which
is far from usual, it was, when he had once mastered his art, as easy for him to
write these novels, so far as the actual putting pen to paper went, as it is for us to
read them. Thus the people who read them swiftly forgot that art such as this must
have been acquired with infinite pains, and did not reflect that these meant more
than the actual writing down of words . . .

Professor Elton, too, notices that »there is more finesse in Trollope
than his plain positive style might seem to accommodate».[33] But Sadleir,
who quotes Pollock with approval, stresses the point in this way in his
Introduction:

The style in which the best of Trollope's work is written, flat and ordinary as
it may at first sight appear, possessess in fact to a supreme degree the art which
conceals art. Only those who have tried know how difficult it is for a writer to
obliterate his personality from the style in which he writes, and at the same time
to preserve what he regards as the necessary forcefulness. It is easier to write
»beautifully» than, while subordinating style to theme, to write expressively.

However, there might be some doubt as to whether a genuine novelist
does 'obliterate his personality'; if the artist should 'participate in his
public's emotions', as Collingwood thinks he should, and as I think
Trollope did, he is supposed to feel at one with his public and then he
adopts a style suited to his subject as a matter of course.

Miss Curtis Brown (writing in 1950) appears to be the next critic to
contemplate seriously the hidden qualities of his style and she is mainly
puzzled:

How he contrived to maintain suspense with so relaxed a style of writing, it is
difficult to explain; but perhaps a good deal by his very method of going back to
go forward. The secret of Trollope's style, in fact, is movement . . .

And in order that others should enter into this world . . . he adopted a style
which almost sucked them into his books; there must be no barrier to their participa-
tion; no difficulty should cause them to hesitate on the threshold. Greatness, for
himself, might be lost — but what he had to tell was so important that personal
greatness did not rank high beside it.

But she finds that »Trollope's notes on writing . . . do not really explain
his secret». They do not »explain how he so skilfully selects the moment
of action on which to forward his story, the faultless way he cuts in on
his characters' lives, the details he picks up to furnish his world» and so
on.[34] It seems that Miss Brown asks for too much; no writer can explain
the ultimate secrets of the process of creating, of which style and the
sense of tact that goes with it forms a vital part.

* * *

However disconcerted criticism has often been by the rapidity of Trollope's mode of working, sensible critics have at least tried to reconcile themselves to the view expressed by Professor Elton that, »of course nothing matters but the result». Still his writing capacity commands respect by itself; it seems to have resembled the very virtuosity of a musician, which he says the author should try to imitate, but which seems a preposterous demand, were it not for the evidence of his own capacity. »He could», Pollock tells us, »sit down in his writing-chair at a given time and get up from it in a given time without ever interrupting the passage of his pen across the paper»; and it is astonishing how little he needed to correct his manuscript. I have seen with my own eyes Trollope's manuscript of *Framley Parsonage* in the Vaughan Library at Harrow; it is written in ink, and only on about every three or four pages might there be found a word or a phrase crossed over.

We remember that this was the novel that really made his fame, made him known to 'the millions' of the readers of the *Cornhill*, and he tells us himself in his *Autobiography* that he wrote the first pages of the story on his journey back to Ireland in a railway carriage. He had only six weeks in which to finish the first instalment of this his first serial, which he wrote to order, and in those six weeks he also removed his household from Ireland to Waltham House near London and took charge of a new postal district. It seems a wonder that anyone could do imaginative work in these circumstances and Trollope must have had much of the story ready in his mind when he started writing. However, thus overburdened with practical work and writing away at pressure, he experienced perhaps the most important thing during his writing career: his vision of Barset took final shape. »As I wrote it», he says of *Framley Parsonage,* »I became more closely than ever acquainted with the new shire which I had added to the English counties. I had it all in my mind, — its road and railroads, its towns and parishes . . .» It was the fourth of the Barset novels. He tells us with great simplicity (no doubt shocking to the aesthetes) of what 'slight elements' he 'fabricated a hodge-podge in which the real plot consisted at last simply of a girl refusing to marry the man she loved till the man's friends agreed to accept her lovingly'. »Nothing», he says, »could be less efficient or artistic. But the characters were so well handled, that the work from the first to the last was popular.»

The story was thoroughly English. There was a little fox-hunting and a little tuft-hunting, some Christian virtue and some Christian cant. There was no heroism and no villainy. There was much Church, but more love-making. And it was down-

right honest love, in which there was no pretence on the part of the lady . . . (or)
on the part of the man . . . Each of them longed for the other, and they were not
ashamed to say so. Consequently they in England who were living, or had lived,
the same sort of life, liked *Framley Parsonage*.

Here I think Trollope himself gives the essentials of the contents and
appeal of this novel, and the reasons of its appeal to posterity appear
to be the same. It may be regarded as in a way representative of the
whole Barset series, of its accidental birth or growth, and its attraction
to readers. Trollope himself took Hawthorne's comment on his novels
(above p. 74) to be just »as true of that work as of any I have written»,
and we may, perhaps, regard his appreciation as especially applicable to
the Barset series. The variations within the series, in conception, modes
of work, and literary qualities, from its tentative beginnings with *The
Warden* to the partly tragical and forcible *Last Chronicle* need not now
be pointed out.

Whatever differences there may be between Balzac's *Comédie
Humaine* and the world in Trollope's novels, the latter has at least
suggested something of the panoramic view of the former to several
critics after the revival — Walpole (1928), Sadleir (1929), MacCarthy
(1931), Cecil (1934), Allen (1954), though Frederic Harrison (1906) was
probably the first to suggest the comparison — but no such idea had
occurred to Trollope's contemporaries, or only to cause some critics to
deny the resemblance.

It is of course true, as Desmond MacCarthy says, that the phrase
'world-creating' is vague because »in a sense, most novelists of the first
order create 'a world'». Still critics persist in pointing out some novelists
as particular 'world-creators' and the idea that Trollope was one had
suggested itself at least to the Dublin Reviewer among his contemporaries
(see above, p. 114). To Harrison's curious statement (and as has been
mentioned the *Dublin Review* had made a similar one) that »the Barsetshire cycle of tales is designed on a scheme which is either a success or a
tiresome failure» Quiller-Couch (p. 230) remarks: »I should prefer to say
that it grew.» It is evident from Trollope's Introduction of 1879, from his
Autobiography, and from the stories themselves that the novels were not
premeditated as a series. He had several other books in hand simultaneously or alternating with the Barset novels but, as some critics have
perceived, the county began to fascinate him more than other themes.
In his *History of the English Novel* (1937) Baker regards the novels that
came between as digressions and says of *Framley Parsonage* for example

that it was »like a return to his own people». Mgr. Knox conjectures that even after the publication of *Barchester Towers* »Trollope found himself suffering from a nostalgia for Barsetshire» and that when writing *Doctor Thorne* he became »committed to a series»; Miss Dunstable in this book »was too good to be dropped, and so we got *Framley Parsonage*». Mgr. Knox also observes the regularity with which the Barset novels appear after *Doctor Thorne;* there were three years between each — »so admirably was Trollope a creature of routine». But in Baker's opinion »he was not a Balzac» evidently because »there is no reason to suppose that Trollope saw at once all the possibilities opening out, or had any scheme for a comprehensive survey of rural England». It must be granted that Balzac eventually had a much more comprehensive world in his mind than Trollope, but Balzac, too, had begun his cycle of novels without any preconceived scheme.[35]

Only when busy with *Framley Parsonage* did Trollope draw the map of Barsetshire reproduced in Sadleir's *Commentary* where we also find a reproduction of Nichols's map already referred to and one drawn by Father (later Mgr.) Knox, which was originally published in the *London Mercury* in 1922. »For a generation», Sadleir writes, »Trollopians wondered where — if indeed it was ever made — that map (Trollope's own) was hidden. Pending its discovery two enthusiasts — Mr. Nichols and Father Knox — tried their hand at a reconstruction of the county as Trollope conceived it. They worked from such (often contradictory) details as are given in the various chronicles of Barsetshire.» All the three maps are curious evidences of the felt reality of the miniature county representing the English world and, simultaneously, 'fairyland' (Knox's expression in 1952). »We know Barset», says MacCarthy, »as well as a county we have lived in all our lives.»

Referring to the parallel between Trollope and Balzac as world-creating novelists, MacCarthy says:

> As far as I know, there is no evidence that Trollope ever took a hint from the *Comédie Humaine,* or had even read Balzac. (By the by, he would have disliked him!) The panoramic view of society, and the device of reintroducing the same characters at different ages and in different connections, were apparently Trollope's own inventions, and the genuine products of his nature, like every other characteristic of his work.

As has been mentioned, James thought that Trollope had borrowed through Thackeray Balzac's device of reintroducing old characters. The *Dublin Review* (1883) had already noticed that Trollope's characters in the Chronicles change when getting older, and that this increases their life-likeness. Sadleir in *A Commentary* (p. 417) only observes that 'certain persons' in the Barsetshire novels »in the manner of their reappearance show Trollope's skill in so drawing his characters as to depict them gradually growing older or altered in nature by altered circumstance». In his Introduction to the Chronicles he totally neglects this point. After the *Dublin Review* it seems that F. G. Bettany is the first to sense its importance; he writes in the *Fortnightly* in 1905:

> Trollope's knack of putting old faces into new frames affords his readers some very vivid sensations. Nearly everybody has known what it is to find himself a cipher in a crowd or to overhear accidentally unpalatable hometruths. It is this sort of experience which we enjoy vicariously with Trollope. He will bring on, for instance, Mary Thorne and her husband, persons who have formerly been exalted to the proud position of hero and heroine, and show them in their right perspective as regards the world they live in. So that we marvel at the insignificant figure which they cut as the Greshams, casual guests at a dinner party. Does not this kind of paradox strike us in actual life? For a time certain people absorb our whole horizon; met after a long interval, they have shrunk to liliputian stature. But besides showing us the true proportions of his *dramatis personae* Trollope can look at them from the different angles of different observers. He is also able, and prided himself on his ability, to exhibit the effects of time upon his characters. It is quite pathetic to note the advance of senility on Mr. Harding, or to observe Lily Dale fast becoming an old maid, just as it is pleasing to see John Eames shaking off his hobbledehoy awkwardness, or the Archdeacon lapsing into a kindly blusterer. Here again the novelist affords us the very illusion of our working-day world, its amusing ironies, it melancholy transformations.

Trollope had 'prided himself on his ability' in the following passage after discussing Plantagenet Palliser and his wife, Lady Glencora, who are most prominent in the 'political novels':

> In conducting these characters from one story to another I realised the necessity, not only of consistency, — which, had it been maintained by a hard exactitude, would have been untrue to nature, — but also of those changes which time always produces. There are, perhaps, but few of us who, after the lapse of ten years, will be found to have changed our chief characteristics. The selfish man will still be selfish, and the false man false. But our manner of showing or of hiding these characteristics will be changed, as also our power of adding to or diminishing their intensity. It was my study that these people, as they grew in years, should encounter the changes which come upon us all; and I think that I have succeeded.

But he doubts that »the game has been worth the candle»:

> To carry out my scheme I have had to spread my picture over so wide a canvas that I cannot expect that any lover of such art should trouble himself to look at it as a whole. Who will read *Can You Forgive Her?* *Phineas Finn, Phineas Redux,*

and *The Prime Minister* consecutively, in order that they may understand the characters of the Duke of Omnium, of Plantagenet Palliser, and of Lady Glencora? I look upon this string of characters as the best work of my life. (*A*, 168—170.)

As Hugh Walker observes of this group of novels, »its special interest lies in the deliberate attempt made in it to trace development of character».

Other novelists had done the same thing before. But few have set themselves so conscientiously and on the whole so successfully as Anthony Trollope to show what is the effect upon character of different circumstances, and how age changes the point of view.

With reference also to the more important Barset novels Walker says that Trollope »probably gave more attention than any other writer to the development of character through a series of years».[36]

In *The Writing of Fiction* Mrs. Wharton discusses as one of 'two central difficulties of the novel' 'the choice of the point from which the subject is to be seen', the shifting of 'the point of vision from one character to another'. In the passage quoted from Bettany we have seen that the shifting of the perspective and also of the onlookers, the witnesses of the drama, is regarded as one of the particularly admirable things in Trollope. »The other difficulty», says Mrs. Wharton, »is that of communicating the effect of the gradual passage of time in such a way that the modifying and maturing of the characters shall seem — — the natural result of growth and experience. This is the great mystery of the art of fiction. The secret seems incommunicable; one can only conjecture that it has to do with the novelist's own deep belief in his characters and what he is telling about them.» Bettany finds that Trollope mastered this secret, and it seems that no one has so far given a better exposition of this aspect of Trollope's art of giving the 'illusion of our working-day world'.

The question of what part of England should be regarded as the model for Barsetshire has awakened much interest. Sadleir makes it out to be 'a blend of Dorset, Somerset, Gloucestershire and Wiltshire, over every portion of each of which he is known to have travelled'. Trollope's contemporaries had not generally thought of Barsetshire, or his imaginary world, as of a peculiar entirety although, from about 1867 on, there was a more or less distinct feeling that such a world was to be found in his novels (cf. above, pp. 115—6). Posterity, which has been more fascinated by the distinguishing elements of this world, has found that his passion for hunting and travels on duty meant a great deal for the growth of the 'new county' or the general scene where his stories are staged, whereas

James had only remarked that the hunting-field in his books 'was excellent material'. Hugh Walker puts it like this:

> One of the great merits of this series of novels (the Chronicles) is the verisimilitude of the imaginary county in which the scene is laid; for though Salisbury suggested to Trollope the idea of *The Warden*, Barsetshire is not a copy of any English county. Its verisimilitude is due to the vivid realisation of it in Trollope's own mind. Long practice in hunting had given him an eye for country (in spite of his short-sightedness it must be thus expressed), which had been improved by his habit of investigating the rural postal system, both in Ireland and in England, on horseback. Few who have industriously plied the pen have spent so much of their life in the open air as he.

Here we find a hint of what, after Sadleir's *Commentary* had been published, Walpole calls Trollope's 'sense of space', which he thinks is 'the first of his great qualities'. Having quoted a passage by Forster on Tolstoy ending in, »Space is the lord of *War and Peace*, not time», Walpole writes (pp. 185—6):

> When we, his (Trollope's) readers, look back on the whole panorama of the Barsetshire and political novels we get something far wider, more generous, more enduring than a mere clever evocation of place. We get not only Barchester and its country roads and lanes, but all mid-Victorian England, and then, beyond that again, a realisation of a whole world of human experience and intention. If it is »the sum total of bridges and frozen rivers, forests, roads, gardens, fields» which give *War and Peace* its sonority and amplitude, so it is the sum total of vicarage gardens, High Streets in sunlight . . . passages in the House of Commons . . . sloping fields of the Hunt driving the fox to his last lair, that gives these Barchester novels their great size and quality. — This art of space is exceedingly rare in the artist's equipment.

»Trollope had the gift», says Walpole further, »because everything was of significance to him. It is true that this significance was material and nothing carried him farther than he could see — nevertheless his vision of material things was infinite and swings us far beyond his immediate characters and narrative.»

We might argue against Forster (and Walpole) that it is not space but the passage of time that is the most prominent of these two effects in *War and Peace*. Forster finds that, while it is a matter 'of course' that we grow old, the sense of space that Tolstoy gives us is more magnificent. Lubbock thinks that, although 'the continuity of space is rendered in *War and Peace* with absolute mastery, the passage of time, the effect of time, belongs to the heart of the subject'. »I suppose», he adds (p. 49), »there is nothing that is more difficult to ensure in a novel.» We have found (p. 209) that Mrs. Wharton agrees with the opinion expressed in the last sentence. However, it does not seem to matter much which effect we think greater in a novel, the sense of space or the sense of the passage of time; a writer may give the one better than the other. What concerns us here is the fact that Trollope has been found to render both and render them well; but perhaps it is safe to say that the critics in general have been more interested in his power to render the sense of space, partly because it is the more obvious quality in him, and partly, no doubt, because it brings out better the English essence of his work.

The sense of space is not limited only to places and topographical conceptions; in its social relations character, too, may be looked upon as a mode of seeing life in space.[37] This aspect seems to be present to Professor Elton's mind when expressing his opinion (before Sadleir) that Trollope's work is free from the bondage to period. In his appreciative and sensible survey of Trollope he writes for the 'twenties:

> His patch of Victorian England has not wholly vanished from old hamlets or townlets remote from the railway, in the hunting shires. Dress and means of transit change, but the mental costume of Doctor Thorne or Bishop Proudie changes little. The English girl, the English lady, remain in forms that Trollope would recognise. His countryside cannot alter much. The topography of Barsetshire remains distinct in the map of fancy.[38]

The Americans no less than the English have been enamoured of Trollope's pictures of mid-Victorian England and of his particularly English characteristics. Hawthorne was one of the first to point out his Englishness, while Trollope's contemporary countrymen perhaps took it too much for granted to attach much importance to it even if they did notice it.[39] Leslie Stephen, however, was rather piqued by the idea of the typical Englishman that Hawthorne evidently entertained and found supported in Trollope (see above, p. 74). Stephen writes:

> Hawthorne's appreciation of Trollope's strain was perhaps due in part to his conviction that John Bull was a huge mass of solid flesh incapable of entering the more etherial regions of subtle fancy of which he was himself a native. Trollope was to him a John Bull convicting himself out of his own mouth, and yet a good fellow in his place. When our posterity sits in judgment, it will discover, I hope, that the conventional John Bull is only an embodiment of one set of the national qualities, and by no means an exhaustive portrait of the original. But taking Trollope to represent the point of view from which there is a certain truthfulness in the picture — and no novelist can really do more than give one set of impressions — posterity may after all consider his novels as a very instructive document.[40]

However much Sir Leslie Stephen may now be valued as a critic 'heaved up from temporary oblivion'[41], he seems to me to give Hawthorne's appreciation an unwarranted twist of meaning. Stephen's posterity has considered Trollope's novels much less as 'a very instructive document' than as literature that is alive and full of current meaning, and, what would perhaps have surprised Stephen even more, his posterity does not only find in Trollope's portrait of the average Englishman 'a certain truthfulness'; it finds in it a representation with whose Englishness it is very pleased indeed.

Paul Elmer More, another American, is also strongly impressed by the national characteristics of Trollope's work. Having remonstrated against Sadleir's 'apologetic note' (see above, p. 140), he declares: »I make bold to say that there is nothing in our language more essentially British than Trollope's *Autobiography* and novels, unless it be Boswell's *Johnson*. And for that spirit I see no cause to be humble.» As if aware of the English sensitiveness expressed by Stephen, he hastens to add: »I know there is another side to the English genius, as exhibited in Shakespeare and Shelley; but I think that a right understanding of the former will bring him closer to Johnson and Trollope than might at first be suspected.» As has been mentioned, Quiller-Couch also compares Trollope's Englishness to Shakespeare's.

Again we find this quality in Trollope very strongly emphasized by a naturalized Englishman, Hilaire Belloc, the excellent miscellaneous writer, who like More read lessons from the past. Belloc writes in the *London Mercury* in 1932:

> Trollope is national in the highest degree. This is not to be said by way of praise, still less by way of blame. It is to be said by way of description. He is as national as a game of cricket; he is as national as a French marching song, or a Spanish ballad. And that in which he is most national is the creation of living souls. It is the peculiar glory of English fiction . . . that it thus evokes not types but individuals, who step out of the world of fiction into a real world and live.

»Trollope's world of fiction», Belloc writes earlier in the essay, »is confirmed, enhanced, expanded, by an element which is all-important to success of this kind — the element of wisdom.»

> Though his remarks on universal mankind are applied only to English men and women of his experience, yet since they have in them the common humanity he can through them judge not imperfectly of mankind. Foreigners he does not attempt to judge, and this is significant.

The greatest emphasis of the importance of Trollope's national genuineness we find undoubtedly in Sadleir, whose notion that 'the very greatness' of Trollope springs from his Englishry' has been quoted on page 139. This notion may at first sight seem an absurdity; at least Sadleir's exposition of the effects of this quality seems rash. It might even be alleged that national aspects do not matter at all in works of art, i.e. do not matter for the artistic effect. This appears to be hinted at, for example, by Lubbock when he says of *War and Peace*, »it does not matter, it does not affect the drama, that they are men and women of a certain race», and more to the same effect. But it cannot be denied that to the genuine feel of the particular kind of work that Trollope wrote, the national spirit is of vital importance, nay, it is indispensable because this spirit with its period characteristics is just what his work sets out to interpret. What is more important than genuineness? He could make his people genuine human individuals only by making them genuinely English, or rather by conceiving them as genuine Englishmen from the beginning. Perhaps he even felt them to be so real, as Baker believes he did, that »they were making history, and (that) the history they made must not be altered», which would account for his unwillingness to change his plots.

Barsetshire could only have come into existence in a genuinely English mind, the mind of a man who did not only know but appreciated the institutions, manners and beliefs of his country and period. Trollope's attitude to these things in England was the same as Balzac's to the French world; both loved their century. The Chronicles of Barsetshire are a social comedy which at bottom reflects the seriousness with which Trollope looked upon the world. As Ronald Knox says in his Introduction: »In the political novels, politics are only a game; in the 'clerical' novels all is in deadly earnest — every contested election, every vacant prebend, begins to matter. He could not save the old order of things, the world of privilege he so intimately loved, but his sympathies have enbalmed the unavailing conflict.» And Mgr. Knox finds that Barsetshire »symbolizes the twilight of an *ancien régime*» and that this is its appeal »to a nostalgic age like our own».

* * *

The heading of Paul Elmer More's essay, 'My Debt to Trollope', published in 1929, heralds a solemnity of approach which is perhaps only what can be expected of one of the 'official humanist critics' as Daiches calls him, but which seems somewhat out of keeping with anything connected with Trollope, even with his attitude to morality, which is More's chief theme. Still his opinions do not appear unreasonable.

Mr. More knows all about the ideas of high-brow literature entertained up to the date of his essay. He agrees with the truism that 'morality
is not art'. But from this does not follow, he says, »that art has nothing
to do with morality», which he calls 'a deadly maxim'.

And it is, doubtless (More continues), under the sway of this seductive article
of faith in the autonomy of art that Mr. Sadleir defends Trollope from the ruinous
charge of preaching, thus: »In his *Autobiography* he speaks of the moral purpose of
his fiction; but no modern reader can take this statement very seriously. It is
merely another example of the influence of his period on his method of
self-expression.» I suspect that Mr. Sadleir, despite his modernism, has suffered
some confusion of ideas between moral purpose and unmitigated preaching, and
that Trollope, whatever the modern reader may say of him, was altogether serious
in his claim to the former.

It seems, indeed, curious that Sadleir should doubt the sincerity of
Trollope on this particular point on which he distinctly professes his
faith in his book on *Thackeray*, too, and in several digressions in his
novels.

Mr. More's main point is that it is the element of religion, the ethical,
that pervades all Trollope's fiction. In ignoring this, in not wanting to
acknowledge ethics as a guiding principle in works of art, Sadleir is not
able, More thinks, to give Trollope his due. More suspects that Sadleir's
'tone of apology' is due to the 'baneful influence of the current theory of
the dehumanization of art'.

Because Trollope's tales are superlatively human, because the very warp and
woof of them is woven out of the loves and hates, the joys and sorrows, the good
and evil, of life, looking to the adjustment of character and circumstance, therefore,
though they may be infinitely entertaining, yet they must be poor art, the product
of a brain devoid of imagination and ideas. So I explain to myself why a reader so
acute otherwise belittles critically what instinctively he admires, and so I am confirmed in my opinion that a theory of art which leads to such a contradiction is
intrinsically false.

This outburst of indignation is partly caused by More's opinion that
Sadleir does not repudiate strongly enough James's verdict of 1866 that
'*The Belton Estate* is a stupid book ... without a single idea'.

More's declaration of what he himself owes to Trollope is an imposing
eulogy on the novelist for the moral comfort to be found in him, and More
thinks he would have liked Trollope still better if he had taken less care
to disguise his instruction in entertainment. »The only question in my
own mind», he says, »would be whether Trollope has not conceded more
than is necessary in this direction, whether the moralist in the writer must

yield quite so much to the entertainer.» But he points out that he is here speaking from his own taste. However, if he exaggerates Trollope's moral zeal, as I think he does, it seems likely that others, like Sadleir, have not only been unjustifiably sceptical of his purpose to teach, but have attributed too little of his appeal to the ethics that pervade his work. As More forms his high opinion of Trollope from the belief that 'ethics and aesthetics are inseparable in art', a survey of the views of some other votaries of this belief seems to be called for.

This belief is strongly at variance with the 'art for art's sake' slogan, which even Henry James rejects when expressing the view that 'the moral sense and the artistic sense lie very near together', and that 'no good novel will ever proceed from a superficial mind'. Professor Koskimies writes (p. 259): *Der Wert eines jeden Kunstwerks und namentlich eines Romans, der künstlerischen Anforderungen genügt, beruht in hohem Masse auf dem Geiste, dem Ethos, das es ausstrahlt.* Having stated that »in vain has it been attempted to set up a water-tight compartment between 'art' and 'morality'», Mrs. Wharton (p. 28), like Koskimies, points out that the great novelists' works, and some of their 'explicit statements', prove that this is their conviction. Mrs. Wharton finds further (p. 171) that the particular defects of Proust »are defects in the moral sensibility, that tuning-fork of the novelist's art», and she thus condemns him on ethical grounds although she otherwise admires him. In her study on Virginia Woolf Miss Rantavaara finds (p. 107) that 'the lack of synthesis in her works and the sense of futility that she is unable to dispel' may be due to her substituting 'some kind of pantheism' for 'orthodox religion'.

Now the sense of futility is exactly what the aesthetic school since the eighteen-nineties conveys for example to Koskimies, who agrees with Richard Hamann's characterization of this school: *Der Eindruck soll nur etwas sein, aber nichts bedeuten.*[42] And it is in his opposition to this school and his irritation even with Thackeray's 'complacent admiration' of some of his 'blundering irresponsible' characters that More writes: »I cannot forget, when the spell of his genius is not upon me, that he is in the direct line of the 'futilitarians' of the present day. To that school Trollope certainly does not belong.»

Lucas finds (p. 228) that modern criticism seems still (in 1951) 'largely influenced' by the 'Art for Art's sake' school. For this school there exists only the 'pleasure-value', but, says Lucas (p. 233), »Since literature influences, can we wholly forget that influence?» He thinks that the critic (as well as the writer) should consider the 'pleasure-value' *and* the 'influence-value' — for »though there can be art without purpose, there cannot be art without result» (p. 302). Like More Lucas believes that »it is impossible to keep Ethics and Aesthetics apart.» In the opinion of the latter, however, ethics did not come from God (p. 316), but from 'the mixture of reason and tradition that forms the moral code of civilized states', and he thinks that we should not disregard ethical codes (in life or in literature), 'because they have become part of ourselves', and that by disregarding them we may be challenging the Erinyes (p. 320). Ethics are thus the most important factor for the 'influence-value' of literature. We find from his reasoning that, even if Trollope were thought a 'demi-pagan', as the Stebbinses style him, the ethical basis of his work could not be regarded as less valuable from the literary point of view. »Man's fate is, in fact», says Daiches (pp. 83—4), »directly or indirectly, the sole subject of art. All great literature breathes a sense of man's fate, whatever attitude to man the writer may take.» This must evidently be taken to imply, 'and whatever attitude to religion the writer may take'.

The massive evidence of the importance of ethics in literature gives, I think, an added pregnancy to a retrospective contemplation of James's statement: »Trollope will remain one of the most trustworthy, though not one of the most eloquent, of writers who have helped the heart of man to know itself.» But like Sadleir More knows nothing of James's essay on Trollope, or ignores it.

Of the practical consequences of a right-minded novelist's attitude to ethics More writes:

Of the intimate relation between ethics and any form of art that deals directly with human nature I do not see how there can be a reasonable doubt. Such a relation, in fact, means no more than that he who would depict life must be familiar with the springs and consequences of action, and that in the large matters of experience the tradition of the ages is probably richer in content than his own limited observation. The problem for the artist, more especially for the novelist, is not how far he shall accept the obligations of this law — his art will gain in depth in proportion to the measure of his acceptance — but how he shall manifest its operation. And just on this point we have the confession of a master of the craft. — — The novelist should screen his ethical theory under the guise of an objective presentation of life. The problem is how to wear the mask. What Trollope has to say on this delicate matter might be summed up in the phrase »poetic justice».

And More finds this to be »the critic's equivalent for the Aeschylean maxim 'he that does must suffer the consequences of his doing', and the

Hindu doctrine of Karma, or for what St. Paul expressed in the language of theism: 'Be not deceived; God is not mocked; for whatsoever a man soweth, that shall he also reap.'»

Belloc (writing about three years later than More) finds in Trollope's novels the same forces at work although he is content to call these forces 'the immanent justice of creation'. Having mentioned as a typical example the 'villain' of *The Small House at Allington* (Mr. Crosbie, who was noted for the same reason by Trollope's contemporaries, see above, pp. 112—3), Belloc writes:

> What is most remarkable of all is the way in which the consequences of wrong-doing come in their natural order, as physical effect follows from physical cause. The immanent justice of creation runs through Trollope and puts just the right amount of life, no more, into the process of destiny: of acute tragedy very little, but of doom a great deal. His gods have woollen feet. In his narratives evil, mixed as it nearly always is with excuses from motives not evil, bears its inevitable fruit.

The point here discussed is not a new discovery, as we know, but it is worth noting for the force with which it is presented especially in More's version. Novelists are usually expected to dispense poetic justice as a matter of course, but More tells us that Trollope's ethics form nothing less than an obsession with him, a passion to dispense poetic justice as if he were showing the works of fate like a Greek drama and were himself acting the chorus.[43] And this is why More does not find Trollope's personal comments to be a fault but a method of heightening the effect of his stories, just as Mrs. Tillotson (p. 251 ff.) sees in Thackeray's constant presence and comments in *Vanity Fair* his 'most important way' of giving 'shape and purpose to his great pictorial mass' — a way 'often under-valued by later readers, because misunderstood'. More finds in other words that contents and form, or better, subject, purpose and method are inseparable in the Trollopian novel.

More thinks that »what is beginning to attract more and more atten-tion to Trollope at the present time is not so much his art in the telling of stories and his discernment into the vagaries of human character, as the incontestable fact that he is, of all the novelists of the Victorian era, the one most contrary to the desolating mood of the 'futilitarians'», not only because of his attitude to morality but because to him »preeminently life presented itself as a game worth the candles». Several critics had pointed out his genuine interest in life before, but More gives in this con-nection perhaps the best answer to the imputations of too low ideals that for example the *Spectator* had made to him in 1883 (above, pp. 129—30):

The goal which his heroes set before their eyes may not always have been of the most exalted type. His Dr. Grantly, scheming to marry his daughter to a marquis, and rejoicing in his success, may be condemned as a worldly snob, and indeed his creator did not deal with him too gently; but even such an ambition, frankly and actively cherished, is something; it is nobler than the flabby indifference of our heroes who drift on the tides of temperament with no rudder at all. — — What he (Trollope) held to be desirable, what he presented always as really worthy of respect, was the slow and unostentatious distinctions that comes normally to strength of character and steadiness of purpose, checked by the humility of religious conviction.

»The objectivity of art and the detachment of the artist from the moral implications of his work», »this law of reticence», is not regarded by More with any great sympathy. »At any rate», he says with great satisfaction, »this certainly was not the method of Trollope. — — There is no indifference in Trollope, some would say no reticence. We are never at a loss to know how he feels towards his characters and their actions.»

Baker (writing a few years later) points out how effectively Trollope breaks in himself in *Barchester Towers* (Ch. IV) after his 'almost spiteful' portraiture of Mr. Slope, the evangelical curate:

I never could endure to shake hands with Mr. Slope. A cold, clammy perspiration always exudes from him, the small drops are ever to be seen standing on his brow, and his friendly grasp is unpleasant.

Baker's comment on this is:

It seems hardly fair for the novelist to interpose like that with his personal dislike ... but as an illicit stroke of sheer actuality it is murderously effective: no one can disbelieve in Mr Slope after that, and everyone watches with bloodthirsty delight the guerilla warfare between him and Mrs Proudie.

Baker rightly points out that Trollope »compels the reader to take sides» suggesting that the reader gets more excited about the story by this means than by an artistically detached method. More declares that by this means Trollope also »converts his readers into accomplices with him in executing the law of poetic justice».

To Sadleir, however, Trollope is 'fundamentally detached'. »Also», he says, »to the point inevitable in detachment, he is cynical.» And when pleased or indignant with his characters, he is »touched in his sense of citizenship rather than in his moral consciousness». He »arrogates to himself no general right of judgment, no knowledge of the true paths of virtue or of social decency more profound than that possessed by any of his characters».[44] But every artist is supposed to be 'fundamentally detached' in his artistic work; 'he is not suffering life', as Scott-James says (p. 343), but 'contemplating it'. A certain amount of detachment was indispensable to Trollope, too, in spite of his apparent zest. And if he does not want to stand above his characters when judging them, it is obviously because he feels at one with them and with his public. This Sadleir feels, although he does not appear to perceive it clearly, when quoting with approval what Ethel C. Mayne had written in 1919: »Trollope achieved his immortality by his perception of the value — the artistic value — of humanity's incompetence.» In this connection Sadleir finds that Trollope's outstanding quality was his tolerance, his understanding of human foibles; that he »was readier to defend the erring than to applaud the virtuous»; that »in his books he is at pains to bring out the good points even of persons in the main contemptible»[45] The last point is also noted by More and Baker.

Trollope's moderation in administering poetic justice had already struck his contemporaries (see above, pp. 112—3), although one of them remarked that 'there is no very broad and palpable system of rewards and punishments' in his novels. His charity and understanding of human frailty may be considered the reason why he could not be too implacable towards the bad ones; his moderation in granting rewards is thus explained by Belloc:

> There are many good men and not a few good women in that multitude of pages, but they do not reap any particular reward — or perhaps I ought to say no adequate reward — that I can remember. For Trollope is not portraying the universal or the eternal, but human life in this world and in that age — and if any one of you reading this remember seeing good deeds well rewarded on earth, you have had an exceptional experience.

Only 'the universal' seems to be a slip of the pen for it is just the universal that Trollope is portraying in his moderation, and this is evidently what Belloc means.

As far as I know Miss Curtis Brown is the only critic so far who has tried to find a philosophical basis common to all Trollope's novels; she has thereby come to suggest a pattern on which, perhaps in most cases, his work relies for its fundamentally serious effect, its message. She penetrates »to a fundamental conflict which is repeated in nearly all his books».

> It is the conflict between what a man or woman wants and what they think they want. The story is the progress of the characters through misapprehensions to the final peace of mind which comes to them when they have found their fundamental desire. This pattern has variation. — — In any case, the »happy ending» for Trollope is not the Victorian happy ending . . . His happy ending was a kind of

spiritual emancipation: a man and woman, having worked through uncertainties, either about their love or their lives, or both, reach a certainty. — — Normality returns, but everyone is a little older and a little wiser. This »happy ending» promises no certain happiness but inward sureness — and this, possibly, was the only happiness which Trollope recognised as lasting. (Brown, 51—2.)

This interpretation could serve as an additional explanation of the problem why Trollope's good men and women do not 'reap any particular reward', which apparently puzzled Belloc in spite of his own off-hand explanation.

* * *

Sadleir, like most other critics in our century, agrees with Trollope's contemporaries in regarding his power of characterization as his 'superlative quality' as a novelist.[46] Lord Bryce writes in 1903: »His clerical portrait-gallery is the most complete that any English novelist has given us. No two faces are exactly alike, and yet all are such people as one might see any day in the pulpit.» Still it is as evident to Bryce as it had been to Henry James that Trollope did not study his characters in the same way as the French novelists studied theirs. Lord Cecil, writing in 1934, does not compare his characters to those of the French writers, but oddly enough finds 'a large number of them' (even Archdeacon Grantly and Mrs. Proudie) individually unconvincing even in comparison with the characters of his English contemporaries; yet he admits that »their social relations to each other are always absorbing». On this point, however, Baker's appreciation seems valuable, and in this connection his explanation of Trollope's allegorical names seems to give them the right perspective (cf. above, pp. 106—7).

Trollope was (says Baker) less of a classifier than Thackeray or even Dickens. Though he was fond of bestowing designations which are labels rather than names upon the undistinguished crowd — a clear sign that these are generic specimens rather than odd individuals or eccentrics — yet his more distinctive characters are very far indeed from being mere variations of a few types. A character out of Trollope means rather such people as Mr Harding, Mrs Proudie ... John Eames, the Signora Neroni ... people who cannot be summarily thrown into the common categories of saints, snobs, fortune-hunters, flirts, wiseacres or nincompoops, or mere eccentrics. Dickens caricatured, and in so doing provided the classifier with unmistakable earmarks. Even Thackeray to a very large extent classified mankind. Trollope, on the contrary, was bent on showing off the infinite differences and the inexhaustible comedy of men's peculiarities of temperament, temper, and mentality, and selfish or generous outlook. — — No novelist was a greater contrast than

Trollope to those of his profession who were mere machines for turning out articles of a stamp that hardly varied, with the same trade-marks on characters, sentiments, and story. (Baker, 127—8.)

I think Baker here gives a good reason why readers had begun to drefer Trollope to Thackeray as a novelist, as MacCarthy said 'not a few' pid (see above, p. 67). This seems to excuse Nichols's putting Trollope above Dickens and Thackeray, and I have myself heard English readers discussing Trollope and Dickens express a preference for the former. 'Because he is not so vulgar as Dickens.' It may be, as Cecil says, 'no service to his reputation' to pretend that he is better than his contemporaries, but it is, of course, a service to criticism if we can find reasons why readers prefer him, as even Cecil has to admit that 'some people' do. Cecil's own explanation of this preference is worth noting:

Indeed, it is at once the final effect of Trollope's realism and the principal cause of his continued popularity that the literary conventions of his time are to him only machinery; they do not modify his conception. His contemporaries, concerned either to create an artistic effect or to illustrate a view of human conduct, conceived a large part of their stories in accordance, not with actual fact, but with some artistic or moral ideal. And since they were of the time, their ideals were the conventional ideals of the period. But Trollope, for all that the general scheme of his novels is the orthodox Victorian scheme, conceives his story not after a conventional ideal, but after his own observation of actual fact. So that the fabric of his book is as uniformly fresh as on the day it was made. The modern reader never has to adjust his mind to a Victorian angle in order to enjoy it. He can sit back and take the book just as it comes to him. No wonder some people find him easier to read than his contemporaries. (Cecil, 253—4.)

A further reason for modern readers to appreciate Trollope is seen by Miss Brown in the change that the rhythm of life has undergone since his day:

Trollope's passionate interest in living, as distinct from Life, has given him a value which he could not foresee. We have come near to losing the art of living by intercourse; conduct has almost ceased to be an art. Also life has become more restricted, paradoxically enough; long office hours and long train journeys, on the one hand, and supplied amusements, on the other, have eaten into the time which was once laid out in the play of relationships. Often enough we live on borrowed feelings. We feel lonely; life is precarious in every sense, and we doubt if we are making the best of it while we have it. Reading Trollope we can know that life on the level of behaviour is now, as it ever was, entirely ours to handle and that, skilfully handled, it can provide a pattern of the most intricate and delightful and even dramatic kind. (Brown, 49.)

To me it seems very doubtful indeed that 'life on the level of behaviour is now entirely ours to handle' and can be made to excite anything like

the interest it could excite in Trollope's day. But Miss Brown's declaration
of her feelings when reading Trollope seems to be good evidence, not
only of the common nostalgia for his world, but of the force with which
his 'passionate interest in living' works on a discriminating reader living
the artificial life of our day.

* * *

'However arbitrary the Stebbinses may seem in *The Trollopes,* their
attempt to interpret much of Anthony's work, definitely not as the
result of superficial observation, but as a product of the novelist's
psychological insight and complexes originating in his unconscious reactions to early experiences, is interesting *per se,* and gives a kind of high-
brow nimbus both to the authors and presumably to Trollope, too. The
chief aim of the Stebbinses, however, is biography, not criticism, and the
most remarkable thing to be noticed in their book as a whole is their
antagonism to Anthony Trollope himself which so strangely contrasts
with their admiration of his work. It is no wonder that Sadleir finds the
book to be 'a curious production', and he is undoubtedly right in saying
that, »as an example of manner unsuited to matter it deserves to become
a classic, for the authors have chosen to write of as solid and unpretentious an English dynasty as could well be imagined in a style so
rompish and dandified as to achieve a sort of nightmare frolic.» I,[49]
Still the book is by no means unvaluable as even Sadleir admits. One
example of its praise of Trollope's artistic genius must suffice. After a
discussion of *Rachel Ray* we read:

> Anthony's understanding of life in half a hundred households showed clearly
> that as a child he had intently observed the ramifications of interests and personali-
> ties among his own relations; no amount of study in later years could account for
> the consummate art which was so germane to him as to be unconscious.

The Stebbinses believe that his feelings towards his father and mother
decisively influenced the creation of some of his characters, for instance
Mr. Crawley and Miss Dunstable. Their psychological reasoning may
be inadequate as Hugh G. Dick tries to show (I,[86]), but something of the
fundamental solidity of Trollope's work can no doubt be explained by
the psycho-analytical method.

In one point of view the Stebbinses differ from all other critics I have
come across: They make out — and I have mentioned it once before
(p. 34) — that he really wanted to write more pretentious work than

became his average. They think his very first novel, *The Macdermots of Ballycloran*, evinces this desire. But after the favourable reception of *The Warden*

Anthony realized that he was exceptionally able in characterization and that he had lighted upon a rich field. The public, who refused to read about the wild Irish, liked characters who resembled themselves and the people they met at parties — with slight improvements in the wit and beauty of the good; with delicate deepening of shadows in the dishonesty and impropriety of the less good. To write thus to order was immensely better than not to write at all; yet it was not what he wanted. His desire was to probe deep into human nature and to publish his discoveries, unrestrained by the shabby-genteel limitations of his age. Such writing, he began to realize, would leave him a poor man and an unread author. The choice was clear, but he was slow to make it. To the end of his life, he never quite abandoned himself to the second-rate career he now chose to follow. (Stebbins, 143—4.)

When in the early 1870's he felt disillusioned in spite of his general success, he sat down to work off his spleen, as the Stebbinses put it, and wrote 'a most brilliant piece of work', 'one of the greatest Victorian novels', *The Way We Live Now*, one of the books which show what a height he could reach when he wanted to. With this book, says Sadleir (p. 399) »he would prove that the old hand could still outmodernise the youngsters, and at the same time expose the new magnificence for the hollow bombast that it was». I have already quoted Walpole's high opinion of the novel (above p. 31). Allen, writing as we remember in 1954, calls it 'one of the remarkable novels of the language'; it is one of Trollope's later books which, Allen thinks, 'have not received the attention they deserve'. There are, indeed, several critics who hold that Trollope was capable of writing fiction on a level above his usual standard, although they do not go so far as to say like the Stebbinses that it was his wish to write such work exclusively. Allen points to his 'recognition of the obsessional that fascinated him the more the older he grew', which is to be seen in *He Knew He Was Right* and even in some of the 'political' novels. (By the way 'the obsessional' is something of a fad with Allen in his critical history of *The English Novel*.) But, says Allen, »Trollope has never received anything like adequate recognition for his sober appraisals of the psychologically abnormal and the part they play in society. Yet they add greatly to the depth of his rendering of the social scene, for, among other things, they hint at the instability underlying the surface of society.»

It seems that critics generally have begun to look for Trollope's greatest qualities in his less known books. To this group of critics we

have to add Mr. A. O. J. Cockshut, the author of what is presumably at
the moment the latest critical study of Trollope, and a reviewer of his
book, Sir Philip Magnus, who applauds the former for insisting upon
»the fact that the much-loved Barsetshire series does not, on the whole,
represent the novelist at the height of his achievement.» (*Sunday Times*,
Sept. 4, 1955.) Thus Trollope's exceptional books maintain or even
increase his reputation among literary specialists, and if these books
reveal 'his sober appraisals of the psychologically abnormal' better than
his 'standard' books, they may perhaps convince the modern sceptic of
his hidden depths. But so far these books have only attracted the attention of a very limited number of readers beyond the Trollope fans and
literary critics.

Miss Brown gives perhaps a correct picture of the common reader's
attitude to Trollope today (she writes in 1950):

> For every ten who have read *Barchester Towers* there is probably one who has
> read *The Prime Minister* and scarcely one in twenty has read *The Way We Live
> Now*. Even *The Last Chronicle* — the greatest of the Barsetshires — is far less
> popular than the others. He was not to be allowed by his public to go beyond the
> bounds of a certain kind of comedy, to rise above a certain level of intensity.
> Trollope has suffered, perhaps more than most novelists, from a reputation arising
> less from the quality of his work as a whole, than from the public's taste for parti-
> cular works. To-day, even, he is suffering from the same limitations on his popularity
> that he suffered from nearly a hundred years ago. To-day he has a potential public
> for what — it is reasonable to believe — he himself rightly considered the best
> qualities in all his works: but the very virtues of *Barchester Towers* are still obscuring
> the achievements of even greater books. (Brown, 38—9.)

It is worth noting that *Barchester Towers* has been the favourite not
only of the common reader; even critics, among them George Saintsbury,
have given it the palm. But like Trollope himself and probably the
majority of his contemporary critics Miss Brown considers *The Last
Chronicle* his best book. In view of the fact that Sadleir makes such a
great point of Trollope's ability to write novels different from his old
genre, and write them 'better than most of those they challenged', it is
rather curious to note his decided preference for *Doctor Thorne*, 'the
proud apex of the pyramid of Trollope fiction' as he calls it (p. 401).
His predilection is rather due to the charming picture of Mary Thorne
than to anything else in the story, and he has devoted a special article
to the book, or rather the girl.[47] His choice shows at any rate that he, too,
like the common reader, finds Trollope's good qualities to be at their best
in the genuine 'Trollopian' novels. Incidentally Mgr. Knox (born in

1888 like Sadleir) also expresses the opinion, as late as 1952, that *Doktor Thorne* is probably Trollope's best book, and it is perhaps natural for a writer of detective stories to think so because it is 'certainly his best plot'.

The psychologically normal then is what the common reader appreciates in Trollope, but it is perhaps only natural that the psychological insight displayed in his popular novels should not attract much special attention in criticism because this usually implies an evaluation or interpretation of his psychology, too. Still it seems that a more conscious psychological approach on the part of the critic could better illuminate Trollope's appeal and eliminate part of his elusiveness, which strikes Sadleir, perhaps, more than other critics. Some such illumination he appears, in fact, to be in want of, to judge from several passages (cf. for example above, p. 140), notably from the following one, written after a conclusion that Trollope does not compare with his great contemporaries in certain respects:

But not by elimination only can the quality of Trollope be appraised. He may be neither teacher nor word-painter, neither pantheist nor social reformer, but he is definitely something. What is he? Wherein lies that strange potency, which renders work so featureless, so sober and so undemonstrative an entertainment than which few are more enthralling? It lies surely in his acceptance and his profound understanding of ordinary daily life. In the tale of English literature he is — to put the matter in a phrase — the supreme novelist of acquiescence. A curious, though not perhaps unnatural, result of Trollope's extreme acquiescence has been to set his work athwart the pattern of modern literary criticism. (Pp. 367, 369.)

What exactly Sadleir means by 'the pattern of modern literary criticism' is difficult to know and he does not become more definite by adding that Trollope's books »— so drab yet so mysteriously alive, so obvious yet so impossible of imitation — evade every criterion of what has become an academic judgment». The criticism quoted in this study shows, I think, that Trollope's books far from 'evade every criterion of academic judgment'. If they violate, as Sadleir says, 'the modish canons of good fiction', they violate also the canons of his contemporary critics, but they do not violate them all, and, besides, all great Victorian novelists violate rules. Now, at any rate, it is hardly any longer legitimate to speak of 'the pattern of modern literary criticism' considering the large prospects of illuminating literature opened by the Freudian analytical method, which is thought by Lionel Trilling to be able to »explain the 'inner meaning' of the work of art and explain the temperament of the artist as man»[48], and further the liberal ideas of literature and criticism entertained by such a modern critic as Trilling himself, to whom a definite 'pattern' of criticism is evidently a horror.

However, beyond the biography by the Stebbinses the psychological approach has so far not been much considered in Trollope criticism.[49] Miss Curtis Brown makes some vague suggestions in that direction in her accentuation of his 'human approach'. In a passage, which could be regarded as an amplification of James's thesis that Trollope's 'inestimable merit was a complete appreciation of the usual', she writes:

> Trollope was interested in how far the internal realities of peoples' natures, their strengths, weaknesses, courage, ambition, fidelity, rapacity and so on, are carried onto the external levels on which behaviour has play. Yet while staying within the limits of behaviour and adjusting his treatment most delicately to this particular pitch among the many on which life is expressed, he implies much of life that lies above and below behaviour and there arises therefore from his work a comprehension of what is noble, dignified and admirable in men and women. By taking this level of living as his sphere, he cut himself off from nearly all adventitious aids. He most deliberately stuck to the normal; he would not touch the unlikely, the eccentric — the character created for its own sake. (Brown, 47—8.)

This last is generally true only as regards his popular novels. Miss Curtis Brown endeavours in her book to suggest that »Trollope's central view of life gave his writing a wholeness, a sort of comprehensiveness, which is perhaps his distinguishing quality as a novelist».

> He stands at the centre of his world and he observes and understands the operation of people on each other and of objects and time and movement and seasons upon people. His direct vision, when he allowed it full play, enabled him to receive emanations of personality and of feeling which usually pass unnoticed except by writers who are concerned mainly with the psychological approach. (Ibid., 86.)

Miss Curtis Brown here praises what James calls 'a capacity for receiving straight impressions', which he thinks is the writer's most important quality.[50]

Baker acknowledges Trollope's 'bent for psychological analysis' but finds, even in his exceptional novels, 'no great complexity or profundity'. Baker is, however, affected with much of the old prejudice against Trollope, and his fifty pages of criticism on various points in him end up in a declaration that »he had not the vision essential to great creative art», but was simply a 'superlative' craftsman 'incapable of wandering off the track of actual experience'. It should be noted that this was written as late as 1937.

In the same year we find another extreme in Trollope criticism, Ashley Sampson's essay 'Trollope in the Twentieth Century' published in the *London Mercury* (Vol. 35). Sampson sees 'the key to Trollope's popularity in artistic circles to-day' in his psychological approach rather to the social group than to the individual. His individual characters, Sampson maintains, cannot compare with those of his great contemporaries; »but as a group, a family, an environment, they move with a sureness and react with a sense of inevitability and sublime artistic conviction that nothing in literature has ever surpassed. The 'team work' of his novels forms one of the marvels of English fiction.» And this, Sampson thinks, makes Trollope anticipate modern fiction.

> Not only has the plot of earlier fiction today thinned out into something that is a pattern rather than a plot, but the vogue for the dominating character has practically gone from English fiction. For the modern novel deals in psychological reaction of groups to their environment, instead of the rather introspective individuals that blotched the canvas of fiction some ten to twenty years ago. Of all the great Victorian novelists, Trollope alone got something of this psychological proportion into his work. His novels owed much to the influence of his masters, unconsciously assimilated and digested; but they began a movement which has almost outgrown our own age.

Sampson refers to 'some pioneer work in this field' done by Katherine Mansfield, Anthon Tchekov, Proust and Edith Wharton. Joad (p. 280) calls the movement begun by the first two the 'Slice of Life' movement, and points out Tchekov's and Katherine Mansfield's inability to construct and tell a story. »But the shifting of the centre of gravidity», says Sampson, »which has occurred in English fiction during the last decade goes back to Trollope more than to any other man — whom the English authors of a later generation have unearthed from the mausoleum of Victorian invective and read for themselves.»

Now this is a wild suggestion, first for the simple reason that Trollope always did tell a story, though often rambling enough, and *could* tell a story as critics often point out; and secondly because his interest in his characters and their individual fates is striking. But it is true that his characters are seldom dominating, one individual does not absorb all the interest of the story, and if Sampson underlines Trollope's interest in the social group too much, this interest has perhaps not been sufficiently noticed by others. 'His central view of life', to borrow Miss Curtis Brown's expression, made him very much interested in the individual character *and* the social groups *and* especially their relations to each other. Cecil, who also thinks that the social relations of his characters are 'always absorbing', almost denies these characters 'psychological complexities'. Trollope 'describes them', says Cecil, 'as he describes everything, not by

analysis, but by exhibiting them in action before us'. We could point to
the psychology exhibited for instance in Trollope's dialogues, too; but
exhibiting psychological motives at work in action is certainly not a bad
way of exhibiting them. There is many a delicate hint in Trollope's
numerous love-stories exhibited in a masterly way in small actions which
I do not think any Trollopian would like to see exchanged for analysis
and which show that he knew his business — the art of the novelist
— better than most of his critics.

It has been maintained that Trollope made 'little contribution to the
development of the novel'[51], which is true in a certain sense: he did not
devise any new tricks or any new manner that could be easily adopted
by other novelists, or pointed out by literary historians. Much of the
essence of his art consists in the inner meaning embedded in his work and
impossible to sum up without doing injustice to his qualities.

Mr. Cockshut's Critical Study

Mr. Cockshut's *Anthony Trollope, A Critical Study* (256 pp.) must be
considered separately here for two reasons: it was issued from the press
when the last twenty pages of the present thesis were being copied out
and was brought within my reach only when the copying was completed;
and it is a really important psychological study although we should
not, perhaps, be quite so impressed with it as the reviewer in *The T. L. S.*,
Sept. 23, 1955.

Sir Philip Magnus (see above, p. 170) and *The T. L. S.* find Mr.
Cockshut occasionally superficial and this, I think, is especially true of
his short chapter called 'The Story of a Reputation'. Mr. Cockshut wants
to distinguish between esteem and popularity, which the reviewer in the
The T. L. S. regards as an 'excellent point' because "there is all the difference in the world' between the two conceptions. This seems to me not at
all a self-evident thing; such a distinction is almost identical with 'detaching the novel as art from the novel as pastime' which is admittedly
difficult to do (see above, p. 141). »The often-repeated story of Trollope's
declining powers in the seventies», Mr. Cockshut maintains, »has no
greater foundation» than the natural preference for the 'crowded, gay,
extrovert, humorous' books of his earlier years over the later gloomier
novels. 'The often-repeated story', however, belongs rather to the
criticism by Trollope's contemporaries than to what I have called
'the New Judgment'.

Mr. Cockshut's book is devoted to a critical interpretation of some aspects of Trollope's work and outlook and to separate studies of seven of his later novels beginning with *He Knew He Was Right* and ending with *Mr. Scarborough's Family*. Mr. Cockshut calls the first one 'The Drama of Loneliness' and his great point is that it marks »the beginning of a new kind of writing, of his (Trollope's) greatest artistic achievements». »The new atmosphere», he says further (p. 197), »is unmistakable, tinged with gloom, sometimes with madness, a world of internal inner feelings, and rare but often terrible external events.» Although he finds that Trollope's break with his old world 'was never complete' (p. 198), he does not set him up as 'the voice of an epoch' because »on the showing of some of his later works he is as little fitted to fill this exalted but limited position as Dr. Johnson is to be considered the representative Augustan» (p. 227); and because »the Barsetshire series, fine as it is, is not fully characteristic of his genius» (p. 9). To me it seems, however, that 'some of his later books' do not invalidate the reasons for calling him 'the voice of an epoch' in the sense I think Trollope deserves this title and which is explained in my 'Conclusion'.

Earlier critics, beginning with Sadleir and ending with Allen, have been seen in the present thesis to entertain high opinions of Trollope's later books, too; but although Miss Brown comes nearest to doing so in her booklet, none of them has had the courage, or the conviction, needed to go the whole length of declaring, what Mr. Cockshut does declare, that they are 'his greatest artistic achievements', by which he obviously means that they are also his greatest literary achievements. Perhaps this point in criticism has now been reached because of the increasing vogue in literature of the conscious utilization of Freud's scientific explorations of man's depravity. We must admit, I think, that Trollope is a much more conscious artist in some of his later books than in the earlier ones, and the votaries of 'pure literature' will be naturally inclined to take a greater interest in the former than the common reader, whose opinion Mr. Cockshut does not care for. He writes (p. 144): »People may quote Johnson's remark about concurring with the common reader, but how many critics either in the nineteenth or the twentieth century have genuinely subscribed to it?» Most of the critics I have quoted have been at least in sympathy with the common reader. Still, if critics do betray their sense of superiority over the common reader often enough especially since the 'nineties, it should be remembered that, as Lucas says (p. 213), 'the critic is only the advocate: the reader is the judge'. And the common reader never admits that the conscious artist is the only kind of artist, or even necessarily a superior kind.

'Progress to Pessimism', the title that Mr. Cockshut has given to the second part of his book, he thinks »may seem unduly paradoxical, but», he says (p. 11), »it is not after all so rare that what was painful or even disastrous to a man has proved a blessing to the same man as a writer.» Anyhow.the present fashion in literature largely favours a gloomy view of life. In such a novel as *The Way We Live Now*, whose title declares its purpose, I do not think we are entitled to resent even exaggerated pessimism or perversity. Mr. Cockshut, like Sadleir and other critics after him (see above, p. 169), appreciates the book deeming that here »formally, Trollope came near to writing a masterpiece». But of all the books he has chosen for his particular study, Mr. Cockshut really appears to take the greatest interest in *The Eustace Diamonds*, as 'perhaps the first' of Trollope's satirical books, for its 'ambiguity about the value of convention', for 'the moral confusion which is the book's real subject', for its complex characters, and for its revelation of Trollope's 'universal pity' in his portrayal of a character (Mrs. Carbuncle) that 'Fielding, Dickens, Thackeray, Conrad, and the rest would have conceived as hard and deliberately cruel'. As has been indicated, the common reader also appreciated this book from the first.

I think Mr. Cockshut's study is useful exactly because of its one-sidedness, because it is almost exclusively concerned with the obsessional and gloomy in Trollope. It brings home to the student of Trollope better than any previous criticism the complexity of the writer whom critics up to the last few years have found it necessary to defend against the charge with commonplaceness, second-rateness. Such a student will no doubt be struck by the fact that much of the quixotic and obsessional for which Mr. Cockshut finds Trollope remarkable in the later novels is to be found in his earlier novels, too, though fortunately with more moderation and more sympathy for his fellow-beings.

Conclusion

Certain outlines and aspects seem to remain the lasting impressions from this survey of Trollope criticism over a hundred years. There is no doubt of his popularity during his lifetime and, in this century, from the early 'twenties with a certain decline in the 'thirties followed by a sensational boom in the 'forties; if he is not equally popular just now, it is perhaps only natural, for no writer can, I think, maintain a long popularity without breaks, and besides, the Trollope vogue has earlier declined some time after great wars. The critics have often been much more uncertain of his value than the readers, and only in 1955 has a penetrating study been published of part of his production, while the part that is the nucleus of his fame has not invited anyone to a really exhaustive study so far. The opinion that he is really a greater novelist than Thackeray has been advanced repeatedly in the last three decades.

Trollope's chief achievement, the Chronicles of Barsetshire, owe much of their popularity to their delineation of clergymen exposed in their frailties and divested of the spirituality of their calling. The subject was not only new but also piquant, and the *Dublin Review* in 1872 suggests that it really ought to have outraged the Protestants: »If the series of novels had been cunningly prepared by an enemy . . . instead of having been written, in perfect good faith, by a respectable member of the Church of England, to amuse his readers . . . it could not have been better adapted to its purpose.» But the stories contained no challenge to the Church as an institution and the majority of Trollope's Protestant readers heartily enjoyed all the fun they offered. No other profession could have offered equally intriguing possibilities as the centre of a social comedy of this kind including all the conflicts of normal life but emphasizing the social strife.

Ronald Knox says that Trollope 'had stumbled on fairyland by accident' meaning the blend of different counties that constitutes Barsetshire. But the 'fairyland' to be found in his novels seems in the last resort to have very little to do with geography. For Trollope's fairyland world, its atmosphere seems much more important, the atmosphere created by the ideals and beliefs of the mid-Victorians, the people with their assumptions and circumstances. These ideals and beliefs were beginning to vanish when Trollope was at the height of his power, and the world he wrote about was just beginning to assume a tinge of fairyland which comes with the sense of the past, and it was a past with a particularly strong sense of manners. Trollope's advantage over later depicters of society was not so much the fact that he had for his model a static world as the fact that this world believed in its own ideals and took its manners and conventions in deadly earnest. Sadleir says (p. 370) that his two predominant qualities were: 'power of characterisation and power of dramatisation of the undramatic'; but what he dramatized was really dramatic in the world the essence of whose life Trollope understood so perfectly. The strong belief in these ideals appeared to his immediate posterity ridiculous, hence in part his oblivion. To later generations these ideals and beliefs are no longer ridiculous, and Trollope's world has again assumed the strange tinge of fairyland — because accepted as a world in which assumption rules.

Today many different publics are catered for by different writers; »since Trollope», says Allen, »it is unlikely that any single novelist has captured them all». The spread of education gradually enabled all layers of society to read, and then it became no longer possible for any single writer to capture them all because their tastes and levels were, and still are, different. Many writers in the eighteen-eighties, or even before, must have felt this and some of them who by their own tastes did not feel at one with the greatest mass of readers did not even try to write for them. The segregation of readers in this way led to a segregation of writers, which contributed to the notion that the conscious artist may write, or even should write, from his own taste regardless of any public at all, the notion of 'art for art's sake', the growth of which has been indicated earlier (p. 39 ff.). Allen (pp. 250—251) observes that when during the 'eighties the three-volume novel was superseded by the one-volume novel the latter »imposed upon the novelist the necessity for a much more rigorous selection of incident and material». All these changes in conjunction with the *Autobiography* contributed to Trollope's temporary oblivion which was practically sensational in its suddenness, extremity, and persistence.

During the domination of the three-volume novel there was, however, hardly any subject better suited for it than a broad picture of society such as *Vanity Fair* and Trollope's social comedy. Trollope's work appealed to his contemporaries very much for its delightful portrayal of themselves and keen interest in their ambitions and daily life, and to later generations as a lifelike and fascinating picture of 'the England that was England when England was England' (Belloc). Sometimes Trollope has been labelled as a faithful delineator of manners with an air of condescension as if 'mere' manners were too simple a theme for an artist. I think Trilling's idea of this theme is the best argument against such a notion:

What I understand by manners is a culture's hum and buzz of implication. I mean the whole evanescent context in which its explicit statements are made. It is that part of a culture which is made up of half-uttered or unuttered or un- utterable expressions of value. They are hinted at by small actions ... by the words that are used with a special frequency or a special meaning. They are the

things that for good or bad draw the people of a culture together and that separate
them from the people of another culture. They make the part of a culture which is
not art, or religion, or morals, or politics, and yet it relates to all these highly
formulated departments of culture. It is modified by them; it modifies them; it is
generated by them; it generates them. In this part of culture assumption rules,
which is often so much stronger than reason.[1]

This is what we find in abundance in the novels of Trollope, admittedly
the best painter of the manners of his period. »The great novelists knew»,
says Trilling further, »that manners indicate the largest intentions of
men's souls as well as the smallest and they are perpetually concerned
to catch the meaning of every dim implicit hint.»[2] Man's fate is the ultimate interest of Trollope as of all great fiction, and his own excitement
about it, always within the modifying frame of manners, is what his
public has been delighted to share. Still there is really a certain reason
for speaking of two publics for, as has been mentioned, the *Dublin Review*
observed in 1883 that »he was fortunate in pleasing both the popular
and the critical taste» of his contemporaries, and the same may be said
of his appeal today when his psychological experiments and later novels
have awakened a greater interest among critics than ever before.

The *Autobiography*, once fatal to his reputation, is now regarded as
the most important of his works and as one of the masterpieces among
the autobiographies of the world.

There is evidently nothing in the *Autobiography* that Sadleir finds
more compromising to Trollope as a great novelist than his reiteration of
the moral purpose of his fiction. He tries to explain it away by saying
that 'no modern reader can take this statement very seriously' and in
one way this seems to be true: no reader has been disturbed by any
didactic purpose in Trollope's novels. From his fiction alone we should
not suspect that he was even thinking of such a purpose were it not for
his deliberate interruptions of his tales to declare his aim, but reading his
stories we are not interested in his digressions, and we simply do not
believe that he really wants to teach us. But if we make a study of his
Autobiography and *Thackeray* we must take him to be serious about it.
Still the discussion may be beside the point; contemplating the appeal
of the work of an author we are, in the last resort, not interested in the
author's beliefs but in his results.

Trollope's 'moral lessons' were, in fact, introduced into his stories
spontaneously because the stories originated in a moral mind. No doubt
the ethical intension is inherent in the work produced by such a man, or,

to quote James once more on this point: »The deepest quality of a work of art will always be the quality of the mind of the producer. In proportion as that intelligence is fine will the novel, the picture, the statue partake of the substance of beauty and truth. To be constituted of such elements is, to my vision, to have purpose enough. No good novel will ever proceed from a superficial mind.»[3] Trollope must have been 'constituted of such elements'; his wisdom and moral sense always lead him right, and he was not afraid of opposing conventional morality when it was too narrow. »Everybody trusted him», says Sadleir. I cannot but think that this trust is still felt by the public, is one of the reasons that has sent readers back to Trollope especially in times of trouble in our century. More is perhaps the most emphatic of those Trollopians who confess to the solace they have found in his books. But because Trollope persisted in sticking to the 'usual', to the unpretentious joys and sorrows of every-day life, his purpose has sometimes been misunderstood: he has been thought to cater only for the shallow reader's demand for amusement, or even to stimulate such a demand. And when he went beyond the range of every-day experience, some earlier critics (even as late as 1920) expressed no appreciation. In fact, his public has largely wanted to see him confined to the genre which made his first fame and which is still its basis. Professor Saintsbury constitutes perhaps the most remarkable instance, not of 'the irresponsibilities of critical judgment' of which Hugh Walpole takes Trollope to have been an outstanding object[4], but of a simple misunderstanding of his quality and purpose. Even in his last reconsideration of Trollope he writes of *He Knew He Was Right* and *Ralph the Heir* that they may be good enough for a circulating library, 'but they have no literary value whatever', and of *The Way We Live Now* he has an almost equally low opinion.

The change in the opinion of his range has been brought about among critics by the increased interest in psychology in our century. Some critics think the amount of psychological insight woven into his work, but overlooked before, must increase our respect for his intellectual stature; they are even inclined to look upon the point as more or less an epoch-making discovery in the criticism of Trollope. No doubt the quality of his mind and the 'influence-value' of his work as well as its 'inner meaning' can be better appreciated in the light of psychological considerations. »It is precisely our own century», says Lucas (p. 222), »which has a chance, thanks to psychology, of judging the influence-value of literature rather better than ever before.»[5]

It seems as if Sadleir and some others, who have thought that Trollope's practice was better than his theory, have been under the impression that he originally wanted to write with his sermon and his audience constantly in his mind; still Sadleir is well aware of the importance of Trollope's declaration that the novelist must 'live' with his characters.[6] On the other hand More, who so warmly defends Trollope's moral purpose and even wishes that he had preached openly, does not seem to understand that, although the moral purpose may be desirable — and I think James's definition of the relation between the novelist and ethics is good — the novelist must forget it and forget his audience. As Mrs. Wharton says, »he will never do his best till he ceases altogether to think of his readers (and his editor and his publisher) and begins to write, not for himself, but for that *other self* with whom the creative artist is always in mysterious correspondence, and who, happily, has an objective existence somewhere, and will some day receive the message sent to him, though the reader may never know it.« Trollope did not forget his readers and publishers all the time he was working at a novel; hardly any of the great novelists did. And work done with an eye on the public inclines to become the work of a craftsman. Daiches obviously states the general truth after mentioning Dickens and Scott as examples of novelists in whose work we find passages written on the strength of mere craftsmanship: »Many artists operate as craftsmen part of the time and as artists only occasionally. The novelist in particular, because of the length of his work and the length of time necessary to complete it, is liable to descend on occasion to the level of the mere craftsman.«[7]

But still Trollope's relation to his public is different from that of so many other writers, and the critics have at least some notion of it as we may find from James's verdict that Trollope's 'great, his inestimable merit was a complete appreciation of the usual', Sadleir's opinion that he is 'the supreme novelist of acquiescence', and Miss Curtis Brown's reflection about 'Trollope's passionate interest in living, as distinct from Life'. No doubt these opinions refer mainly to his attitude to his subject but I take them to imply his relation to his readers, too, which is that he feels at one with them and regards them as his collaborators. (Cf. further e.g. the opinions of More and Baker, above p. 164.) Collingwood's idea of the ideal attitude of the artist towards his audience seems to be written just as if he had had Trollope for his model:

In so far as the artist feels himself at one with his audience . . . he (will take) it as his business to express not his own private emotions, irrespectively of whether any one else feels them or not, but the emotions he shares with his audience. He will conceive himself as his audience's spokesman, saying for it the things it wants to say but cannot say unaided. Instead of setting up for the great man who (as Hegel said) imposes upon the world the task of understanding him, he will be a humbler person, imposing upon himself the task of understanding the world, and thus enabling it to understand itself.[8]

The cult of 'genius' says Collingwood further, is dying away, but if we 'look at the facts, whatever airs they may give themselves, artists have always been in the habit of treating the public as collaborators' though only in 'the attempt to answer the question: is this a genuine work of art or not?' But the audience's collaboration 'must be admitted further'. 'The artist's business is to express emotions', and he should take care that his expression of them 'is as valid for the audience as it is for himself'. Some of Collingwood's ideas may be arguable, but I think the point about collaboration is illuminating as to the appeal of such a writer as Trollope. James spoke of the unpretentiousness that had endeared Trollope to many readers; it seems that the collaboration idea places this unpretentiousness in a proper light, gives it a greater importance than when looked upon only as an endearing quality.

In the light of the collaboration idea Hugh Walpole's appreciation of Trollope also acquires a deeper meaning. He has hardly any notion of such an idea when writing that Trollope considered the novel 'first as an impulse for his own entertainment and happiness; secondly as a means of livelihood; thirdly as his principal proof of self-justification'. But when he proceeds to expatiate on 'his impulse of creation', he says things that Collingwood could very well have chosen as illustrations of his idea:

The first great quality of his charm and power lies just in this, that he is as deeply pleased as we are at the acquaintances and friendships that he is for ever making. We are there with him at the very moment of the first meeting. — — we can see just why he is pleased, excited, amused, indignant. — — We know him to be an honest man, not easily deceived, unlikely to be taken in by something of no sort of value, and so, as we watch him thus deeply absorbed, we want to share his discoveries.[9]

That is to say, his public trusts him, looks upon him 'as his audience's spokesman' who will express the emotions this audience shares spontaneously, and his own excitement about it all carries away his readers. As Miss Curtis Brown says, he 'contrives by his writings to give an added substance to the existing world'.

The artist to be an artist, the novelist to be a genuine novelist, should have originality as is expounded for example by Mrs. Wharton

(p. 18) and Daiches (p. 126), but it seems that Gottfried Keller, Trollope's great Swiss contemporary, supplies a definition which, though at bottom not different from theirs, is better applicable verbatim to Trollope: *Das Neue wird überhaupt nicht von einzelnen auszuhecken und unwillkürlich von aussen in die Welt hinein zu bringen sein; vielmehr wird es darauf hinauslaufen, dass es der gelungene Ausdruck des Innerlichen, Zuständlichen und Notwendigen ist, das jeweilig in einer Zeit und in einem Volke steckt, etwas sehr Nahes, Bekanntes und Verwandtes, fast wie das Ei des Kolumbus.*[10] This is equal to saying that 'true originality is a power to express happily the primary emotions of one's epoch'. This is the greatest originality that Trollope has been found to possess, and this is apparently what Sadleir sees in him, too, although his expressions might sometimes be misleading, as for instance when he says (p. 16) that »his achievement can now be regarded as having a significance beyond the purely literary» because his fiction 'mirrors social fact'. The designation of Trollope as 'the Voice of an Epoch' should not be given him for anything 'beyond' his literary significance; those who know Trollope must find it to be a most happy expression for just his literary significance, the significance of a novelist whose greatest originality consisted in his ability to feel more at one with his period than any of his contemporaries and express its emotions in work which may be said to have passed the test of immortality.

Bibliography

ALLEN, WALTER, *The English Novel*. A Short Critical History. Phoenix House Ltd. London 1954.

ALLEMANDY, VICTOR H., *Notes on Kingley's 'Alton Locke'*. Third Edition. The Normal Press, Ltd. London.

BAILY, F. E., *Six Great Victorian Novelists*. MacDonald & Co. (Publishers) Ltd. London 1947.

BAKER ERNEST A., *The History of the English Novel*. VIII. H. F. & G. Witherby Ltd.. London 1937.

BATHO, EDITH, and BONAMY DOBRÉE, *The Victorians and After 1830—1914* (Introductions to English Literature Edited by Bonamy Dobrée. Vol. IV.) The Cresset Press London 1938.

BAUGH, ALBERT C., *A Literary History of England*. Routledge & Kegan Paul Ltd. London 1950.

BENNETT, ARNOLD, *Books and Persons*. Being Comments on a Past Epoch 1908 —1911. Chatto & Windus London 1917.
From the Prefatory Note: »The contents of this book have been chosen from a series of weekly articles which enlivened the *New Age* during the years 1908, 1909, and 1911, under the pseudonym 'Jacob Tonson'.»

BOOTH, BRADFORD A., *The Letters of Anthony Trollope*. Oxford University Press London 1951.

BOWEN, ELISABETH, *Anthony Trollope*. A New Judgement. Oxford University Press London 1946. (A Radio Play first broadcast by the B.B.C. in 1945.)

BRIGGS, ASA, *Victorian People*. Odhams Press Limited London 1954.

British Authors of the Nineteenth Century. Edited by Stanley J. Kunitz. The H. W. Wilson Company New York 1936.

BROWN, B. C., *Anthony Trollope*. (The English Novelists Series.) Arthur Barker Ltd. London 1950.

BRYCE, JAMES, VISCOUNT, *Studies in Contemporary Biography*. Macmillan & Co. Ltd. London 1903.

The Cambridge History of English Literature. XIII. Edited by Sir A. W. Ward and A. R. Waller. Cambridge University Press 1916.
Article on Anthony Trollope by W. T. Young.

CECIL, LORD DAVID, *Early Victorian Novelists*. Constable & Co. Ltd. London 1948 (1934).

Chambers's Cyclopaedia of English Literature. III. New Edition by David Patrick and J. Liddell Geddie. W. & R. Chambers, Ltd. London 1927.
Article on Anthony Trollope by Robert Aitken.

CHESTERTON, G. K., *The Victorian Age in Literature*. Oxford University Press 1947 (1913).

COCKSHUT, A. O. J., *Anthony Trollope*. A Critical Study. Collins London 1955.

COLLINGWOOD, R. G. *The Principles of Art*. Clarendon Press Oxford 1938.

COOPER, THOMPSON, *Men of Mark*. Sampson Low, Marston, Searle, and Rivington London 1878.

CROSS, WILBUR L., *The Development of the English Novel*. The Macmillan Company New York 1949 (1899).

CRUSE, AMY, *The Victorians and Their Books*. George Allen & Unwin Ltd. London 1936 (1935).

CURTIUS, ERNST ROBERT, *Kritische Essays zur europäischen Literatur*. A. Franke AG. Verlag Bern 1950.

DAICHES, DAVID, *A Study of Literature*. For Readers and Critics. Cornell University Press Ithaca, New York 1948.

Dictionary of National Biography. LVII. London 1899.
    Article on Anthony Trollope by Richard Garnett.

DISRAELI, BENJAMIN, *Sybil or the Two Nations*. Longmans, Green, and Co. London 1871.

ELTON, OLIVER, *A Survey of English Literature 1830—1880* I—II. Edward Arnold &Co. London 1948 (1920).

The English Catalogue of Books. Sampson Low, Son, and Marston London.

The English Novelists. A Survey of the Novel by Twenty Contemporary Novelists. Edited by Derek Vershoyle. Chatto & Windus London 1936.

ESCOTT, T. H. S., *Anthony Trollope, His Works, Associates and Originals*. John Lane, The Bodley Head London 1913.

Essays and Studies by Members of the English Society. Vol. VI. Clarendon Press Oxford 1920.
    Pp. 41—66: 'Trollope Revisited' by George Saintsbury.

EVANS, B. IFOR, *A Short History of English Literature*. Penguin Books Ltd. Harmondsworth, Middlesex 1950 (1940).

FESTER, LOTTE, *Anthony Trollope als Beurteiler der politischen und gesellschaftlichen Zustände seiner Zeit*. Diss. Giessen 1939.

FORSTER, E. M., *Aspect of the Novel*. Edward Arnold & Co. London 1949 (1927).

FRISWELL, J. HAIN, *Modern Men of Letters Honestly Criticised*. Hodder and Stoughton London 1870.

GEROULD, W. G. and J. T. GEROULD, *A Guide to Trollope*. Princeton University Press 1948.

GOSSE, SIR EDMUND, *A Short History of Modern English Literature*. William Heinemann Ltd. London 1923 (1897).

—»— *Father and Son*. A Study of Two Temperaments. William Heinemann Ltd. London 1937 (1907).

GRAVES, ROBERT, and ALAN HODGE, *The Long Week-end*. A Social History of Great Britain 1918—1939. Faber and Faber Ltd. London 1950 (1940).

The Great Victorians I—II. By Various Authors. Penguin Books Ltd. Harmondsworth, Middlesex 1938 (1932).
    Article on Anthony Trollope by Hugh Walpole.

HALEVY, ELIE, *Victorian Years 1841—1895*. (A History of the English People
— IV.) Ernest Benn Ltd. London 1951.

HARDY, EVELYN, *Thomas Hardy*. A Critical Biography. The Hogarth Press London
1954.

HARRISON, FREDERIC, *Studies in Early Victorian Literature*. Edward Arnold London
& New York 1895.

HARVEY, SIR PAUL, *The Oxford Companion to English Literature*. Clarendon Press
Oxford 1948 (1932).

HAWTHORNE, JULIAN, *Confessions and Criticism*. Ticknor and Company Boston 1887.

HEYWOOD, J. C., *How They Strike Me, These Authors*. J. B. Lippincott & Co.
Philadelphia 1877.

Ideas and Beliefs of the Victorians. Sylvan Press Ltd. London 1950 (1949).

IRWIN, MARY LESLIE, *Anthony Trollope, a Bibliography*. The H. W. Wilson Company
New York; Sir Isaac Pitman & Sons Ltd. London 1926.

JAMES, Henry, *The Art of Fiction and Other Essays*. Oxford University Press New
York 1948.

—»— *The Art of the Novel*. Critical Prefaces. Charles Scribner's Sons New York
1950.

—»— *Partial Portraits*. The Macmillan Company New York 1888.

JOAD, C. E. M., *Guide to Modern Thought*. Faber and Faber Ltd. London 1948
(1933).

KETTLE, ARNOLD, *An Introduction to the English Novel* I. Hutchinson's University
Library London 1951.

KOSKIMIES, RAFAEL, *Theorie des Romans*. (Annales Academiae Scientiarum Fennicae, B XXXV.) Helsinki 1935.

LEAVIS, Q. D., *Fiction and the Reading Public*. Chatto & Windus London 1939
(1932).

LEGOUIS, E. and L. CAZAMIAN, *A History of English Literature*. J. M. Dent and Sons
Ltd. London 1947. (Modern Times, 1660—, by L. Cazamian, first published
1927.)

LIDDELL, ROBERT, *A Treatise on the Novel*. Jonathan Cape London 1947.

LUBBOCK, PERCY, *The Craft of Fiction*. (The Traveller's Library.) Jonathan Cape
London 1932 (1921).

LUCAS, F. L., *Literature and Psychology*. Cassell & Co. Ltd. London 1951.

MACCARTHY, DESMOND, *Portraits I*. Putnam London & New York 1931.

MAUROIS, ANDRÉ, *Disraelis liv*. Holger Schildts Förlag Helsingfors 1927.

MORE, PAUL ELMER, *The Demon of the Absolute*. (New Shelburne Essays. Vol. I.)
Princeton 1929.

MUIR, EDWIN, *The Present Age from 1914*. (Introductions to English Literature
Edited by Bonamy Dobrée. Vol. V) The Cresset Press London 1939.

—»— *The Structure of the Novel*. (The Hogarth Lectures on Literature No. 6.)
The Hogarth Press London 1949 (1928).

NICHOLS, SPENCER VAN BOKKELEN, *The Significance of Anthony Trollope*. Douglas
C. McMurtrie New York 1925. (Printed 490 copies only.)

PHILLIPS, W. C., *Dickens, Reade, and Collins, Sensation Novelists*. A Study in the
Conditions and Theories of Novel Writing in Victorian England. Columbia
University Press New York 1919.

PINTO, V. DE SOLA, *Crisis in English Poetry 1880—1940.* Hutchinson's University Library London 1951.

PRIESTLEY, J. B., *The English Novel.* Thomas Nelson & Sons Ltd. London 1935 (1927).

QUILLER-COUCH, SIR ARTHUR, *Charles Dickens and Other Victorians.* Cambridge University Press 1925.

RANTAVAARA, IRMA, *Dickens in the Light of English Criticism.* (Annales Academiae Scientiarum Fennicae, B. LIII, 1.) Helsinki 1944.

—»— *Virginia Woolf and Bloomsbury.* (Annales Academiae Scientiarum Fennicae, B 82, 1.) Helsinki 1953.

RICHARDS, I. A., *Principles of Literary Criticism.* Routledge & Kegan Paul Ltd. London 1949 (1924). (International Library of Psychology Philosophy and Scientific Method.)

ROUTH, H. V., *England under Victoria.* (English Life in English Literature.) Methuen & Co. Ltd. London 1941 (1930).

—»— *English Literature and Ideas in the Twentieth Century.* Methuen & Co. Ltd. London 1950 (1946).

SADLEIR, MICHAEL, *Things Past.* Constable & Co. Ltd. London 1944.

—»— *Trollope, a Bibliography.* Constable & Co. Ltd. London 1928.

—»— *Trollope: A Commentary.* Constable & Co. Ltd. London 1945 (1927).

SAINTSBURY, GEORGE, *Corrected Impressions.* W. Heinemann London 1895.

—»— *The English Novel.* J. M. Dent & Sons Ltd. London 1913.

—»— *A History of Criticism and Literary Taste in Europe.* II—III. William Blackwood and Sons Edinburgh and London 1902 &1906.

—»— *A History of Nineteenth Century Literature.* Macmillan & Co. Ltd. London 1910.

—»— *A Short History of English Literature.* Macmillan & Co. London 1907 (1898).

—»— 'Trollope Revisited', see *Essays and Studies.*

SCOTT-JAMES, R. A., *The Making of Literature.* Secker & Warburg London 1953 (1928).

SICHEL, WALTER, *The Sands of Time.* Recollections and Reflections. Hutchinson & Co. London 1923.

SMITH, V. P., *The Parliamentary Novels of Benjamin Disraeli and Anthony Trollope.* (An Abstract of a Thesis.) Ithaca, New York 1953.

SOMERVELL, D. C., *English Thought in the Nineteenth Century.* Methuen & Co. Ltd. London 1950 (1929).

SPEARE, M. E., *The Political Novel.* Its Development in England and America. Oxford University Press New York, London etc. 1924.

STEBBINS, L. P. and R. P., *The Trollopes. The Chronicle of a Writing Family.* Columbia University Press New York 1945.

STEPHEN, SIR LESLIE, *Hours in a Library.* I—III. Smith, Elder, & Co. London, I (Second Edition) 1877, II 1876, III 1879.

—»— *Studies of a Biographer.* IV. Duckworth and Co. London 1902. Article on Trollope reprinted from the National Review, 1901—2, Vol. 38.

STRACHEY, LYTTON, *Eminent Victorians.* Chatto & Windus London 1924.

—»— *Queen Victoria.* The Continental Book Company AB Stockholm 1943. (London 1921.)

STREET, G. S., *A Book of Essays*. Archibald Constable and Co. Ltd. Westminster 1902.
Article on Trollope reprinted from the *Cornhill Magazine*, 1901, New Ser. X.
TILLOTSON, KATHLEEN, *Novels of the Eighteen-forties*. Clarendon Press Oxford 1954.
Tradition and Experiment in Present-day Literature. Adresses delivered at the City Literary Institute. Oxford University Press London 1929.
TREVELYAN, G. M., *British History in the Nineteenth Century and After 1782—1919*. Longmans, Green and Co. London etc. 1948 (1922).
—»— *English Social History*. A Survey of Six Centuries, Chaucer to Queen Victoria. The Reprint Society London 1948 (1944).
TRILLING, LIONEL, *The Liberal Imagination*. Essays on Literature nad Society. The Viking Press New York 1951.
TROLLOPE, ANTHONY, *An Autobiography*. (With an Introduction by Charles Morgan.) Williams & Norgate Ltd. London 1946 (1883).
—»— *Thackeray*. (English Men of Letters.) Macmillan and Co. London 1879.
WALKER, HUGH, *The Literature of the Victorian Era*. Cambridge University Press 1921 (1910).
WALPOLE, HUGH, *Anthony Trollope*. (English Men of Letters.) Macmillan & Co. Ltd. London 1929 (1928).
WELLS, H. G., *Tono-Bungay* I—II. Bernhard Tauchnitz Leipzig 1909.
WHARTON, EDITH, *The Writing of Fiction*. Charles Scribner's Sons New York & London 1925.
WILDMAN, J. H., *Anthony Trollope's England*. Brown University Providence, Rhode Island 1940.
WILLEY, BASIL, *Nineteenth Century Studies*. Chatto & Windus London 1949.
WILLIAMS, T. G., *English Literature*. A Critical Survey. Sir Isaac Pitman & Sons Ltd. London 1951.
WILMAN, GEORGE, *Sketches of Living Clebrities*. Griffith and Farran London 1882.
WOOLF, VIRGINIA, *The Common Reader* I—II. The Hogarth Press London 1948 (I 1925, II 1932).
—»— *The Moment and Other Essays*. The Hogarth Press London 1947.
WOTTON, MABEL E., *Word Portraits of Famous Writers*. Richard Bentley & Sons London 1887.
YOUNG, G. M., *Victorian England*. Portrait of an Age. Oxford University Press London 1949 (1936).

Periodicals and Newpapers

(* = American)

Academy
* *Atlantic Monthly*
Bentley's Quarterly Review
Bermondsey Book
Blackwood's Edinburgh Magazine
* *Bookman*

* *Century*
* *College English*
Contemporary Review
Cornhill Magazine
Dickensian
Dublin Review

Edinburgh Review
English Review
Fortnightly Review
* *Forum*
Good Words
* *Harper's New Monthly Magazine*
Library
Listener
* *Littel's Living Age*
London Mercury
London Society
Macmillan's Magazine
* *Nation*
National Review
New Monthly Magazine

Nineteenth Century (and After)
* *North American Review*
Pall Mall Gazette
Quarterly Review
* *Queen's Quarterly*
Saturday Review
Spectator
Sunday Times
Temple Bar
Times
Times Literary Supplement
Trollopian
Truth
Westminster Review

Notes

A = Trollope's *Autobiography*. *Letters* = Booth, *The Letters of A. T.* *Caz.* = Legouis & Cazamian, *A Hist. of Eng. Lit.* *Part Port.* = Henry James, *Partial Portraits*. *Br. Hist.* = Trevelyan, *British Hist. in the 19th Cent. and After.* *Soc. Hist.* = Trevelyan, *English Social Hist.* — Names of authors refer to works mentioned in the Bibliography.

Introduction

[1] *Trollopian*, 1945, No. 1, Preface 1. [2] Cecil, 245. [3] Somervell, 167. [4] Caz., 1091. [5] *Trollopian*, 1945, No. 1, 'Trollope at Harrow School', 44. [6] Willey, 52. [7] Elton I, Preface; II, 370. [8] *Fortnightly Rev.*, 1927, Vol. 122, 'Trollope and Mid-Victorianism'. [9] Cf. Liddell (p. 49) who thinks that a creative writer is likely to »use his experience of many years past« because he is unable to »keep pace with the world«; and further K. Tillotson, 91 ff., on the 'great tradition' of writers, from Scott to I. Crompton-Burnett, who prefer a setting 'in a period from twenty to sixty years earlier' than their own day. [10] Cf. *Soc. Hist.*, 375, 535—6; *Br. Hist.*, Introd. XVI; Young, 50. [11] *Soc. Hist.*, 516. [12] Cf. *Fortnightly Rev.*, 1869, V, 'Mr. Anthony Trollope's Novels,' 197—8: »We know how the English clergy appear to many. They are country gentlemen,. who always wear white neck-ties and never swear; they are a kind of better behaved squires, who don't drink much, and who read the Bible. But that fairly described the majority twenty years hence.« [13] Quiller-Couch, 175. [14] Allemandy, 11—15; *Br. Hist.*, 267. [15] Allemandy, 15. [16] Quiller-Couch, 176—7. [17] Booth, Introd., XXV. [18] If we are to rely on Escott, Trollope actually found a likeness between Mr. Micawber and his own father: »As for my father,« once said Trollope, »while the soul of honour and unselfishness, after he gave up the Bar he showed a want of ballast, a fickleness, and an inability to make both ends meet, really reminding one of Micawber in *David Copperfield*.« Escott, 20. [19] *Soc. Hist.*, 376. [20] *Br. Hist.*, 289. [21] *Soc. Hist.*, 545. [22] Escott, 48—50; Sadleir, *Commentary*, 144. [23] Stephen Gwynn on 'Trollope and Ireland' in the *Contemporary Rev.*, 1926, Vol. 129, p. 77. [24] Gwynn, op. cit., 72. [25] Somervell, 17—18; *Soc. Hist.*, 515—6. [26] *Soc. Hist.*, 517. [27] Ibid., 519. [28] Somervell, 21. [29] »Men of letters dislike the Evangelicals for their narrow Puritanism, men of science for their intellectual feebleness.« Somervell, 101, from Halévy's *History of the Eng. People in the 19th Cent.*, III, 165. — Wildman, 53—4, mentions Dickens and Thackeray, besides Trollope, as examples of such men of letters. [30] Cf. *Soc. Hist.*, 520. [31] Ibid., 519. [32] Halévy, 352 ff.; Somervell, 104—110; Harvey, 145. [33] *Soc. Hist.*, 521. [34] Cf. Gwynn, op. cit. (above n. 23), 78: »In the Ireland which he knew, the Roman Catholic was, as such, regarded as 'inferior in standing' even though he were, like Sir Nicholas Bodkin in *The Land Leaguers*, a baronet of long-established family. 'It was the business of a Protestant to take rent, and the busi-

ness of a Catholic to pay rent.'» [35] Wildman, 49. [36] Somervell, 112. [37] Willey, 52. [38] Cf. Somervell, 85. [39] Young, 78, 87. [40] *Soc. Hist.*, 538—9. [41] Young, 83. [42] *Soc. Hist.*, 528. [43] Young, 81. [44] *Soc. Hist.*, 554. [45] Young, 78. [46] *Soc. Hist.*, 497—8. [47] Somervell, 103—4. [48] Cf. *Soc. Hist.*, 554; *Ideas and Beliefs*, 351, 362; Cruse, 16, 353. [49] Routh, *England under Victoria*, 154—5. [50] Soc. Hist., 492, 554. [51] Cruse, Ch. XVI, 'The New Woman'; *Ideas and Beliefs*, 254—60; *Soc. Hist.*, 557. [52] Somervell, 98. [53] Young, 91. [54] Quoted by Cruse, 340. [55] *Ideas and Beliefs*, 264. [56] Ibid., 352. [57] *Br. Hist.*, 274—5. [58] *Soc. Hist.*, 550—51. [59] Cf. Young, 81—2; Batho & Dobrée, 140. [60] In *Soc. Hist.*, 493, Trevelyan speaks of »a snobbish society like England, where those below were always seeking to imitate those just above them» as existing already in the early Victorian days. — Sadleir, 35, comments on 'the subtle taint of snobbery creeping into social atmosphere with the coming of middle dog between dog and underdog.' [61] Wildman, 79. [62] Young, 59, 88. [63] Cf. *Soc. Hist.*, 522—3; Somervell, 82; *Ideas and Beliefs*, 307; *Blackwood's*, May 1870, 'The Education Difficulty.' [64] *Soc. Hist.*, 523—5. [65] Young, 89. [66] *Soc. Hist.*, 525; *Culture and Anarchy* (1869) quoted by Routh in *England under Victoria*, 134. [67] Somervell, 158; Willey, 261; *Ideas and Beliefs*, 308. [68] *Soc. Hist.*, 525. [69] Somervell, 56—7, 159. [70] Cruse, 129—130. [71] Quoted by Phillips, 3—4, and Rantavaara, *Dickens*, 18. [72] Phillips, 38—9. [73] Cruse, 310—12. [74] Cruse, 408.

Part I

[1] Cecil, 198. [2] Cruse, 412—3. [3] Leslie Stephen quoted by Somervell, 8. [4] Giles Hoggett, the old brickmaker in *The Last Chronicle of Barset*. [5] Cf. Quiller-Couch, Preface: »His bulk is part of his quality.» [6] By April 1863, when this number of the *National Review* was issued, the *Cornhill* had serialised *Framley Parsonage* and *The Small House at Allington*, both belonging to the Barsetshire series, and further, between the two, *Brown, Jones and Robinson*, Trollope's greatest failure. [7] Sadleir, 298 ff. — In his *A*, 313 n., Trollope expresses his sentiments on the reception of the novel: »Writing this note in 1878, after a lapse of nearly three years, I am obliged to say that, as regards the public, *The Prime Minister* was a failure. It was worse spoken of by the press than any novel I had written. I was specially hurt by a criticism on it in the *Spectator*. The critic who wrote the article I know to be a good critic, inclined to be more than fair to me; but in this case I could not agree with him, so much do I love the man whose character I had endeavoured to portray.» [8] »Such puerilities.» *Letters*, p. 386. [9] See *Letters*, p. 386. [10] Cruse, 321. [11] E. Hardy, 98. [12] Phillips, 38. [13] *Edinburgh Rev.*, Jan. 1884, pp. 209—10. Cf. also Stebbins, 289—90 (in regard to Trollope's contract for *The American Senator* in 1875): »So many elements entered into the market that falling prices did not necessarily mean decline in popularity.» Further Leavis, 160—61, about the cheap novels that »ultimately drove out the expensive three-decker»; by 'ultimately' Leavis seems to mean 'towards the end of the century', but the effect of the competition was felt much earlier as is indicated by the *Edinburgh*. Allen, 250, maintains that the three-volume novel was 'finally displaced' by the onevolume novel during the 'eighties. [14] Batho & Dobrée, 140. [15] *Part. Port.*, 100, 102. [16] Cf. Sadleir, 394. [17] Cf Henry M. Trollope's preface to the *A*, 17, and Sadleir, 316. [18] *Letters*, p. 394. [19] *Letters*, p. 495. [20] *Letters*, p. 441. [21] Reeve

wrote: »Once, at least, he has apparently laid himself out to alienate our sympathies and take liberties with good taste, as in that unfortunate production 'The Way We Live Now.'» *Edinburgh Rev.*, 457. [22] Cf. Stebbins, 291. [23] Somervell, 183. [24] Batho & Dobrée, 35. [25] Cf. Cecil, 245; Sadleir, 366—70; Walpole, 198. [26] *Part. Port.*, 101. [27] Cf. Harrison, 36: »The novelist must draw from the living model and he must address the people of his own age. — — What sons of their own time were Fielding, Scott, Dickens, Thackeray, Trollope: how intensely did they drink with both hands from the cup of life.» [28] Somervell, 194; Cf. also *Br. Hist.*, 340 ff. [29] Young, 116. [30] Cruse, 106. [31] *Soc. Hist.*, 557. [32] Trollope's conviction of the inferiority of woman to man is conspicuous in most of his stories. It is expressly stated in a letter to Adrian H. Joline, Apr. 4 1879: »The necessity of the supremacy of man (over woman) is as certain to me as the eternity of the soul. There are other matters on which one fights as on subjects which are in doubt, — universal suffrage, ballot, public education, and the like — but not, as I think, on these two.» *Letters*, p. 418. [33] *Br. Hist.*, 341. [34] *Soc. Hist.*, 531. [35] Ibid., 557 ff. [36] Cf. *Blackwood's*, Feb. 1883, p. 317: »It is of course a matter of present controversy as to what place Anthony Trollope's work will ultimately take; but it may be at once conceded, that when the last pages of the 'Land Leagers' were left unfinished, the writer had no living rival.» [37] Cf. Batho & Dobrée, 98. [38] Batho & Dobrée, 95. [39] Caz. Book VII. Ch. I—II. [40] Quoted by Cruse, 379. [41] Leavis, 168. [42] Quoted by *Blackwood's*, Jan. 1883, p. 142; the English journal comments on this: »We don't doubt that, even in America, the old gods will outlive the temporary dazzling of Mr. Henry James's fine style, and delicate power of analysis, and even the setting down given to them by the critics.» [43] Quoted by E. Hardy, 208. [44] To take a few instances: R. H. Hutton of the *Spectator* is only mentioned as a critic whom Trollope respected in the *A*, 185, 313, but not at all in the *Letters;* Richard Littledale of *The Academy* is mentioned in neither book; Henry Reeve of the *Edinburgh* occurs in the *Letters* but not as a personal acquaintance, at least not of any intimacy. [45] Stebbins, 291. [46] *Eng. Rev.*, 1923, Vol. 37, p. 38. [47] Quoted by *The TLS*, Nov. 11 1953, p. 744, from G. K. Chesterton's *A Handful of Authors*. [48] For »the foolish and insolent things said of Trollope's work by criticasters» Sadleir (p. 364) refers to an essay, 'A Great Victorian' by A. Edward Newton, published in 1920; it is a rewritten version of a booklet printed in 1911. — The dates of the critiques referred to are not given by Newton, and only two 'criticasters' (Americans) are mentioned by name. [49] Introd. to the *A*, 1947, The World's Classics. [50] Caz., 1297—8. [51] Somervell, 202, 211. [52] Cruse, 418 ff. [53] *Br. Hist.*, 401—5. [54] *Soc. Hist.*, 565—6. [55] Cf. *Br. Hist.*, 404. [56] Ibid., 405. [57] Speaking of the great public, Leavis, 38—9, says: »The contemporaries of Hardy, Gissing, and Meredith clung to their Dickens, Thackeray, and Trollope.» [58] Cf. Cruse, 378 ff. and Caz., 1279—80. The quotations are from Caz. [59] Quiller-Couch, 139, 143. [60] Walter Crotch in *The Dickensian*, July, 1919, p. 121. [61] Quiller-Couch, 142. [62] Cf. Saintsbury's *Short Hist. of Eng. Lit.*, 752: »In the years which have passed since her death her repute with the critics has decreased out of all proportion to her real merits.» [63] The essay had appeared earlier in *The Forum* (New York), March-Aug. 1895, with the heading 'Anthony Trollope's Place in Literature'. [64] *Dickens*, 131. [65] Loc. cit. [66] Pinto, 32. [67] Somervell, 182—3. [68] Young, 164—5. [69] Somervell, 189; Pinto, 32. [70] Routh, *Eng. Lit. and Ideas*, p. 8. Routh has it

that the »newcomers perceived only too well that a world of intellectual refinement
existed, just barely within their reach», that they themselves »fully realized that
the readiest approach was through the literature which the Victorian middle-
class had created», and that the publishers wanted to »facilitate this approach».
[71] Elton, II, 370: »There was not nearly so much good writing of all kinds from
1880 to 1900 as there had been from 1860 to 1880. Those last twenty years mark
an ebb in English literature, an ebb which begins to be felt about 1880, in spite
of the survival of several great men.» Saintsbury in *The English Novel*, 273,
regards the early 'seventies as marking the beginning of what he calls »that slightly
downward movement of the nineteenth-century novel». [72] Harrison, 20, 25. [73] The
D. N. B. was begun in the year of Trollope's death. Trevelyan in *Soc. Hist.*, 574,
calls it »the best record of a nation's past that any civilization has produced».
To be included in this work is, of course, *per se* a distinction. [74] *Fortnightly Rev.*,
Jan.—June 1905, Vol. 77, pp. 1000—1001: »Our true-blue 'Young England' Tory,
Mr. G. S. Street, who revels in the old Liberal's pictures of the manners of the
'sixties and boldly dubs him a great realist.» [75] Young, 168. [76] Cf. further e.g.
Edinburgh Rev., 1877, Vol. 146, p. 482 (in regard to Phineas Finn): »We cannot
help thinking that the son of an Irish provincial doctor must have been deficient
in those little points of social education that help such a *parvenu* to such a rise as
his.» Etc. *Spectator*, Oct. 27 1883, p. 1379: »Mr. Trollope was not an able political
writer . . . life in Parliament would certainly have been waste of life to him.»
[77] Still Trollope himself does not mention Escott at all in his *A* and only in one
of his *Letters*, p. 489; in that letter of Aug. 18 1882 to his grand-daughter Rose
Muriel Trollope, Tom (Anthony's brother) is said to have met Mulford (?) and
Escott. »The great man was all smiles, as was also the less great man who is to be
the new editor of the Fortnightly.» 'The less great man' refers to Escott. [78] *Br.
Hist.*, 441; Cf. further ibid., 438; Muir, *The Present Age*, 23; Batho & Dobrée, 35.
[79] Muir, *The Present Age*, 27—8. [80] Graves & Hodge, 113, 150. [81] *Gaz.*, 1357.
[82] *Eng. Rev.*, Vol. 37. [83] In his Introduction to the *A* published by the University
of California Press in 1947, Professor Booth says: »In world literature there are
only a few masterpieces of autobiography. It is generally conceded that Anthony
Trollope's is among them.» [84] Rantavaara, *V. Woolf and Bloomsbury*, 43, cf. also
46. [85] Street, writing in 1901 in the *Cornhill*, »after a year of public excitement»,
had also expressed his pleasure at contemplating »the social English as they were
in a quiet time», that is to say in Trollope's novels, but, as Trollope had not yet
revived by that time, Street may be said to mark an early isolated case of the
phenomenon that became common with the reading public at large after and
during the two World Wars. [86] Hugh G. Dick reviewing *The Trollopes* in *The
Trollopian*, March 1946, p. 30. [87] Cf. Brown, 103. [88] Elizabeth Bowen's statement in her New Judgment (p. 3) that »in the early nineteen-hundreds Trollope
was so stone dead, so utterly off the map, that he might just as well not have
been born at all» is thus, besides being exaggerated, somewhat misleading as regards the specification of time.

Part II

A.

[1] See V. Woolf, *The Common Reader* I, 11.   [2] »The cruel, hard-hearted, indifferent public must be the judge.» Letter to Miss Badham, May 9 1881. *Letters*, p. 455. See further *A*, 214 and *passim*.   [3] Cf. Liddell, 21.   [4] *Hours in a Library* III, 161.   [5] *A History of Criticism* II, 574.   [6] *Hours in a Library* III, 161—2.   [7] *The Moments*, 79.   [8] Liddell, 46.   [9] *A*, 137; Sadleir, 240.   [10] Tillotson, 87.   [11] *Books and Persons*, 94, 96.   [12] Op. cit., 96.   [13] *Part. Port.*, 133.   [14] Quoted by Liddell, 37.   [15] *Edinburgh Rev.*, 467.   [16] Cf. Cruse, 61—2.   [17] Escott, 110—11.   [18] *Part. Port.*, 111—2.   [19] *Part. Port.*, 127—9.   [20] *Edinburgh Rev.*, 1877, p. 471.   [21] Cf. Escott, 255: »(Hence) his mortification at the indifference largely manifested to the *dramatis personae* of the political novels that followed *Phineas Finn*.» According to Escott, 270—71, the Americans appreciated the political novels far more cordially than the British public.   [22] *Part. Port.*, 131.   [23] If Disraeli in his trilogy »intended to set forth his views of political, social, and religious problems», as Leslie Stephen writes, his intention was not in the first place to write fiction. Stephen speaks of »the inconvenience of combining politics with fiction». *Hours in a Library* II, 358, 367. — Mrs. Tillotson, 210, speaking of the social evils represented in *Sybil*, says: »No one would belittle the value of such stimulus; but the only reason why it should be made through a novel is that it will reach a wider audience.» Cf. further Walpole, 103—4.   [24] *Edinburgh Rev.*, 1877, p. 463.   [25] *Edinburgh Rev.*, 1877, p. 480.   [26] Ibid., 481.   [27] 'Reg. v. Mason' by F. Newbolt in the *Nineteenth Cent.*, Jan.—June 1924, Vol. 96. — In *Phineas Finn*, Ch. XXIX, Trollope himself laments over »those terrible meshes of the Law» which a novelist can hardly avoid »in these excited days» if he wants to »create the needed biting interest». Escott, 194, writes with reference to *Orley Farm*: »Trollope justly prided himself on the accuracy with which, thanks to the experts he consulted, are presented in the legal details in the trial and in all the business connected with it, Here Escott himself is flagrantly inaccurate. But Trollope consulted a legal authority for *The Eustace Diamonds*. *A*, 114. Cf. Sadleir, 389.   [28] Forster, 68.   [29] *The Structure of the Novel*, 141.   [30] Two years later *The Times*, Aug. 10 1877, apparently influenced by the indignation of some other critics, gives as its opinion that Trollope in this novel »sinks below his ordinary level, and grows dull over a disagreeable theme».   [31] *Hours in a Library* III, 72.   [32] *Part. Port.*, 101.   [33] Hardy quoted by Liddell, 34.   [34] *The Art of Fiction*, 15.   [35] *The Common Reader* I, 194.   [36] Wharton, 26—7.   [37] *Part. Port.*, 100—101.   [38] *Edinburgh Rev.*, 1877, p. 461.   [39] *Hours in a Library* III, 163.   [40] *Part. Port.*, 132.   [41] Cf. e.g. Batho & Dobrée, 78.   [42] Cf. e.g. Saintsbury, *The English Novel*, 305—6; Cross, 236.   [43] Liddell, 46; Kettle, 98, says about the same.   [44] Daiches, 123.   [45] Cf. V. Woolf, *The Common Reader* I, 194: ». . . there is no limit to the horizon, and . . . nothing — no 'method', no experiment, even of the wildest — is forbidden, but only falsity and pretence.»   [46] *Part. Port.*, 99—100.   [47] *Theorie des Romans*, 86—7, 92—3.   [48] *Part. Port.*, 101.   [49] *The Art of Fiction*, 14.   [50] Ibid., 9.   [51] Ibid., 8.   [52] *Part. Port.*, 132.   [53] Ibid., 123.   [54] Liddell, 26.   [55] Cf. Rantavaara, *Dickens*, 189.   [56] In the *A*, which James had not yet read, Trollope wrote the admirable epigram: The writer should write, »not because he has to tell a story, but because he has a story to tell». *A*, 206.   [57] *Part. Port.*, 105.   [58] *Part. Port.*, 106.   [59] »A story», says

Forster, »is not the same as a plot. It may form the basis of one, but the plot is an organism of a higher type.» — »'The king died and then the queen died», is a story. 'The kingd died, and then the queen died of grief' is a plot. The time-sequence is preserved, but the sense of causality overshadows it». Forster, 31, 82. [60] *Part. Port.*, 106.   [61] One passage in *Part. Port.*, 131—2, evinces the curious fact that James finds the social tension in Trollope to be rather exceptional, to be found in some books only: »There is in *Doctor Thorne* and some other works a certain crudity of reference to distinctions of rank — as if people's conscious-ness of this matter were, on either side, rather inflated. It suggests a general state of tension. It is true that, if Trollope's consciousness had been more flaccid he would perhaps not have given us Lady Lufton and Lady Glencora Palliser.» This goes to show that James is practically blind to the perpetual strife for prece-dence depicted or hinted at in practically all Trollope's novels.   [62] Cf. Batho & Dobrée, 79.   [63] *Part. Port.*, 112—3.   [64] Ibid., 105.   [65] In the article referred to on page 80, *Blackwood's* confesses »to having felt a sense of injury in our national pride» after such an attack by the 'Revue des Deux Mondes' »in one of its recent numbers», but acknowledges that »the Frenchman was right» in regarding the bad writers as »purely, characteristically English». The essayist turns with relief to Trollope as a representative of 'the higher ground' in English fiction, »to the better fare which is still set before us». — For the continuation see above, p. 80.   [66] Cf. Lucas, 201—2.   [67] *Part. Port.*, 103.   [68] *Part. Port.*, 126.   [69] *Edinburgh Rev.*, 1877, p. 463.   [70] *Part. Port.*, 117.   [71] *Part. Port.*, 109.   [72] *Edinburgh Rev.*, 1877, pp. 487—8.   [73] *Part. Port.*, 108—9.   [74] Trollope, *Thackeray*, 202—3.   [75] *Fortnightly Rev.*, 1869, p. 193.   [76] *Dublin Rev.*, 1869, p. 363.   [77] *Part. Port.*, 129.   [78] E.g. *The Times* and the *Dublin Rev.*, 1872.   [79] *Part. Port.*, 133.   [80] *Part. Port.*, 131.   [81] According to Allen, 263.   [82] *Edinburgh Rev.*, 1877, pp. 459—60.   [83] Wharton, 47.   [84] *Edin-burgh Rev.*, 1877, pp. 461—2.   [85] *Part. Port.*, 109.   [86] *Part. Port.*, 106—7. — Daiches, 41, asks himself: »If the artist is concerned with the cumulative effect of his work, can we pass judgment until we have allowed the whole work to unfold itself?» And answers: »On the whole it is possible to recognize and to appreciate the liter-ary use of language even in part of the work, though a full understanding and appreciation must, of course, await a full reading. Nevertheless, there are more cases where one cannot do this than are generally imagined.»   [87] Cf. Daiches, 34—8.   [88] Cf. *The Art of Fiction*, Introd., XIII.   [89] *Part. Port.*, 107—9.   [90] *Fort-nightly Rev.*, 1869, p. 196.   [91] *Part. Port.*, 121—4.   [92] *The Art of the Novel*, 45.   [93] Ibid., 340.   [94] *The Art of Fiction*, Introd., XVIII; cf. also Daiches, 133.   [95] *Part. Port.*, 104.   [96] *The Art of Fiction*, 12.   [97] Lucas, 215.

B. *Trollope in the Eyes of Posterity*

[1] *Dublin Rev.*, April 1883.   [2] Liddell, 57.   [3] The Review here alludes to a pas-sage by Matthew Arnold on Johnson.   [4] See e.g. the working table for *The Claver-ings. A Commentary*, 351.   [5] *Things Past*, 18.   [6] Arnold Bennett, 269, has »no hesitation in de-classing the whole professorial squad — Bradley, Herford, Dow-den, Walter Raleigh, Elton, Saintbury», that is to say as critical writers, but as the best of them he regards Saintsbury.   [7] *Letters*, p. 457.   [8] Bennett, 44.   [9] Ibid., 264.   [10] I cannot help expressing once more my failure to understand Sadleir's omission to mention James's essay on Trollope. A footnote in the first edition of

A *Commentary*, however, seems to indicate a genuine and invincible suspiciousness of James's critical ability and of 'the school and period he represented'. Here Sadleir with apparent satisfaction quotes extensively an essay published in 1926 and called 'The Weakness of Henry James'. [11] Harrison, 206. [12] James had written: »He was the great *improvisatore* of these latter years.» *Part. Port.*, 98. [13] The Stebbinses note that he weighed 225 pounds in 1878. [14] Quoted in Mary Irwin's Trollope Bibliography from A. Edward Newton's book *The Amenities of Book-Collecting*, published in 1920. [15] Curtius, 117. [16] Op. cit., 387. [17] This does not seem to be Saintsbury's opinion of James. At least he appears to include him among 'some of our Zarathustras, especially those coming over the sea' who, he thinks, are not understood by 'the people' because their 'discussion of what fiction ought to be' is unnecessarily complicated. 'Trollope Revisited', 51. [18] Walpole, 180. [19] Quiller-Couch, Preface. [20] Ibid., 222. [21] *London Mercury*, 1932, Vol. 27, 'Some Reflexions of a Popular Writer'. [22] *Part. Port.*, 111. [23] Allen, 191. [24] *English Rev.*, 1923, Vol. 37. [25] Trollope wrote to Alfred Austen in 1871: »My doubt as to finding a heaven for myself at last arises from the fear that the disembodied and beatified spirits will not want novels.» *Letters*, p. 286. [26] See e.g. E. Wrangel, *Dikten och diktaren*, pp. 80—83, and Scott-James, 199. [27] Wharton, 77—8. [28] Introduction to the Barsetshire Novels in *The Warden*. The Oxford Trollope Crown Edition. Oxford University Press 1952. [29] *The Art of Fiction*, 15. [30] Quoted from Sadleir's *Things Past*, 32—3. [31] Collingwood, 331—2. [32] *National Rev.*, 1901—2. [33] Elton, II, 281. [34] Brown, Ch. III. [35] Cf. Curtius, 103. [36] Walker, 774—6. [37] Cf. Muir, *The Structure of the Novel*, 63. [38] Elton, II, 281. [39] It is mentioned for example by Stack, Reeve, and, for special reasons (see p. 157), by the *National Review*, 1863. [40] *National Rev.*, 1901—2. [41] Rantavaara, *V. Woolf*, 68. [42] Koskimies, 260. [43] More's attitude must be connected with the fact that, when writing his essay at the age of about sixty-five, he was an old student of Greek philosophy, Sanskrit, religious problems, and literature. *Who Was Who*, III. 1929—40. Adam & Charles Black London, 1947. [44] Sadleir, 368—9. [45] Ibid., 342—3. [46] Ibid., 366. [47] *Nineteenth Century and After*, 1924, Vol. 96. [48] Trilling, 47. [49] When this was written I had not yet seen Mr. Cockshut's study or any thorough review of it; see p. 174. [50] *The Art of Fiction*, 17. [51] Evans, 168; Baker says about the same regarding it as one of the reasons why Trollope should be considered a craftsman and not an artist.

Conclusion

[1] Trilling, 206—7. [2] Ibid., 211—2. [3] *The Art of Fiction*, 21—2. [4] *The Great Victorians*, II, 510. [5] If Lucas, in his *Literature and Psychology*, judges Trollope only by his working-methods as he evidently thinks some passages of the *Autobiography* reveal them and speaks of Trollope's 'happy craftsmanship', it is because Trollope seems to illustrate Lucas's points, but, in fact, he appears to belong to those people to whom Trollope is only known as 'the man who wrote by the clock'. I have met several Englishmen who have designated Trollope thus, which shows what an adhesive label his *Autobiography* put on him. [6] Cf. Sadleir, 353. [7] Daiches, 88. [8] Collingwood, 312. [9] Walpole, 178—9. [10] Quoted from G. Keller's essay 'Am Mythenstein' in Felix Rosenberg's Introduction to *Die Leute von Seldwyla* I. Deutsche Bibliothek in Berlin, 1921.

Index

The figures in boldface refer to notes.

Academy, 41 **44**, 41, 51

Aestheticism, 39—42, 46—7, 57, 64, 67, 121, 123, 130, 143, 144, 146, 160—2, 178

Allen, Walter, 31 **13**, 144, 145, 146, 148, 152, 169, 175, 177

American interest and criticism (excl. H. James), 8, 18 **29**, 19 **35**, 32—5 *passim*, 40, 43, 56—9 *passim*, 68—70, 74—5, 83 **21**, 92, 105, 129, 130, 133—4, 138—40 *passim*, 144, 145, 149—50, 153, 157, 158, 159—64, 165, 168—9, 181

The American Senator, 28

Arnold, Matthew, 20, 24, 36, 46, 131 **3**

Arnold, Thomas, 19, 23, 112

Atlantic Monthly, 56

Austen, Jane, 25, 57, 65, 93, 125

Autobiography, 32, 41—3, 56, 57, 59, 65—6, 66 **83**, 69, 73, 126 ff., 137, 142, 179

Bagehot, Walter, 28, 34

Baker, Ernest A., 152, 153, 159, 164, 165, 166—7, 172, 174 **51**, 181

Balzac, 25, 39, 114, 141, 142, 144, 152, 153, 159

Barchester Towers, 17, 28, 75, 78, 79, 81, 93, 97, 103, 105—7 *passim*, 116, 153, 159, 164, 170

Batho and Dobrée, 31 **14**, 34 **24**, 38 **37**, 38, 39, 44, 60 **78**, 93 **41**, 98 **62**, 130

Belloc, Hilaire, 60, 158, 163, 165, 166—7, 178

The Belton Estate, 112, 121, 160

Bennett, Arnold, 59, 60, 76, 134 **6**, 134

The Bertrams, 110

Besant, Walter, 73, 124

Bettany, F. G., see *Fortnightly Rev.*

Blackmore, R. D., 11

Black, William, 11

Blackwood's Magazine, 38 **36**, 40 **42**, 80, 100 **65**, 108, 115, 119

Boer War, the, 47, 52—3, 70

Bookman, E. W. Harter, 'The Future of AT', 57—8

Booth, Bradford, 8, 14, 66 **83**, 69, 144, 145

Bowen, Elisabeth, 68, 70 **88**

Box, H. Oldfield, 68, 69

Miss Braddon, 11, 80, 81

British Imperialism, 44, 52, 126

Brontë, Charlotte, 26, 40

Brontës, the, 30

Brown, B. C., 70 **87**, 150, 165—6, 167—8, 170, 172, 173, 181, 182

Browning, E. B., 13

Brown, Jones and Robinson, 27 **6**

Bryce, James, Viscount, 54, 166

Burn, W. L., 84

Butler, Samuel, 60

Can You Forgive Her? 51, 154

Carlyle, 13, 24, 27, 45

Castle Richmond, 16

Cazamian, 8, 10, 25, 39, 44 **50**, 47 **58**, 60, 62 **81**, 79

Cecil, Lord David, 8, 10, 34 **25**, 35, 80, 96, 122, 152, 166, 167, 173—4

Century, 40, 54

Chartism, 13, 20
Chesterton, G. K., 42 **47**, 59, 60
'The Chronicles of Barsetshire', 11, 48,
  51, 58, 59, 62, 68, 78, 103, 114—6,
  137, 145 ff., 177
Church of England, 12, 17—9, 36,
  54, 91, 177
The Claverings, 66
Cockshut, A. O. J., 170, 172 **49**, 174—6
Coleridge, 72
College English, John Wildman, 'AT
  Today', 68
Collingwood, R. G., 141, 146, 147, 148,
  150, 181—2
Collins, Wilkie, 11, 26, 30, 57, 96
'The common reader', 67, 71, 78, 93,
  94, 116—7, 130, 170, 175, 176
Conrad, Joseph, 40, 60, 115, 176
Contemporary Review, Stephen Gwynn,
  'AT and Ireland', 16 **23**—4, 18 **34**,
  83
Cornhill Magazine, 27 **6**, 33, 54, 68 **85**,
  99, 100, 111, 140, 151
Criticism, views on, 64—5, 67, 71—4,
  141—2, 146—8, 171—2, 173
Crotch, Walter, see *Dickensian*
Cruse, Amy, 10, 21 **48**—30 **10** *passim*,
  36 **30**, 39 **40**, 45 **52**, 47 **58**, 79 **16**
Curtius, E. R., 141, 147, 153 **35**
Daiches, David, 90, 93 **44**, 93, 100,
  119 **86**, 120, 124, 159, 162, 181, 183
Darwin, 36, 39
Daudet, 121
'Decadentism', 47, 49—51 *passim*, 53,
  57
Defoe, 98
Dickens, 13, 14, 15, 24, 25, 26, 27, 35
  27, 40, 45, 46 **57**, 49, 51, 52, 57, 58,
  62, 65, 75, 93, 94, 96, 102, 105, 111,
  116, 119, 120, 126, 128, 130, 138,
  139, 142, 166, 167, 176, 181
Dickensian (Walter Crotch), 47 **60**, 51,
  52
Dick, Hugh G., 70 **86**, 168
Disraeli, 13, 14, 22, 26, 83, 83 **23**, 84
Doctor Thorne, 17, 23, 98 **61**, 106, 112,
  153, 170—1

Dr. Wortle's School, 33, 113
Dublin Review, 10, 11, 19, 27, 28, 35,
  37, 55, 83—95 *passim*, 102—118
  passim, 124, 127 **1**, 145, 152, 153—4,
  177, 179
The Duke's Children, 33
Dumas, 25, 142
Edinburgh Review (Henry Reeve), 26—
  31 *passim*, 33 **21**, 38, 41 **44**, 42,
  55 **76**, 78, 81, 83 **20**, 84 **24**—6, 89—90,
  92, 106—10 *passim* 114, 116, 117,
  126—9, 157 **39**
Eliot, George, 10, 25, 26, 28, 30, 38,
  40, 48, 49, 57, 67, 93, 121
Eliot, T. S., 61
Ellis, S. M., 11
Elton, Oliver, 10, 47, 53 **71**, 53, 134 **6**,
  150, 151, 157
English Review (Charles Whibley), 42.
  66, 144
Escott, T. H. S., 7, 15 **18**, 16 **22**, 58,
  59 **77**, 59, 79 **17**, 83 **21**, 84, 84 **27**
The Eustace Diamonds, 29, 84 **27**, 84,
  176
Evangelicalism, 17, 18, 20
Evans, B. Ifor, 174 **51**
Fielding, 25, 35 **27**, 40, 49, 88, 90, 94.
  98, 176
FitzGerald, Edward, 28
Flaubert, 39, 78, 121, 144
Forster, E. M., 86, 97 **59**, 141, 156
Fortnightly Review, S. M. Ellis, 'T
  and Mid-Victorianism', 11 **8**; Her-
  bert Stack, 'Mr. AT's Novels', 12 **12**,
  79, 81, 89, 90—1, 93, 105, 110, 111,
  119—20, 124, 125, 157 **39**; F. G.
  Bettany, 'In Praise of AT', 54, 56—7,
  154, 155; T. H. S. Escott, 'An Ap-
  preciation and Reminiscence', 58—9;
  Wilfrid L. Randell, 'AT and His
  Work', 62
Forum (Frederic Harrison), 49 **63**
Framley Parsonage, 14, 25, 27 **6**, 33,
  151—3
Freud, 171, 175
Friswell, J. Hain, 35, 37
Garnett, Richard, 54, 144

Gaskell, Mrs., 14, 25, 26
George, Henry, 45
Gissing, George, 45, 46, 46 **57**, 51
Good Words, 132
Gore, Mrs., 75, 136
Gwynn, Stephen, see *Contemporary Rev.*
Hamann, Richard, 161
Hardy, Thomas, 30, 38, 39, 40, 46, 46 **57**, 51, 89
Harper's New Monthly Magazine (W. H. Pollock), 120, 136, 149—50, 151
Harrison, Frederic, 28, 35 **27**, 38, 47—57 *passim*, 134, 135—8, 146, 148, 149, 152
Harter, E. W., see *Bookman*
Hawthorne, Julian, 43, 130
Hawthorne, Nathaniel, 57, 74—5, 89, 98, 130, 152, 157
He Knew He Was Right, 30, 87, 91, 111—2, 116, 125, 169, 175, 180
Hook, Theodore, 48
Hood, T., 13
Hopkins, G. M., 40
Howells, W. D., 49, 57
Hutton, C. H. (of the *Spectator*), 41 **44**, 81
Industrial Revolution, the, 12, 17, 18, 37, 44, 61
Irwin, Mary Leslie, 59, 133—4
Ireland, 16, 18
James, Henry, 31, 35 **26**, 40, 46, 49, 54, 57, 73—4, 78, 79, 81—2, 83, 88—99 *passim*, 98 **61**, 102—15 *passim*, 118—28 *passim*, 133, 134, 134 **10**, 136 **12**, 142; 142 **17**, 143, 146, 147, 153, 156, 160, 161, 162, 166, 180, 181, 182
Jeffrey, Francais, 72, 90
John Caldigate, 63
Johnson, Dr., 71, 72, 131, 175; Boswell's *Life of*, 126, 158
Joyce, James, 61, 67
Keller, Gottfried, 183
Kingsley, Charles, 13, 14, 19, 26
Kipling, Rudyard, 44, 52, 60
Knox, Ronald, 145, 152, 159, 170, 177
Koskimies, Rafael, 94, 104, 144, 161
The Landleaguers, 16, 18, 45

The Last Chronicle of Barset, 27 **4**, 33, 34, 35, 69, 86, 91, 105—6, 111, 115, 152, 170
Lawrence, D. H., 61
Leavis, R. D., 31 **13**, 40 **41**, 40, 46 **57**, 71
Lever, Charles, 16, 30
Lewes, G. H., 103
Liddell, Robert, 11 **9**, 71 **3**, 71, 74 **8**, 80, 83, 88, 92, 93 **43**, 93, 96 **54**, 96, 112, 122, 130
Listener, H. Oldfield Box, 'The Decline and Rise of AT', 68
London Mercury, J. B. Priestley, 143, 146; R. Knox, 153; H. Belloc, 158; A. Sampson, 'T in the 20th Century', 172—3
London Society, 132
Lord, W. F., see *Nineteenth Century*
Lubbock, Percy, 141, 142, 156, 159
Lucas, F. L., 71, 100, 101 **66**, 115, 125, 126 **97**, 141, 147, 161—2, 175, 180, 180 **5**
Macaulay, 24, 56, 104, 131
MacCarthy, Desmond, 67, 70, 97, 152, 153, 167
The Macdermots of Ballycloran, 86, 169
Magnus, Sir Philip, 170, 174
Mansfield, Katherine, 173
Marion Fay, 32, 52
Martineau, Harriet, 75
Maugham, Somerset, 61, 143
Maurice, F. D., 19, 21
Mayne, Ethel C., 165
Melville, Herman, 8
Meredith, George, 26, 30, 38, 39, 46, 46 **57**, 49, 51, 63, 93
Mid-Victorian prosperity, 19—20
Milford, Sir Humphrey, 65, 67
Mill, John Stuart, 21, 34, 36, 46
More, Paul Elmer, 140, 158, 159—164, 165, 181
Morgan, Charles, 32, 69
Moore, George, 40
Morris, William, 13, 39
Mr. Scarborough's Family, 175
Mudie's Library, 25, 27, 90
Muir, Edwin, 60 **78**, 61, 86, 157 **37**

'Municipal socialism', 45—6
Nation, 33
National Review, 27, 56, 76, 81, 84—5,
   87, 88, 99, 100, 101, 103—6 passim,
   110, 112, 123, 125, 135, 157 39
New Age, see Bennett, Arnold
Newbolt, F., 84 27
Newman, Cardinal, 18, 33
New Romanticism, 39, 46—7, 49, 50
Newspapers and periodicals, 24—5, 46
Newton, Edward A., 43 47, 138
Nichols, Spencer van B., 139, 153, 167
Nineteenth Century (and After), W. F.
   Lord, 54—6; M. Sadleir, 62, 66,
   170 47; W. L. Burn, 84; F. Newbolt,
   84 27; H. Paul, 134—5
North American Review, 92, 105, 129
North British Review, 19, 76—8, 79,
   82, 84, 85—6, 87, 88, 89, 96, 97,
   112—3, 123
Nostalgia for AT's world, 8—9, 67,
   68, 68 85, 115—6, 152, 159, 168
Orley Farm, 29, 76, 84—5, 99, 101,
   102, 104, 106, 111, 112, 135, 137
Oxford University Press, publishers of
   The World's Classics, 65—8 passim
Pall Mall Gazette, 113
Pater, Walter, 39; 64
Paul, Herbert, 134—5
Phineas Finn, 55, 55 76, 83, 83 21,
   84 27, 85, 108, 137, 154
Phineas Redux, 137, 154
Prices of books, 24—5, 30—1, 31 13, 69
Priestley, J. B., 67, 68, 143, 146 21
The Prime Minister, 29, 29 7, 33, 83,
   155, 170
Proust, Marcel, 161, 173
Psychological approach, 93, 168—176,
   180
Publising, 24—5, 30—1
Punch, 25, 27, 75
Quarterly Review, 41, 51, 58
Queen's Quarterly, 69
Quiller-Couch, Sir Arthur, 13, 13 13 &
   16, 14, 27 5, 27, 47, 47 59 & 61,
   106, 143, 152, 158
Rachel Ray, 168

Ralph the Heir, 35, 83, 105, 108, 180
Randell, Wilfred L., see Fortnightly Rev.
Rantavaara, Irma, 51, 67 84, 157 41
Reaction against Victorianism, 8, 34—
   40 passim, 46—8, 50, 61—2, 65,
   136—7, 142
Reade, Charles, 26, 30, 40, 57
Reeve, Henry, 29—30, see further
   Edinburgh Rev.
Reform Bills, 12, 35—6, 55
Religion and science, 36, 39, 46
Richardson, Samuel, 40, 81
Roberts, Morris, 118, 123
Roman Catholicism, 18
Rousseau, 127
Rural England, charge of, 37
Ruskin, John, 13, 27, 39, 45
Sadleir, Michael, 7—12 passim, 16, 17,
   22, 29—35 passim, 40—3 passim,
   43 48, 58, 59, 62—4, 65; origin of
   Trollope: A. Commentary, 66; 69,
   105, 112, 121, 130—3 passim, 134 10,
   139—40, 147—55 passim, 158—9,
   160—171 passim, 176, 177, 179, 180,
   181, 183
Saintsbury, George, 47—9, 50, 53 71,
   59, 63-5, 72, 133, 134, 134 6, 142 17,
   142, 170, 180
Sampson, Ashley, see London Mercury
Saturday Review, 33, 41, 67
Scandal at Barset, 69
Schools, 23—4, 36
Scott-James, R. A., 139, 164—5
Scott, Sir Walter, 24, 25, 27, 49, 65,
   94, 128, 181
Stratification of fiction, 53, 54, 61, 178
Sentimental readers, 42, 126, 130, 131,
   137
Shakespeare, 82, 143, 158
Shaw, Bernard, 45, 51, 52, 60
Shelley, 13, 158
The Small House at Allington, 27 6,
   100, 110, 112, 129, 163
Somervell, D. C., 8 3, 17 25, 18, 18
   28, 29 & 32, 19 36 & 38, 20 47, 21 52,
   23 63, 24 67 & 69, 24, 34 23, 34, 44,
   45 51, 52 67, 53 69, 163

Socialism, 44—5, 60
Space, the sense of, 155—7
Spectator, 29 7, 41 44, 41, 55 76, 81, 86, 129—30, 163—4
Spencer, Herbert, 21
Stack, Herbert, see *Fortnightly Review*
Stebbins, L. P. and R. P., 31 13, 32, 33 22, 34, 35, 42 45, 42 58, 69—70, 131, 162, 168, 169, 172
Stebbins, R. P., 8
Stephen, Sir Leslie, 27 3, 54, 56, 72 4, 72, 83 23, 88, 90 39, 148—9, 157—8
Stevenson, R. L., 28, 38, 49
Strachey, Lytton, 44, 62, 64
Street, G. S., 54, 57, 66, 68 85
Subject, the matter of, 89, 94, 146—8
Sunday Times (Sir Philip Magnus), 170, 174
Swinburne, A. C., 39, 46
Taste, individual, 71—2, 101, 125, 126. 170, 178
Tchekov, 173
Thackeray, 25, 26, 28, 33, 35 27, 40, 46 57, 47, 49, 51, 57, 58, 59, 65, 67, 75, 77, 82—3, 92, 93, 98, 102, 103, 104, 106, 114, 117, 119, 120, 128, 138, 139, 145, 153, 161, 163, 166, 167, 177
Thackeray, 98, 106, 107, 109, 149, 160
The Three Clerks, 16, 52, 88, 99, 104, 112
Tillotson, Kathleen, 72, 73, 74, 75, 83 23, 103, 104, 141—2, 163
Times, 41, 73, 75, 80, 84, 85, 87 30, 91, 93, 99, 100, 101, 105, 109, 110, 116, 125, 126, 127, 136
Times Literary Supplement, 59, 61, 139, 174
Tolstoy, 145, 156, 159
Trevelyan, G. M., 12 10—1, 16 19—21, 17 25—7, 18 30—1 & 33, 20 40, 42, 44 & 46, 21 48, 50 & 51, 22 57, 23 58, 60, 63 & 64, 24 66 & 68, 25, 34, 36 33, 37, 37 35, 46 53—6, 54 73, 60 78
Trilling, Lionel, 171—2, 178—9
Trollope, Anthony
— Biography: 14 ff., 32—3, 80, 126—7, 151

— Criticism of his work, and his own opinions and attitudes: a representative (interpretor) of his period, 8, 9, 10, 11, 12, 19, 27, 28, 34—5, 65, 74—5, 76—8, 85, 95, 114—5, 156, 159, 167, 183; clergy, 11, 12, 17, 18, 75—6, 78—80, 91, 122, 166, 177; women, 11, 21, 36, 82, 105, 110, 136—7; a 'photographer', 11, 56, 87—9; the poor, 14, 22, 95; the middle class, 14, 23, 35, 55, 75—7, 97, 145, 146; Irish subjects, 16; modes of work, 17, 41, 42, 59, 128, 131—3, 137, 151; historical interest of his novels, 17, 56, 138, 157—8; Barsetshire, 18, 27, 67, 68, 103, 114—5, 145, 151—9, 177—8; politics, 22, 83, 159, political ambition, 55, 55 76, 83, 'political' novels, 83—4, 154—5, 159; the aristocracy, 23; social strife, 23, 97, 98, 98 61, 177; realism, 25, 77 ff., 117—8, 120, 124, 165, 167, 172; competitors, 26—7, 38, 60—2; painter of ordinary (commonplace) life, 27, 48, 74, 76—7, 85—91, 95, 100—1, 147, 178—9; noteworthy contemporary admirers, 28, 33; characters (characterization), 28, 43, 76—8, 86, 88—90, 96 ff., 101—3, 111—2, 114, 115, 121, 122, 127—8, 129, 148, 153—5, 157, 164, 165, 166, 168, 169, 173—4, 176, 177, 181; decline of reputation, 29, 30, 31, 31 13, 33, 37, 40—3, 51, 125; attitude towards sensationalism, 29, 85, 95; limits, 29, 90—2, 95; psychology, 30, 32, 69, 92, 122, 168—76, 179, 180: publishers, 30, 41; satire, 32, 121, 174; love of his art, 33, 42, 144, 168—9; (lack of) depth, 34—5, 41, 77, 90—3, 99—100, 111, 140, 168; acceptance of the Victorian barriers, acquiescence, 34—5, 94—5, 171; chronicler of manners, 34, 43, 86, 87, 97, 177—9; attitude towards socialism, 35; getting old-fashioned, 35, 37; obituary notices, 40—1, 42;

(not) a man of genius, 41, 48, 54, 122, 127, 128, 140, 143; future 'life' of AT prophesied, 41, 50, 56, 58, 62, 90, 95, 137, 138; length of novels, 41, 106, 129; inspiration, 41, 128, 131—3; mundane ideals, 41, 129—31, 142, 144, 163—4; ethics (and art), 43, 80—1, 84, 92, 98—101, 100 65, 110, 112—3, 120, 122, 129—30, 159—164, 165, 176, 179—80, 181; hunting scenes, 43, 156; peculiar names of characters, 47, 106—7, 166; a craftsman (craftsmanship), 48, 131, 133, 172, 181; vulgarity, 48, 104—5, 106, 167; dawn of revival, 52. ff., 138, definite revival, 62 ff., 142, height of revival, 68—9; 'not an artist', 56, 88, 172; instrusion into the story, 62, 106, 129; style, 62, 117—20, 135—6, 148—50; unpretentiousness, 66, 77, 93—5, 182; novels as radio plays, 68, 69; the wars and AT's reputation, 70, 116, 177; AT on criticism, 72—3; range, 74—95, 170, 180; human nature, a guiding principle, 74—5, 96, 116—7, 118, 148, 160, 165; Englishness, 74, 81, 95, 100. 139. 151—2, 157, 158—9; at one with his readers (and characters), 77, 85, 94, 150, 165, 181—2; tone and atmosphere, 77, 88—9, 119—20; knowledge — imagination, 78—9, 80—1, 86, 103, 124, 137; knowledge of the world, 79, 86, 89, 120; girls in love, 80—3, 91, 108, 110; delicacy of feeling, 81—2, 99, 137; young men, 82, 88; law, lawyers, 84—5, 84 27, 104; lifelikeness, 'impression of life', 85, 88, 95, 98, 102—3, 114—5, 119, 120, 124, 158; moderation, 86—7 102, 138, 163—6, 170—1; plot and character, 87, 88, 96 ff., 138; accuracy, fidelity to facts, 87—9, 120; difference from other Victorian novelists, 96, 101, 105, 155, 166—7, 173, 183; story, 97—8, 105—6, 107—8, 111, 148; moral lessons, 98—9, 108—13,

129, 160—1, 162, 179—80, 181; novelist's first duty to please, 98, 107, 115—6, 117; cumulative effect, 98, 118, 118 86, 144; pathos, 99—100, 111—2, poetic justice, 99, 112—3, 162—5; against social prejudice, 99, 113, 180; love and love-making, 100—1, 107—111, 151—2, 174; appeal to popular taste, 101—2, 111, 125—6, 151, 170; seriousness, zest, 102—3, 104, 119, 163—5, 182; a worl-creator, 102, 114—5, 144, 146, 151—9; digressions, 104, 105, 108—9, 160; social comedy, 105—8, 159, 177, 178; humour, 107, 125; not sentimental, 110; imagination, 113, 118, 120—4, 127, 130, 131; dialogue, 117—8, 136, 174; an unconscious artist, 121—3, 168; elusiveness, 121, 139—40, 141, 171; 'the Tupper of fiction', 125, two publics, 125, 170, 179; sacrificed quality to quantity, 129, 143; serious view of the novelist's vocation, 131; creator of the demands which he supplied, 135, 180; map of Barsetshire, 139, 153; sincerity, 142, 143, 144, quantity a merit, 142—5; a conscious artist, 149—50, 154—5, 175; onlooker's point of vision, 154—5; wisdom, 158, 180; detachment, 164—5; gay early novels — gloomy later ones, 174; pessimism, the obsessional, 175—6

Trollope, Frances, 15, 105, 145
Trollope, Henry Merivale, 33 17, 66
Trollope, Thomas Anthony, 14, 15
Trollopian (Nineteenth-Century Fiction), B. A. Booth, 7; R. P. Stebbins, 8; H. O. Box, 69; foundation of, 69; H. G. Dick, 70 86, 168
Values: 'Insight' and pleasure of 'recognition', 'influence value' and 'pleasure value', 100, 115. 119, 161—2, 180
The Vicar of Bullhampton, 108, 118, 119
Victoria, Queen, 12, 20, 21, 44, 55
Vincent, C. J., 69
Walker, Hugh, 59, 155, 156

Walpole, Hugh, 31, 32, 34 **25**, 83 **23**, 142, 144, 152, 156, 169, 180, 182

Ward, Mrs. Humphry, 39

The Warden, 7, 14, 16, 17, 25, 28, 33, 62, 75, 78, 79, 93, 98, 99, 106, 111, 127, 152, 156, 169

The Way We Live Now, 31, 32, 33, 42, 73, 87, 125, 131, 169, 176, 180

Wells, H. G., 60, 61

Westminster Review, 33, 41−2, 43, 126, 131

Wharton, Edith, 89, 96, 97, 116 **83**, 119, 133, 141, 144, 145, 155, 156, 161, 173, 181, 182

Whibley, Charles, 42, 66, 144

Wilde, Oscar, 39, 46

Wildman, J. H., 18 **29** & **35**, 23 **61**, 68

Willey, Basil, 9 **6**, 19 **37**, 62

Woman, Victorian, 21, 22, 36, 46, 80−1, 82, **1**05, 136−7

Woolf, Virginia, 61, 67, 71 **1**, 74, 89, 90, 93 **45**, 115, 141, 148, 161

World War I, 58, 59, 60, 61, 67, 70, 138

World War II, 68, 70

Yellow Book, 47

Yonge, Charlotte, 79.

Young, G. M., 12 **10**, 20 **39**, **41**, **43** & **45**, 21 **53**, 23 **59** & **62**, 24 **65**, 36 **29**, 44, 52 **68**, 55